VMware®
Infrastructure 3
FOR
DUMMIES®

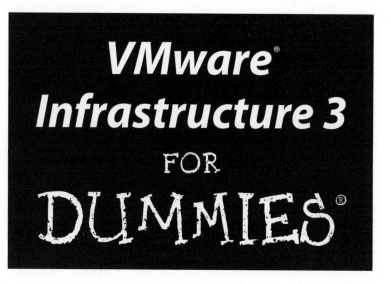

VMware® Infrastructure 3 FOR DUMMIES®

by William J. Lowe

WILEY

Wiley Publishing, Inc.

VMware® Infrastructure 3 For Dummies®

Published by
Wiley Publishing, Inc.
111 River Street
Hoboken, NJ 07030-5774

www.wiley.com

WILEY

About the Author

Bill Lowe was tinkering with computers as a hobby long before it became his career. He has been working with computers in various capacities for nearly twenty years. He has been a system administrator, consultant, and held various hands-on technical management positions in several companies. Bill has several industry certifications and a Master of Science degree in Computer Networking from New Jersey Institute of Technology. He is currently pursuing an MBA in Finance at Monmouth University.

Bill is available for speaking opportunities. Please contact him via email at virtualwilliamj-contact@yahoo.com.

Author's Acknowledgments

First, I would like to thank Mark Zegarelli for introducing me to the Dummies people. One look at me and he said "You are truly Dummy material!" Mark is the person who took the idea for this book to the Dummies group.

Next I would like to thank Katie Feltman, Blair Pottenger, Teresa Artman, and David Marshall whose sage advice helped make this book far better than I ever could have on my own. Additionally, I would like to thank everyone at Wiley Publishing for all the effort expended putting this book together.

I would also like to thank my parents, Jack and Joan Lowe; my wife's parents, Howard and Gail Sturdevant; and Duane Flaherty for their encouragement and support.

Additionally, Stephen Foskett has been both inspirational and motivational to me. Stephen, you are the one who got me started on the path that led to this book.

Mervin, Murray, Ross, Jack, and Kathy: You have become more than just mentors to me - I feel like you are family.

Finally, I have saved the best for last. I want to give special thanks to my loving bride, Michele, who can correct grammatical mistakes at the speed of light and spot a typographic error from space. Thank you, I could not have done this without your love, help, and support.

Publisher's Acknowledgments

We're proud of this book; please send us your comments through our online registration form located at www.dummies.com/register/.

Some of the people who helped bring this book to market include the following:

Acquisitions and Editorial

Project Editor: Blair J. Pottenger

Senior Acquisitions Editor: Katie Feltman

Senior Copy Editor: Teresa Artman

Technical Editor: David Marshall

Editorial Manager: Kevin Kirschner

Editorial Assistant: Amanda Foxworth

Sr. Editorial Assistant: Cherie Case

Cartoons: Rich Tennant
(www.the5thwave.com)

Composition Services

Project Coordinator: Kristie Rees

Layout and Graphics: Reuben W. Davis, Shane Johnson, Christin Swinford, Christine Williams, Erin Zeltner

Proofreaders: John Greenough, Linda Seifert

Indexer: Broccoli Information Management

Special Help: Richard Meyer

Publishing and Editorial for Technology Dummies

Richard Swadley, Vice President and Executive Group Publisher

Andy Cummings, Vice President and Publisher

Mary Bednarek, Executive Acquisitions Director

Mary C. Corder, Editorial Director

Publishing for Consumer Dummies

Diane Graves Steele, Vice President and Publisher

Joyce Pepple, Acquisitions Director

Composition Services

Gerry Fahey, Vice President of Production Services

Debbie Stailey, Director of Composition Services

Contents at a Glance

Table of Contents

Introduction

Mainframes, PCs, networks, and the Internet all drastically changed the computer industry. Virtualization based on the x86 platform is another industry reshaper, but what exactly is it?

Your standalone PC comprises hardware and software. You have a CPU, memory, and disk resources. A single operating system sits on top of your hardware resources and controls access to them. On top of your operating system sit applications such as e-mail and word processing. To access the hardware, your applications ask the operating system to perform hardware actions on their behalf. Say you want to save a Word file, like this chapter: You click the Save button, and the word processor says to the operating system, "Please write this data to the hard disk and let me know when you are done."

The operating system takes the data and calls the disk hardware drivers to write the data to the disk drive. The drivers write the data and tell the operating system that they're done. Then the operating system tells the word processor that the data has been written to disk. Suddenly, after a few breathless seconds, you happily see that your document has been saved without error.

While you continue writing, your computer has very little to do. In fact, it's just sitting there waiting for you to type your next character. To understand the wait, you need to understand Hertz (Hz). One Hz is one cycle of something every second. The second hand on a clock moves at a speed one tick a second. Each movement is a complete cycle, so the second hand runs at a speed of one cycle per second, or 1 Hz.

Similarly, you type at a certain number of bits per second (bps). Say that you're a slow typist like me, and you can type only two characters per second. I don't know how many words per minute that translates to, but I know that I am a slow typist! Because each character is 8 bits, your data input speed is 16 bits per second (8 bits per character × 2 characters). In other words, your typing speed is 16 Hz.

Your computer is likely running at the speed of at least one billion (1,000,000,000) Hz. If you type as slowly as I do, you're using only 0.0000016 percent of your computer's potential resources (16 ÷ 1,000,000,000). In other words, the computer is spending most of its time waiting for you. So, until you can type one billion bits per second, your computer will be eagerly waiting for your next character.

In fact, most computers run at low utilization rates because best practices often dictate using a single machine for a single function. As machines got faster, though, single-purpose machine hardware utilization rates dropped. However, the practice of using single purpose machines continues because it limits the effects of failures and outages to a single application. In fact, even a misbehaving program can't interfere with another application because they're on different machines. In this case, a machine is the combination of hardware and software that performs a task for you.

So where am I going with all this? *Virtualization* simply separates the hardware from the software. A *virtual machine* is the combination of your applications and operating system. The virtual machine is tricked into thinking that it has its own hardware. However, the hardware is actually shared with several other virtual machines. When one virtual machine is doing nothing, another virtual machine can use the first machine's share of the hardware. CPU, memory, and disk resources are all split between many virtual machines. This offers a much better utilization rate for your expensive server hardware while still isolating applications by virtual machine. You can read more about this in detail in Chapter 1.

But for now, just know that using virtualization allows you to separate your applications by virtual machine without underutilizing your hardware. When implemented properly, you can run many virtual machines on one piece of hardware. This translates into savings on hardware and hardware maintenance contracts, as well as the cost of server room space and the electricity needed to run the hardware and cooling systems in your server room. Additional savings are achieved by simplified management. Using virtualization is extremely economical.

About This Book

This book is a full and complete introduction to VMware Infrastructure 3. It provides you with all the information you need to design and install a virtual infrastructure. *VMware Infrastructure 3 For Dummies* explains the components in VMware Infrastructure 3. In addition, planning, designing, installing, and configuring your first VI3 environment is covered. Using VI3 requires you to understand a lot of information, which isn't difficult when you break it into its most basic parts.

Computer scientists make great use of the term *primitive* — and not to describe a nonindustrial culture. Computer scientists use *primitive* to describe the simplest base unit used to create more complex items. For instance

- ✔ Programming languages use *primitive data structures* to describe the built-in data types, such as integers.
- ✔ CPU designers use *primitive* to describe a single processor instruction, such as *add*.

VI3 is made of thousands of easily understood primitives combined in groups. These groups are mixed and matched to create a rather complex system.

To help you understand this concept, this book covers

- ✔ The VI3 components
- ✔ The functions of the VI3 components
- ✔ Planning a virtual infrastructure
- ✔ Installing and configuring a highly fault-tolerant virtual infrastructure
- ✔ Managing your virtual infrastructure
- ✔ Backing up and troubleshooting your virtual infrastructure

By explaining the primitives of VI3, how the primitives are grouped into functionality, and how all that functionality is combined into a complex system, this book explains VI3 in a friendly and easily digestible way. You've likely read other *For Dummies* books, and I'm proud to continue in the true *For Dummies* tradition. In fact, my wife has been referring to me as a dummy for years. This book finally proves it!

Conventions Used in This Book

VI3 encompasses a huge amount of information. No single piece of it is too complex, but the sheer volume of information might make mastering VI3 seem a bit daunting. Because each complex concept is formed by linking many simpler concepts — or primitives (see the preceding section) — I try to introduce concepts in the *For Dummies* conversational manner and move from complex and general to simple and specific. Here are some ways I break this down for you:

✔ Bulleted lists, I bold any concept that is followed by a definition.

✔ If a list is just general information that does not require further definition, regular text is used.

✔ The main steps of numbered lists appear in bold while step explanations are regular text.

✔ Command paths, Web addresses, code, and onscreen messages are presented in `monofont`.

What You're Not to Read

This book caters to three different audiences with different informational needs:

✔ **Non-technical managers** who want a simple overview of virtualization need not read the entire book. The Introduction through Chapter 2 will suffice for an overview. I recommend reviewing Chapter 12 for an understanding of fault tolerance, and Chapter 20 is a good chapter to read for an understanding of virtual appliances.

✔ A **technical manager** who isn't implementing a virtual infrastructure but wants to understand how it works should read the entire book but can skip lists and information denoted with a Technical Stuff icon.

✔ A **system designer or implementation person** should read the entire book. Sorry, implementers, but you have the most reading to do. I'll try to make it concise and as painless as possible.

Foolish Assumptions

In the interest of time and space, I've made several assumptions about you, the reader:

✔ You've mastered using a personal computer and moved on to server installation and administration.

✔ You have a conceptual understanding of networking concepts and storage area networks (SANs). (For a little brush-up reading, check out *Storage Area Networks For Dummies,* 2nd Edition by Christopher Poelker, Wiley.)

✔ You prefer using a GUI interface to the command line, which is good because VI3 makes the same assumption!

For more on these topics, I recommend finding other *For Dummies* books as your guide. Specifically, look for *Virtualization For Dummies, Networking For Dummies, Windows Server 2003 For Dummies,* and perhaps one of the *For Dummies* books about Linux.

How This Book Is Organized

VMware Infrastructure 3 For Dummies is divided into six parts. Each part builds upon the information covered in the part before it. If you're brand-new to VI3, your best bet is to read this book sequentially. If you already have a pretty solid understanding of the subject, feel free to jump to whatever chapter you fancy. Here is what you can find in each part.

Part I: Ready, Set, Go with VMware Infrastructure 3

Part I provides the information needed to understand what VMware Infrastructure 3 is and what you need to do before you begin virtualizing your physical machines.

Part II: Setting Up ESX Hosts

The heart and soul of a virtual infrastructure is the ESX host. ESX hosts are the foundation of your virtual house. This part covers the anatomy and installation of ESX hosts.

Part III: Connecting the Physical to Your Virtual Environment

ESX hosts can't exist in a vacuum. Connecting them to storage and data networks is a necessary step in any virtual system. Networking and external storage are covered in this part of the book.

Of course, the fun doesn't stop there. After networking and storage are configured, you need to license and manage your servers. One of the best ways is by using VMware VirtualCenter. At this point, you'll have all the pieces in place to start easily creating and managing powerful virtual machines.

Part IV: Fault Tolerance and Data Centers

For production systems, fault tolerance is a necessity. This is especially true when you virtualize since a single failure can interrupt several machines. This part describes VirtualCenter, creating and managing virtual machines, and making everything fault tolerant with cluster technology.

Part V: Playing Virtual Administrator

Part V delves into the administrative functions of virtual infrastructures. Security, resource utilization and monitoring, backups, and troubleshooting are all covered in this part.

Part VI: The Part of Tens

This traditional *For Dummies* part devotes the concluding chapters to finding more information about VI3, other VMware products, and the world of virtual appliances.

Icons Used in This Book

All *For Dummies* books have an array of useful and explanatory icons. Here are the ones I use in this book.

This icon highlights information that can make your life far easier. For example, version 3.5 of VMware Infrastructure 3 was released during the writing of this book, and I use this icon to draw your attention to those things new or different from version 3.0.x.

The Remember icon points to a fact or issue you'll likely need.

This icon highlights potentially nefarious conditions. Pay particular attention when you see this icon, for danger is near.

When you see this icon, you're about to delve into the inner technical workings of something. And although understanding the inner workings is important, you can skip these sections if you've already absorbed enough information to meet your goal.

When you see this icon, you know a story follows. These stories illustrate points in the text and have actually happened to me or one of my friends. It's better than learning something the hard way!

Where to Go from Here

If you're already familiar with VI3, you can jump to any part of the book that catches your interest. However, if you're not familiar with VI3, you should read the book from start to finish.

Having said that, keep this in mind while reading this book: Computer systems and software are always in a rapid state of change, which means some items in this book might quickly become dated. Always review the VMware Web site or one of the other sites mentioned in Chapter 18 to make sure that you're armed with the latest knowledge.

Part I

Ready, Set, Go with VMware Infrastructure 3

The 5th Wave   By Rich Tennant

"I'm not saying I believe in anything. All I know is since it's been there our server is running 50% faster."

In this part . . .

*T*his part introduces you to virtualization, using VMware Infrastructure 3. Chapter 1 covers Infrastructure 3's many tools and the advantages of using VMware's flagship product.

Chapter 2 introduces you to capacity-planning concepts and tools so you can adequately plan the hardware you need to implement your virtualization effort. This part concludes with Chapter 3, providing a review of the different storage options to choose from.

Chapter 1

Exploring VMware Infrastructure 3 as Your Virtual Solution

*V*Mware Infrastructure 3 (VI3) is a robust, feature-rich, fault-tolerant, and highly reliable platform for virtualization. In fact, VMware created x86-based virtualization. (Now that I got that out of my system, it's time to explore the possibilities of saving time and money with your virtualization project.)

Most x86 computers don't use their hardware to the fullest capacity because *de facto* system design often dictates that you use a single server for a single purpose. As I mention in the book's Introduction, virtualization simply uses "smoke and mirrors" to separate your programs and operating systems from the hardware on which they run. That way, many virtual machines use common hardware, and the hardware is far better utilized.

In this chapter, virtual machines, ESX hosts, the benefits of virtulization, and VI3 are covered. Additionally, the last section describes the major steps in implementing your virtual infrastructure.

Knowing What You Must About Virtual Machines

Making as many of your physical machines as possible become virtual is the end game of virtualization. The more you *virtualize* (convert physical to virtual machines), the more benefits you see, and the more you realize how reliable and stable a platform VMware Infrastructure 3 is. Being skeptical by nature, I went slowly at first, but I quickly began to trust VMware the more I worked with it.

Virtual machines: The non-physical workhorses

For all intents and purposes, virtual machines are just like physical machines. You can log on to them; and they have BIOS, hard disks, memory, CPUs, operating systems, and applications. In fact, if you connect remotely to a machine, you'll never know that it's virtual unless someone tells you. Virtual machines work and behave just like physical machines. Even the machines themselves don't even know they are virtual!

Virtual machine pluses and minuses

Aside from all the general benefits of virtualization (covered in the "Benefitting from VMware Infrastructure 3" section, later in this chapter), here are the major pluses for using virtual machines:

- ✔ **They can be rebooted much faster than physical machines.** I was able to reboot one server in 15 seconds!
- ✔ **They are more simpler than their physical counterparts.** For instance, there are no array controllers to configure in the virtual machines.
- ✔ **They are easy to back up and restore.** The entire machine is stored in a set of files.

Unfortunately, there are also downsides. However, you can easily minimize the downsides:

- ✔ **Support can be a gray area.** Some software vendors might tell you, "Hey, it's on a virtual machine. We don't support that." Pay for VMware support and know your own operating systems to mitigate this risk.
- ✔ **Troubleshooting can be a little tricky.** People troubleshooting a problem on a virtual machine might incorrectly deduce the problem is caused because the machine is virtual. As long as you hone your own troubleshooting skills, this risk is minimized.

   I had a consultant tell me that the most likely problem with a report running slowly and having connectivity issues was because the server was virtual. I had to prove to her that it was the report — not the virtual machine — before we could resolve the issue.

✔ **Inherent flaws are transferable.** Flaws in a virtual infrastructure design can affect all virtual machines. This, in turn, will affect all users of those machines. Watch where you make your trade-offs, and design your system with ample capacity to avoid this risk.

✔ **Some apps can be troublesome for time syncs.** For example, I have one application that throws off the virtual machine's time sync. You can compensate for this by synching the virtual machine's time to the *ESX (Engagement Simulation Exercise)* host. (An *ESX host* is a server that your virtual machines run on. It provides access to all the hardware resources your virtual machines share.) In turn, sync your ESX host to your network's time source.

Symmetrical multiprocessing and why you care

Commonly, physical machines use multiple processors. In fact, you'd be hard pressed to find a server that doesn't come with at least a dual-core processor. Each core is treated as a separate CPU, so a machine using a single, dual-core CPU is taking advantage of *symmetrical multiprocessing (SMP)*. In the physical world, multiple CPUs can greatly aid in processing speed. Things are a little different in the virtual world, however.

Your ESX host will most likely have multiple processors with multiple cores. Whenever your virtual machine needs the CPU, the VMkernel (covered in the next section) can send the work to any CPU in your ESX host. Your single CPU virtual machine is, therefore, getting benefits similar to SMP without even knowing it.

If you have a license for SMP, you can assign multiple processors to a virtual machine. However, just because you *can* do something doesn't mean that you *should.* Dual, virtual CPU machines force co-scheduling of physical processors.

With *co-scheduling,* if one physical processor is scheduled, a second one is as well. This can take resources away from your other virtual machines. Additionally, if Process 1 on virtual CPU1 is waiting too long for Process 2 on virtual CPU2 to finish, both processes might get *scheduled out* (finish their allotted share of CPU time and lose the processor until their next turn) before completion. This can negate the benefits of using multiple CPUs.

Best practices dictate adding multiple CPUs to a virtual machine *only* if you can prove an increase in performance. This is because multiple virtual CPUs can have some negative side effects:

✔ **Potential performance hit:** If you give a virtual machine multiple CPUs, you remove some of the scheduling flexibility available to the VMkernel. This trade-off might (no guarantee) give a few machines a performance boost, but at the cost of your other virtual machines losing performance. If you really need one machine to have a performance boost, you might want to try using a resource pool instead of SMP. Resource pools are covered in Chapter 14.

✔ **Prevent processor fragmentation:** If you have two, single-core processors or two, dual-core processors, you can create a processor fragmentation scenario using SMP. If you create a dual-CPU virtual machine, it might experience *processor starvation.*

Say a single CPU virtual machine is running on one processor, and the dual CPU machine has two active threads ready to run. Both threads need to be co-scheduled, but one physical CPU is in use, so neither thread is scheduled. Meanwhile, only one physical CPU is in use, and the other is just sitting there: doing nothing. Enabling *hyperthreading* (making a single processor appear as two processors to an SMP-aware operating system to make the CPU run more efficiently) allows a single-core CPU to act like two physical CPUs for a virtual machine. Enabling it alleviates the processor fragmentation problem in systems that have more than one processor.

Understanding the Role That VMkernel Plays

Even though each of your virtual machines thinks that it has its own dedicated hardware, the machines actually share a common pool of hardware. The magician creating this illusion is the VMkernel that runs on each ESX host. The simplest way to think of the *VMkernel* is as a scheduler: It schedules virtual machines access to resources. The VMkernel even schedules the management console that you use to configure and operate your ESX hosts. The VMkernel virtualization model is shown in Figure 1-1.

As shown in Figure 1-1, there are three layers to the VMkernel virtualization model:

✔ **Virtual Machine layer:** Here all your operating systems and applications are neatly housed in separate virtual machines. Each virtual machine thinks it is a physical machine with its own hardware, but this is not the case. The ESX tricks all the virtual machines.

✔ **ESX layer:** The VMkernel is the boss of this layer. The kernel schedules hardware for the virtual machines as well as the management interface. The VMkernel is a liar. It tells all the virtual machines that they are physical entities and have access to their own hardware.

✔ **Shared Resources layer:** This layer consists of all your hardware subsystems. It includes your physical and storage area networks.

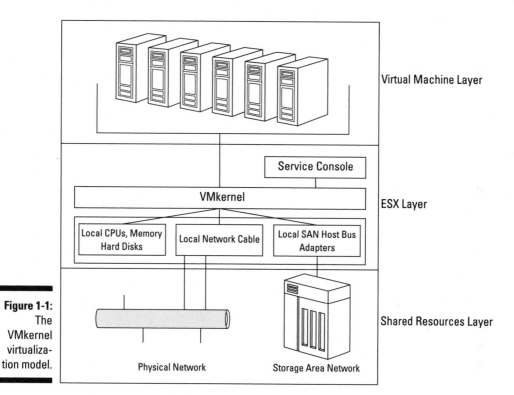

Figure 1-1:
The
VMkernel
virtualiza-
tion model.

VMware Infrastructure 3

Using the VMware Infrastructure product suite enables you to virtualize servers, storage, and networks. In addition, the suite offers you ways to add extreme fault tolerance as well as centralized management, load leveling, and centralized backup.

VMware always offers several different ways to purchase their products. Below are the offerings for version 3.5 (the offerings for 3.0 were entirely different):

✔ **Single ESX:** You can buy the plain ESX that you install on a hard drive or ESXi, which has the operating system on a chip instead of a hard drive.

✔ **VMware Infrastructure Foundation:** This is ESX with a few bells and whistles and offers you automated updates, a VirtualCenter Agent, and Update Manager.

✔ **VMware Infrastructure Standard:** This is ESX with more bells and whistles and offers everything in the Foundation level plus High Availability. This allows you to essentially create an active-passive cluster and would be the minimum level of fault tolerance that is acceptable for production systems.

✔ **VMware Infrastructure Enterprise:** Every available option — If you want it all, then this is for you. This package provides every possible feature to enable active-active fault tolerance and dynamic load balancing across servers. If you are virtualizing datacenters, you want the Enterprise package.

Benefitting from VMware Infrastructure 3

Virtualization simply makes life easier from a technical and administrative viewpoint. Fortunately, it also makes life easier from an economic viewpoint, so everyone can agree that virtualization is a good thing. Before you decide to virtualize, consider some of its many benefits:

✔ **Better hardware usage rates:** This translates to needing less hardware to do the same amount of work.

✔ **Lower hardware-maintenance costs:** You need fewer physical servers, which means less maintenance contracts to pay for.

✔ **Lower cooling costs:** Less heat is generated, so less cooling is needed.

✔ **Lower electric costs:** You have fewer physical servers so your electric bill drops. VMware is a very green technology.

✔ **Lower space costs:** Your server room can be much smaller, which leaves more room for offices. And face it, it is the people in the office that produce your company's income. The server room is an expense that you can help minimize.

✔ **Longer infrastructure run time from UPSes:** If you virtualize all your physical servers and keep the same UPS system, think how much longer it can run during an outage — especially if you are condensing twenty or thirty virtual machines onto one physical machine.

✔ **Faster server deployment:** You can deploy a new server in as little time as about 15 minutes. And you don't need to spec-out hardware and wait for delivery. In fact, deploying a server from a template is as easy as right-clicking and answering a few simple questions.

✔ **Simplified management:** All your virtual servers use the same drivers, and servers are just a collection of files on a hard disk. Whether you're installing a program or adding virtual hardware to a server, all servers are managed through the same client.

I've added "hardware" to a virtual server in New Jersey remotely from a beach in Sarasota. Nice!

✔ **Easy backup and fast recovery:** Again, your servers are just a bunch of files.

✔ **The ability to freeze your server in time through snapshots:** You can take a snapshot before applying a Service Pack. If you have problems after the update, you can go back in time to before the service pack was applied instead of rebuilding your server and restoring your data. Fixing a bad update takes only minutes instead of hours.

✔ **Quality-of-life improvement:** All the time and effort saved makes your IT life much better! All the money you save makes management extremely happy as well. Everyone benefits from virtualization.

After reading this list of benefits, you likely think that using virtualization can prevent many IT headaches — and you're right! Time to meet the components of VI3.

After you start to virtualize machines, it can become very addictive. You might even get the overwhelming urge to create far more virtual machines than you actually need. You should resist that urge! In fact, this is called *virtual machine sprawl.* While it does not take up as much space as physical server sprawl, it can be detrimental from an efficiency, resource, and management point of view. As a rule of thumb, only create a virtual machine if you would have created a physical machine to accomplish your goal in the past.

Meeting the pieces and parts of VMware Infrastructure 3

Many pieces make up VI3, and each has a specific purpose to help create a seamless whole. Although you can purchase different parts separately, buying them as a package costs less. If you're virtualizing your infrastructure, you will want the entire product suite.

Here's a list of what's included in the VI3Enterprise Suite:

✔ **VMware ESX:** This comprises the operating system that you put on your server hardware that allows you to create virtual machines and share hardware resources between them. Your physical servers are referred to as *hosts.* The virtual machines run *guest operating systems.*

A new version — ESXi — is also available. This preinstalled version can be configured by non-technical people via menus at boot-up. This version supports everything that the ESX supports, but it lacks a Service Console. This version is designed for remote deployment and management. And did I mention that it runs on a chip? You don't even need any hard disks in your ESXi server.

- **VMware Virtual SMP:** *Virtual SMP (symmetric multiprocessing)* enables a virtual machine to use up to four physical processors simultaneously. To benefit from multiple virtual CPUs, your operating system and application need to support SMP. However, VMware is very good at scheduling resources and you should only use multiple virtual processors if you can prove a performance increase.

- **VMware VMFS:** Virtual Machine File System is a file system that allows multiple ESX hosts to access the same data storage concurrently. This allows any host to run any virtual machine and provides the ability to switch between hosts on the fly using VMotion.

- **VMware VMotion:** *VMotion* is the resource that actually moves running machines from one host to another with no loss of connectivity. In version 3.0.x, if you shut down a virtual machine, you can also change where its files are stored.

- **VMware Storage VMotion:** While VMotion allows you to move your virtual machine from on ESX to another to better utilize hardware resources, Storage VMotion allows you to move the virtual machine files from one storage location to another to better utilize storage resources. The virtual machine stays on the same ESX host while its files are moved to a new location. Again, this can be done while the virtual machine is running.

- **VMware Distributed Resource Scheduler (DRS):** Use *DRS* monitors your resources and decides which host is best to run a virtual machine on. It provides system wide load leveling. DRS uses VMotion to move virtual machines off hosts that are under heavy loads and onto hosts that have more resources available.

- **VMware High Availability (HA):** This high-availability resource can restart virtual machines on a new host if the host on which they were running fails.

- **VMware Consolidated Backup (VCB):** A centralized way to backup virtual machines through a backup proxy server.

- **VMware Update Manager:** This feature is designed to manage patches for your ESX hosts as well as the guest operating systems running on them.

- **Distributed Power Management (DPM):** DPM attempts to consolidate virtual machines onto the least number of hosts in a cluster as possible so the remaining hosts can sleep and save power. The hosts automatically wake up again if they are needed later.

- **VMware VirtualCenter:** *VirtualCenter* (VC) is a centralized management framework that lets you create fault tolerant clusters (clusters are covered in Chapter 12). It controls HA, DRS, and VMotion for an entire cluster. Additionally, VirtualCenter provides one spot for you to configure all hosts and virtual machines in your virtual infrastructure.

You need VirtualCenter to take advantage of load-leveling and fault tolerance. VirtualCenter is a separate purchase and is not included with VI3.

Two other useful products fall outside the realm of VI3, but you might want them anyway.

✔ **VMware Converter:** You will use this product over and over again. With it, you can easily convert physical Windows machines into virtual machines. Additionally, if you use Virtual Consolidated Backup to back up images of your virtual machines, you can restore those images by using VMware Converter. This is also the product to use to convert between various virtual machine formats from VMware and third-party products.

The two versions of VMware Converter are

- *Starter Edition:* Use this free version to convert physical machines into virtual machines on an ESX from the physical machine itself while it's running. It also enables you to convert physical machines to other VMware formats remotely.

- *Enterprise Edition:* Use this version to convert physical machines to virtual machines remotely and run multiple conversions simultaneously. You can also schedule migrations if you want to run them off-hours. Another benefit is migrating a machine that is powered off, which allows you to create a boot CD for cold cloning. The cold-clone command line interface (CLI) can be used to convert SUSE and Red Hat Linux machines.

✔ **Capacity Planner:** This product is designed for consultants to quickly gather comprehensive data about your IT infrastructure. It is a hosted application service that gathers data without the use of agents, and it's designed to get all the information you need to correctly design your virtual environment.

Planning Your VMware Solution

After you decide to virtualize, there are four distinct stages to bringing your plan to fruition. You start by defining your capacity requirements and figuring your return on investment (ROI). Then it's time to design and build your virtual infrastructure. Then, after you virtualize your physical machines, back up your hard work and investment.

Stage 1: Capacity planning and return on investment

Start off by determining how much capacity you need today as well as how much growth you anticipate. Today's needs, obviously, determine what hardware you have to buy to get started. Your anticipated growth needs determine how much you will save by not purchasing physical servers.

Even without taking the electricity, cooling, and space savings into consideration, you can usually find a ROI just by the savings generated through not buying future servers and their associated hardware maintenance contracts. For example, I designed my system with a minimum virtual-to-physical ratio of 15:1. As I need more capacity, I can add a single physical machine and build at least 15 more virtual servers.

Think about the math behind that for a moment: You can spend $12,000–$15,000 on each server 15 times — or just once. Additionally, you can spend roughly $500–$1,000 per year for maintenance contracts 15 times — or once. Say that you're going to roll out 15 servers ($12,000 each for a physical server) in a year; also assume each server costs $500 per year for a maintenance contract. And, say that the expected lifetime is five years. Look at the following three options:

Plan	Expenses	Total Costs
Physical infrastructure	Hardware: $12,000 × 15	$180,000
	Maintenance: $500 × 15 × 5	$37,500
		$217,500
Adding to an existing virtual infrastructure	Hardware: $12,000	$12,000
	Maintenance: $500 × 5	$2,500
		$14,500
Building a two-node virtual infrastructure from scratch	N+1 fault-tolerant server hardware: $12,000 × 2	$24,000
		$120,000
	SAN hardware	$7,500
	Maintenance: $500 × 3 × 5	
		$151,500
	By using N+1 you have enough excess capacity to absorb a single system failure without an outage.	

In these scenarios, regardless of whether you're rolling out a new virtual infrastructure or expanding an existing one, it pays to virtualize because of hardware and maintenance alone. And that's not even taking into account easier management, space savings, or the electrical savings from not having to cool and power as many physical servers.

I talk about capacity planning in depth in Chapter 2.

Stage 2: Designing and building your virtual infrastructure

After you know the hardware you need and can show that it more than pays for itself, you need to design your virtual infrastructure. This can include the following:

✔ Your ESX, VC, and VCB design

✔ Your virtual networking design

✔ Your backup strategy

✔ Possibly your storage area network (SAN) design

✔ Possibly your IP network design

✔ Possibly your Windows domain design

If you carefully plan ahead and design your infrastructure well, building it will be a piece of cake. Building consists of connecting the hardware and installing the software. That part is easy!

Stage 3: Virtualizing your physical machines

Converting your physical Windows servers to virtual machines is easy: Just use either the VMware Converter Starter or Enterprise edition. Converting Linux machines takes a little more work: You need to buy the Enterprise edition, make a boot disk, and convert via the CLI. This is currently only supported experimentally.

Converting Linux machines without VMware Converter Enterprise edition requires making a disk image, applying that disk image to a virtual machine disk, booting to a recovery CD, and modifying configuration files to replace the SCSI drivers with Buslogic drivers. Many different ways exist to convert Linux to a virtual machine. Try googling "P2V Linux" or "Converting Linux to virtual" to see what other people have done.

Stage 4: New ways to protect your data

If you back up your physical machine, you want to continue backing it up after it becomes virtual. I have good news for you: The method you use to back up your physical machines will work exactly the same after you virtualize them. However, you now have a new backup option that uses virtual machine snapshots.

Snapshots take a picture of your machine at a moment in time. Any changes to a machine or its data after that point in time can either be applied or discarded. The choice is yours. This creates a lot of possibilities to prevent IT headaches.

You can backup an image of your machine to tape for rapid restore using snapshots. This is how VMware Consolidated Backup works. You can use VMware Converter to restore machines backed up using snapshots. It works really well and greatly speeds disaster recovery.

Additionally, snapshots can be used to safely and easily test an upgrade without the risk of destroying your machine. Simply take a snapshot and then apply your update. If it works, apply the snapshot. If not, discard the snapshot.

Of course, you can also get into trouble with snapshots:

 ✓ If your virtual machine is a database server, shut down the database before doing anything with snapshots to prevent database corruption.

 ✓ Snapshots can be used in your backup strategy, but they do not replace your backup strategy. Do not accumulate multiple snapshots over a long period of time. They are designed to be used temporarily. This is covered in more detail in Chapter 16.

Chapter 2

Getting the Scoop on Capacity Planning

*W*hen I first looked for information on capacity planning to design my virtual environment, I was surprised how little there was. In fact, various vendors offer capacity planning services but seem to cover the concept in a shroud of mysticism.

The concept of capacity planning is simple, though. You'll soon see capacity planning is no more difficult than thinking of traffic on a highway. You might even be able to do your own capacity planning for small and even larger networks. However, on larger networks, it may be far more time effective to use capacity planning software and/or a consulting company.

In this chapter, we discuss why capacity planning is so important and what you need to cover in order to put in the right equipment the first time.

Planning: Why You Have to Do It

If you're driving somewhere, chances are you don't want to sit in traffic. Data is the same way. If you have traffic jams in your flow of data, users come away from the system with a bad experience. Users don't want to deal with a slow system, and they shouldn't have to. Because you're going to save a lot of money by virtualizing, use some that money upfront to make sure you have enough hardware capacity to support your needs.

What you need to know about tightly coupled systems

Tightly coupled systems are dependent. A problem in one system can cause trouble in another. VMware Infrastructure 3 (VI3) is a tightly coupled system that consists of storage, networking, processor, and memory subsystems. A slowdown in any one of the subsystems can affect your VI3 system as a whole.

For example, if your pool of memory runs low, at least some of your virtual machines (if not all) will run slowly. Users will be upset. If you can't read or write to disk fast enough, the best case scenario is a slowdown. And, as you can guess, a slow network means a sour user experience. Beyond that, the worst case scenario is filled with application errors and crashes.

Network Congestion

Here's a real life example: I volunteered to look at an animal shelter's network because everything was running so slowly. After five minutes of capturing network traffic with a sniffer, I saw that the problem was attributable to NETBIOS broadcast storms. There were roughly 50 nodes on the network, using NETBIOS over TCP/IP, with no WINS or DNS name server resolution. Every time one machine wanted to find another machine, it broadcast its request to every machine on the LAN. Thus, roughly 85–95 percent of the network traffic was

NETBIOS-related, which made everything run extremely slow. Implementing WINS and DNS resolved the issue.

The symptom was everything running slowly, which caused disgruntled users. The problem was an infrastructure design that was not planned properly. If you do not plan properly ahead of time, you will have a sluggish system and disgruntled users. At that point, it will not matter how much money you wound up saving, it will not be viewed as worth it.

With tightly coupled systems, a problem in one part affects the overall system performance and can leave your users extremely unhappy. Problems can be avoided with proper capacity planning and good system-design practices.

Where you are today

Chances are that your system isn't getting any smaller! And one of the beautiful things about virtualizing is that *you can add capacity as you grow*. To get to that point, though, you need to assess the capacity you're using now for your initial rollout. Put on a civil engineer's hat for a moment.

When doing capacity planning, think of your VI3 as a collection of highways, and think of yourself as a civil engineer who specializes in preventing traffic jams.

Using a traffic analogy is the easiest way to envision capacity planning. If you live near a metropolitan area, you probably understand the differences between driving into the city during rush hour and early on a Sunday morning. If I drive into Manhattan on a Sunday morning, I can be there in 35 minutes. If I drive in during rush hour, it will take at least an hour, if not two or more.

Just like computers, roads have capacity limits. The more lanes on a road, the more cars it can handle. Still, no matter how many lanes you have, there is a point at which too many cars cause the flow of traffic to slow. And if you keep adding cars, traffic begins to stop. It's all a function of volume, which itself is a function of time. Here's another factor that affects traffic: bottlenecks. Think tollbooths, construction, and accidents. In computer systems, the bottlenecks are the slowest part of the subsystem.

- ✔ **Disks:** Actually writing the data
- ✔ **Networks:** The speed of the network card or backbone
- ✔ **Processors:** Whether you have more instructions to run over a period of time that can physically run in that period of time
- ✔ **Memory:** Whether you need to use a swap file

Think of your tightly coupled VI3 as a series of highways. The more lanes on the highways, the more cars they can handle. The cars themselves are data. In fact, the entire function of the data highways is to work with your users to manipulate, store, and retrieve data.

You have the following system data highways to work with:

- ✔ Storage
- ✔ The network
- ✔ Processor power
- ✔ Memory

Figure 2-1 shows how the above components relate to physical and virtual machines. Notice the physical machines each have their own storage, networking, processing power, and memory, whereas several virtual machines share all the hardware.

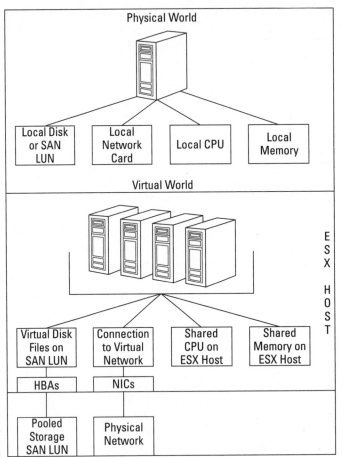

Figure 2-1:
Comparing
data
processing
resources
in physical
and virtual
worlds.

Table 2-1 provides you with a template to gather data on your servers if you
are manually planning capacity. I like to look at both the average utilization
and peak utilization per machine. While all your machines probably won't hit
peak utilization at the same time, it is good to know the worst case scenario.
After collecting information for each server, you can average it all together to
create an average server specification to use for planning.

Table 2-1	Physical Server Usage Template	
Metric	*Average*	*Peak*
Total Disk Utilization	MBps	MBps
Network Utilization	MBps	MBps
Processor Utilization (Total/Number of processors)	%	%
RAM Used	Gigs	N/A

Big takeaway: You need to know how much each of the preceding you're using *today* to design your virtual infrastructure for *tomorrow*. Your goal is to make sure there are never any traffic jams on any of your system data highways.

Where you want to be tomorrow

As I mentioned in the previous section, your system probably isn't getting smaller: It's staying the same size or getting larger. And if you're thinking about virtualizing, I bet the latter is true.

After you get past the first step (the preceding section) in figuring out where you are, it's time to look into the future and decide where you want to be. This isn't a one-size-fits-all approach, but here are a few things that can contribute to your growth rates:

- ✔ An increase in the size or number of people in your company
- ✔ An increase in the amount of storage capacity you need
- ✔ Legal and governmental regulations that may affect what data you need to store
- ✔ New systems you plan to roll out
- ✔ Your company's strategic plans
- ✔ Economic shifts that affect your company in some way

All these issues can influence

- ✔ What systems you need to add
- ✔ How much data you need to store

These two factors affect how much data your network needs to be able to push at any given time as well as how much processing power and memory you need.

Government regulations

Here's a real-world example. Look at the effect that Sarbanes-Oxley and electronic discovery have had on today's computer systems: more data to store, and more systems to govern the storage of that data. I know I always need to expand the capacity and capabilities of my Enterprise Resource Planning (ERP) and my Electronic Data Interchange (EDI) systems (all which are virtualized).

Additionally, older systems need to be updated to the latest and greatest, and new systems always need to be brought online to support business goals.

You should have an idea of the number of systems you will need to add over the next one to five years. This will affect your VMware design today as well as tomorrow. The two goals to meet are to

- **Design your system so it has more capacity that you actually need today.** How much more depends on how fast you plan to grow and will vary from situation to situation.

- **Pick the right hardware to allow you to modularly increase capacity as you need it.** Again, this will greatly vary from situation to situation.

What worked for me

I designed my system to initially allow me to add seven to ten new virtual servers before I needed another physical server and the ability to double the size of my storage area network (SAN) modularly as needed. I can also supplement my system with network attached storage (NAS) as tier-three data storage if I need to reclaim some of my second-tier serial ATA (SATA) SAN storage.

My capacity planning showed me that I needed a 2 Gbps–second SAN with Fibre Channel primary storage and SATA secondary storage. I bought half the SAN capacity up front and can add the rest as needed. Also, when I need tertiary storage, I can supplement the system with NAS. My system was designed to meet my company's needs for five years. At that point, I will have achieved a return on the investment and reassess the situation.

Capacity planning lets you know where you are today and how you will grow tomorrow. In turn, this enables you to evaluate the hardware you need to reach your goals in a cost-effective manner. Get the lowest cost yet reliable hardware that will meet your goals today and tomorrow.

What can happen if you don't plan ahead

If you fail to take the time to plan your capacity, you risk falling victim to

- **Poor performance**

    I have consultants come in to work on my ERP system. They say to me, "Wow, your system runs really well. I have seen this run extremely slow when virtualized." Most VI3 problems can be traced back to configuration and/or design flaws. Don't fall victim to poor performance because of either of these issues.

> ✔ **Overspending on hardware**
>
> If you don't plan your capacity, you can wind up spending more money than you have to on hardware. Knowing what you need and having an idea of what you will need allows you to right-size your solution right now. It also allows you to break up your capacity costs over time by adding capacity in chunks.

Live by the five Ps: Proper Planning Prevents Poor Performance.

Capturing the Right Stuff

Just like driving on a highway, you need to watch more than just the car in front of you. You need to watch traffic patterns over time and be aware of potential bottlenecks. The only way to do this is to look at what's happening on each machine over time and summate the results. This gives you your average and your maximum resource usage and also identifies when each tend to occur. Additionally, you can garner an idea of how long things stay maxed out before they normalize to average resource usage.

Record your usage patterns for at least one week to get an idea of when your machines maximize their hardware usage. A month that includes an end of quarter or end of fiscal year will likely yield much better information for your design.

Sizing up storage needs

The two aspects you need to consider when planning your storage needs are

> ✔ How much storage you need
>
> ✔ How much data you write to your storage over time (known as *disk throughput*)

From the disk throughput side, the amount of data written to and read from your hard disks over time is what counts. For Microsoft's Performance Monitor, this is disk bytes per second (Bps). Of course, transfer rates are often measured in bits per second (bps), so you need to multiply your Bps by 8 to get bps.

You should watch this metric for at least one week on each of your servers. For an even more accurate picture of your disk throughput, record this metric for a full month.

Here's how to come up with your storage design parameters:

1. **Set up your operating system's performance monitor to look at disk throughput in Bps or bps.**

   Implementing this step will vary by OS.

2. **Find the average and maximum disk throughputs over a period of time for each machine.**

   Throughputs need to be measured in bps, not Bps.

3. **Sum the average disk throughputs for each machine.**

4. **Sum the maximum disk throughputs for each machine.**

5. **Note any spikes in disk throughput and try to figure out why they happen.**

   Do spikes happen first thing in the morning when everyone logs in? Or when your databases make an online backup? Or when your nightly backup runs?

   Depending on your discoveries, you'll know whether you need to design your system to

   • Consistently handle the maximum disk throughput

   • Just handle the average disk throughput with some room to spare for temporary spikes

6. **Adjust your storage design to account for your anticipated growth.**

   The only thing you can do here is to decide what system any new server will match closely and add that throughput into your numbers from Steps 3 and 4.

   You should now have a good idea of how much disk throughput your storage subsystem needs to be able to support.

Disk throughput spikes

When I measured my network, I found that my maximum disk throughputs all happened at night: The backups take the most disk throughput. With this knowledge, I could design around average disk throughput with room for bursts and growth. My SAN has a 2 Gbps backplane, but the fabric and Fibre Channel cards can handle 4 Gbps. This gives me room to add another 2 Gbps storage enclosure if I need to — but without paying a higher price for a 4 Gbps SAN upfront.

I have a medium-sized network that's accessed from locations around the world. However, most of my systems are centralized in a corporate headquarters. That architecture allows me to use the built-in monitoring tools that come with Windows.

There is, however, the philosophical debate on whether it's better to run the monitoring tools on the system you're monitoring or to run them on a separate system. The arguments go something like this when considering whether to run monitoring tools on the same system you're monitoring:

- ✔ **Con:** You artificially increase your readings because the monitoring tools themselves use system resources.

- ✔ **Pro:** The other side argues that you *should* monitor from the local system because even though your readings are a little higher, planning for extra capacity is always a good thing.

I fall on the side of using local monitoring because I would rather have the readings slightly inflated and have a little too much capacity as opposed to possibly not having quite enough. I believe in being conservative and erring on the side of caution.

Knowing networking needs

When assessing your networking requirements, you need to know the total number of bits per second (bps) transmitted by each machine, both as a maximum and on average. You also need to know

- ✔ **What your production network equipment is rated for.** If your network equipment is 100 Mbps and your servers generate 90 Mbps of traffic, you need to upgrade to meet expansion requirements. The last thing you want is a sluggish network — that will make any networked applications appear slow to your users.

- ✔ **How saturated the network is outside your servers.** Not all your network traffic is bound for your servers. People are accessing the Internet and perhaps your utilizing VOIP. The point is, you don't just need to know how busy your servers are, but also how busy your network is to see whether you need to upgrade equipment to meet expansion goals.

Use the same six steps to gather your network metrics as you did for your disk metrics as shown here:

1. **Set up your operating system's performance monitor to look at network bytes total per second.**

   Implementing this step will vary by OS.

2. **Find the average and maximum network throughputs over a period of time for each machine.**

Throughputs need to be measured in bps, not Bps. Multiply your Bps by 8 to get bps.

3. **Sum the average network throughputs for each machine.**

4. **Sum the maximum network throughputs for each machine.**

5. **Note any spikes in disk throughput and try to figure out why they happen to see whether you need to design for the maximum throughput or average throughput with spikes.**

6. **Adjust your storage design to account for your anticipated growth.**

   Again, the only thing you can do here is to decide what system any new server will match closely and add that throughput into your numbers from Steps 3 and 4.

If your company has a separate network group, sit down with it and share your anticipated needs. You need their help to decide whether the network infrastructure can handle those needs or whether it needs to be modified.

Big takeaway: Your objective here is to see how much network capacity your servers use and how much spare capacity your network has. Combine this information with your anticipated growth to see whether you need to upgrade your network capacity.

In larger companies, interdepartmental politics can be one of the first hurdles to overcome. One way to deal with the political aspect is to develop a cross-functional design and implementation group with representational leaders from the server, networking, and storage groups.

Plan ahead

My network is wired to support 10 Gbps connections to the desktop. My company built a new building, so I wired it as 10Gig IP because that was only marginally higher in price than 1Gig IP. Currently, desktop connections are switched at 100 Mbps. Each desktop switch has a full-duplex 1 Gbps uplink to a 1 Gbps switched backbone. All the local servers connect at full duplex 1 Gbps to the backbone. Multiple NICs are used for fault tolerance and bandwidth aggregation when applicable. This setup gives me room to grow. If I ever need 10 Gbps for the servers and backbone, I just need to swap out slower switches and NICs for faster ones. I have some time before that happens.

Counting on processor power

CPU usage is the other metric to watch. This is likely the hardest part to calculate because your new ESX host servers will probably have much faster CPUs and bus speeds than your current physical servers. Additionally, newer CPUs tend to run instructions a lot more efficiently by keeping the instruction pipeline full where there used to be stalls. If you're conservative in your designs, you can discount the CPU performance increase from newer technology and design from what you already know you have. This will allow you to run more virtual machines on an ESX host than you initially thought possible.

Here's how to calculate CPU usage:

1. **Look at the overall processor utilization average and maximums for each physical server.**

2. **Calculate the averages of both.**

For example, say you have two servers — one with four CPUs and one with two CPUs, as shown in Table 2-2. The table sums the average and maximum CPU usage per CPU and then finds the average of the sum by dividing by the number of CPUs in the system. This provides an average of the mean CPU and maximum CPU usage per CPU. *Note:* In this table, I use numbers that represent underutilized machines to make a point that I share with you at the end of this section.

Table 2-2		CPU Metrics Calculation	
Server1	*CPU #*	*Average Utilization*	*Maximum Utilization*
	1	0.03	0.25
	2	0.02	0.30
	3	0.04	0.21
	4	0.01	0.27
Total		**0.10**	**1.03**
Average per CPU		**0.025**	**0.2575**
Server2	*CPU #*	*Average Utilization*	*Maximum Utilization*
	1	0.06	0.42
	2	0.07	0.44
Total		**0.13**	**0.86**
Average per CPU		**0.065**	**0.43**

The max: At this point, the data is open to some interpretation. For Server1, the average of the mean per-processor usage is 2.5%, and the average of the maximum per-processor usage is 25.75%. The number you use depends on how often the processors hit their maximums and how long they stay there.

In my example, the maximums are quick, random, and infrequent blips on the chart. This fact is actually reflected by the averages being so much lower than the maximums. I can go with the average usage for my design. If the averages are closer to the maximums, you're be better off using the maximums for your design.

The average: The average usage per processor for Server1 is 2.5%, and the average processor utilization for Server2 is 6.5%. But because the servers will be virtualized and will share hardware, you can take a weighted average to figure out what you can expect the two servers to do to a single physical processor. Assuming a total of six processors, the weighted average calculation is as follows:

$$(4/6 \times 2.5\%) + (2/6 \times 6.5\%) = 3.8\% \text{ average processor usage}$$

You can apply the same logic to the maximum usage as well:

$$(4/6 \times 25.75\%) + (2/6 \times 43\%) = 31.5\% \text{ maximum processor usage}$$

Now you have a range to work between — 3.8% and 31.5%. For this example, say you know you'll be closer to the 3.8%. With that in mind, and with a four-processor system (giving you 400% processing power), you can run quite a few virtual machines matching this profile. Calculate the range like this:

Low end = 400% / 31.5% = 12 virtual machines

High end = 400% / 3.8% = 105 virtual machines

Knowing your limits

The point that I allude to earlier in this section is something else will become a limiting factor before you can put 105 virtual machines on a single physical host. I expect that your memory, disk or network requirements will give you a much lower virtual-to-physical ratio. My system will support roughly 15 to 20 virtual machines per dual Xeon Core Duo ESX host with 16 GB of RAM. So what does that matter? Do the math: A savings of 15:1 or 20:1 on hardware and hardware maintenance costs each year translates into significant savings.

Utilizing memory

Memory has the widest allowance for a margin of error because VMware uses it so efficiently and because it is fast and easy to add more physical RAM to a machine. When it comes to assessing your memory needs, you have two choices: averaging or monitoring.

Assessing memory needs: Averaging method

The simplest way to assess your memory needs is to

1. **Sum the amount of physical memory in each server.**

2. **Divide that number by the number of servers you have.**

   That gives you the average physical memory per server. Then, after you adjust that number for growth, you know how much RAM each physical host needs as a function of the number of virtual machines you plan to run on each host.

   The downside to this approach is you will probably be designing with more memory than you actually need. However, RAM is such a small part of a server's price tag, it may be worth the speed and simplicity of using this approach.

Take a two server example again. Say one server has 1 Gig of RAM and the other has 2 Gigs. This gives you a total of 1+2 = 3 Gigs of RAM or 1.5 Gigs per machine. If you are adding 8 machines, you can put at least 10*1.5=15 Gigs of RAM in your ESX host. Again, this will be more than you need, but having some extra RAM to go with the extra CPU boost from the previous section will allow you to add more virtual machines than you initially thought you could to a single ESX host.

Assessing memory needs: Monitor method

The second way to assess your memory needs is to monitor how much available memory each server has during your monitoring period.

1. **After looking at the memory usage over your monitoring period, pick the point where the least amount of memory available.**

2. **Subtract the least amount of available memory from the total physical memory you have in each server to get the maximum amount of memory the server used during the monitoring period.**

For example, say you have a server with 4 GB of RAM (4,000 MB) that you monitor for one month. You look at the available memory in MB and find that the lowest point is 2,000 MB free. You know that your server likely has nearly twice as much RAM as it needs because the maximum amount of physical RAM that it used in a month was only half of what it had available.

After you get the maximum RAM required for each server, add it up and divide by the number of physical servers you have. This will give you the average RAM required per virtual machine. Take the number of physical machines you will virtualize, add in the new systems you plan to deploy, and multiply the total times the average RAM per virtual machine to get the total amount of physical RAM you need in your ESX host.

For example, say the average maximum amount of RAM used per physical machine is 1 Gig. You have two physical machines and plan to add 8 more. You would need a total of 1*10=10 Gigs of RAM in your ESX host.

While each method comes up with an average amount of RAM required per server, the monitor method gives you a much more accurate picture of how much RAM a server really uses. This method will let you right size your memory much better.

After you measure: Now what?

Through methods like transparent memory page sharing and balloon memory (described in Chapter 10), VMware has ways of stretching physical memory allocation for virtual machines much farther than you can with physical machines.

And, seeing as how RAM is relatively inexpensive, you can always add a percentage increase if you're nervous about not having enough. I know I did, but I still haven't needed it.

Finding Data-Gathering Tools

Many free as well as pay-for tools are available that you can use to analyze your system. The bigger the system, the more you want to use automated software or consulting services to run the analysis.

Freebies

You can find free sniffers online and use the hardware analysis tools that are built in to most operating systems, start them all up, monitor them for several weeks, and then gather and crunch all the numbers yourself. Aside from the monitoring tools built in to your OS, here are a two free network analysis tools worth checking out:

- **Network Probe: www.objectplanet.com**
- **Ethereal: www.ethereal.com**

Not for free

You can contact VMware or their partners to use VMware's capacity-planning tool. This tool performs a complete infrastructure analysis without installing any agents on your physical machines. You can also model different scenarios to see what type of impact they have. If you are doing a large scale virtualization project, you should utilize this tool. You can buy it yourself and take a class on using it or hire a VMware partner to utilize this tool to help you design your system.

Making life easier

I wanted to do my own capacity planning so I'd get experience doing this as well as getting to really know the minute details and test my modeling theories. However, the next time I undertake this, I think I'd hire someone or buy and learn how to use VMware's capacity planning tool. To me, once you understand the underlying theory, it is just easier to utilize a tool that helps automate your capacity planning than tracking and calculating everything out yourself. However, both methods work so the choice is yours.

Where the Money Hits the Pavement: Hardware

After you understand your current storage, networking, processor, and memory needs, you have to adjust them for growth. That's what this chapter has shown so far.

Then, it's time to find the hardware that meets your specifications, deciding what hardware will fit best in your situation. I offer the following general tips:

- ✔ **Know exactly what you want to accomplish before talking to salespeople.** This will prevent you from buying the wrong solutions or spending too much.

- ✔ **Grill the salespeople until you feel comfortable their solution will meet your needs.** If not, you can rule it out. VMware can require a sizable price when you build everything from scratch. You need to know that the solution you choose will work in your environment.

- ✔ **Right-size your hardware to economize.** You do not want to underspend and not have enough hardware. Similarly, you do not want to overspend and have a great deal of unused capacity.

✔ **Look at each piece of hardware with an eye for expanding your resources modularly as you need to.** This will let you buy less hardware up front and expand it as your business requires it.

✔ **Make sure anything you want to buy is on the VMware-certified Hardware Compatibility List (HCL).** While the technical support people at VMware are extremely helpful and would likely give their best to solve a problem, they are under no obligation to support hardware that has not been certified.

✔ **Always buy with an eye for high fault tolerance (Discussed in Part IV).** All your hardware will fail at some point. Be prepared for hardware failures ahead of time.

✔ **Understand the bottlenecks and limitations of any hardware before you buy it.** Every system has a bottleneck that limits its capacity. You need to know where this is ahead of time.

✔ **Buy from a company you know and trust.** I have called companies inquiring about buying something only to have a salesman call me back weeks later. With that lack of interest in selling, imagine what the customer service is like after you buy. You want a vendor you can count on.

✔ **Whatever you buy, make sure you get a support contract with it that includes fast hardware replacement if something fails.** Generally, the faster and more available during off hours the response time is, the more it costs. I like fast technical support by phone and four-hour turn-around times myself. For Dell, I usually purchase silver or gold support. That allows me to bypass L1 technical support and speak directly with someone who can help me solve my problem quickly. Additionally, when a piece of hardware dies, I lose my fault tolerance, so I like to be able to replace the faulty hardware within four hours.

Chapter 3

Knowing Your Storage Options

The type of storage you choose to run your virtual infrastructure on makes a big difference in how well your system will work. You have several choices for protocols and drive technology, and all of them have their advantages and disadvantages. You need to decide what is the correct fit for your situation. This chapter describes the various options available. Before discussing any options, you need to understand SCSI anatomy.

SCSI Anatomy 101

To fully understand your storage options and make informed decisions, you need to understand SCSI. The rest of this chapter has some technical details, but they shouldn't be too painful.

Like the Open Systems Interconnection (OSI) networking model, SCSI makes use of several layers offering different functionality. The official name for this model is the *SCSI Architecture Model (SAM),* and a simplified version is shown in Figure 3-1. This three layer model consists of commands, transport protocols, and interconnects:

✔ **SCSI commands:** The commands are actual directives to send or retrieve data from a SCSI device. Commands can be shared and common to all SCSI devices, or they can be specific to a particular type of SCSI device like a hard drive.

✔ **SCSI transport protocols:** These protocols are responsible for grouping data into chunks for transmission, monitoring the transmission for success, and picking what data blocks go to which device. Some protocols you'll likely be interested in are iSCSI and Fibre Channel, both of which are covered later in this chapter.

✔ **SCSI interconnects:** These — the actual SCSI cards in a system — are responsible for the signaling that actually transmits the data. All SCSI devices are identified by a three-part name comprising a bus, a target, and a LUN:

- *Bus:* A *bus* is a SCSI card in your system. It can be a parallel card connecting to a local disk, a Fibre Channel card, or a NIC connecting to iSCSI storage.

- *Target:* These are single storage resources.

- *LUN: Logical Unit Numbers* are the SCSI client living inside the target. A LUN can be a single disk or a group of disks in some sort of RAID configuration.

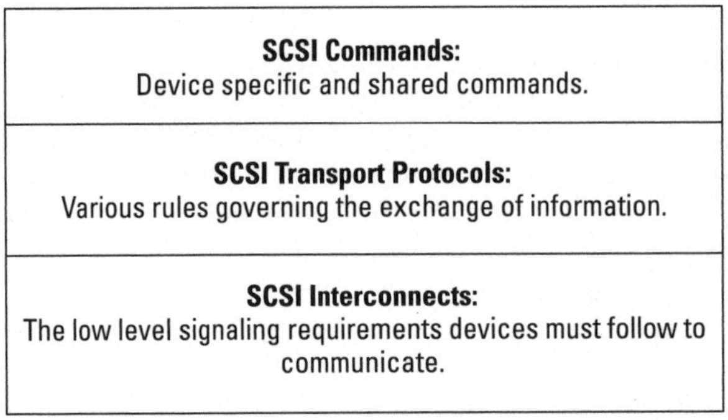

SCSI Commands:
Device specific and shared commands.
SCSI Transport Protocols:
Various rules governing the exchange of information.
SCSI Interconnects:
The low level signaling requirements devices must follow to communicate.

Figure 3-1:
The SCSI
architecture
model.

SCSI communications are considered client/server. The clients are called *initiators,* and the servers are called *targets.* If an application wants to write to a SCSI disk, the initiator issues a write command. The command is routed over the appropriate interconnect, using that interconnect's protocol. The target executes the command and sends back a response to let the initiator know whether its request was successful.

Files, blocks, and protocols

When you store data on a hard disk, it is stored in blocks. Blocks are simply a fixed size amount of data. A file is a variable size object that consists of several data blocks. When transferring data, you can use either a block level or file level protocol. SCSI is referred to as a block level protocol, whereas Network Attached Storage generally uses file level protocols.

Here's how to compare block-level and file-level protocols:

✔ **Block-level:** SCSI is a block-level protocol. That is, your data is dealt with how it's stored on the hard disk — in fixed-size blocks. SANs and iSCSI transmit data in blocks.

✔ **File-level:** File-level protocols, on the other hand, read and write data in variable length files. Your files are later broken into blocks and stored on disk, but only after they're transferred as variable length files. Network Attached Storage (NAS) uses file level protocols (either NFS or CIFS).

To boot or not to boot from a SAN: That is the question

You'll need to decide whether or not you want to boot ESX from a SAN before you install the server. (ESX installation is covered in Chapter 5.) You can boot from SAN with both Fibre Channel and iSCSI (each have a section in this chapter). The only iSCSI catch is that you need to use a hardware initiator instead of a software initiator (covered later in this chapter in the section on iSCSI).

No matter how you boot your system, you will likely be using the SCSI command model. The only difference in your SAN options is how the commands reach your disks. If using local SCSI, the commands travel through your SCSI controller cart to your disk. If you are using Fibre Channel or iSCSI, the commands are encapsulated in a communication protocol and sent to remote disks. This is described in more detail in the sections on Fiber Channel and iSCSI.

Here are the pros and cons of booting from a SAN:

✔ **Pro:** The advantage of booting from a SAN is you don't necessarily need hard drives in your server. Local drives probably won't be Fibre Channel and will therefore have a higher probability of failure.

✔ **Con:** The disadvantage of booting from a SAN is your that ESX doesn't have local drives because it's now sharing bandwidth with the rest of your SAN traffic. Also, you won't be able to boot your server if you have SAN issues that prevent you from reaching the boot LUN.

Using Local SCSI: Why It Works Well

Local SCSI refers to booting your ESX on a local hard disk instead of booting from SAN. Both methods work and the one you pick will depend on your situation and personal preferences. If you use ESXi, you can even boot from a chip and configure your system for the first time through a menu-driven interface.

Why I like local SCSI

I like using local SCSI. This is a my preference, though, and might not be right for your situation.

I prefer clean delineations. I like my server's operating system to reside on a mirrored drive on my server. I don't want to be dependent on an external subsystem to boot my server. Admittedly, all these reasons are preferences, but all in all, I feel that a system is simpler if the server OS is local.

Simple systems have less problems and are easier to troubleshoot when things go wrong.

I've helped others troubleshoot poorly designed complex systems that they somehow inherited. It's never pretty. You should always strive to design as simple a system as possible to meet your needs. To me, that means using local SCSI to boot the server from.

Lastly (and this is a good logical reason to use local storage), you have greater flexibility. If you suddenly decide to use a shared storage Microsoft cluster with VMware, a local boot drive is the only supported configuration.

As of version 3.5, you can boot from local serial ATA (SATA) drives instead of only SCSI drives.

Fibre Channel: The Speed Demon

Fibre Channel SANs are a fast, fault-tolerant, and mature technology. Fibre Channel started in 1985 and got ANSI approval in 1994. A Fibre Channel SAN can be deployed in three physical topologies:

- **Point-to-point:** In this setup (shown in Figure 3-2), two devices are connected directly to each other. Think of an Ethernet crossover cable connecting two computers.

- ✓ **Arbitrated loop:** Device 1 connects to Device 2, which connects to Device 3, and so on until the *n*th device connects back to Device 1 (see Figure 3-3). Think of a Token Ring network.

- ✓ **Switched fabric:** All the devices are connected to Fibre Channel switches that provide optimized data paths (see Figure 3-4). Think of a modern, switched Ethernet network.

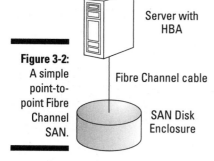

Figure 3-2:
A simple point-to-point Fibre Channel SAN.

Figure 3-3:
An arbi-trated loop of disks.

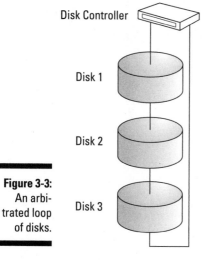

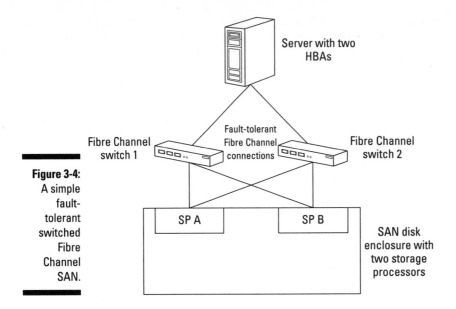

Figure 3-4:
A simple
fault-
tolerant
switched
Fibre
Channel
SAN.

The first SAN on the block

Switched Fibre Channel SANs were the first SAN technology fully supported by VMware. Figure 3-5 shows a simple VMware configuration with a switched Fibre Channel SAN.

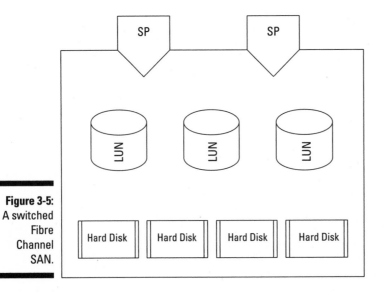

Figure 3-5:
A switched
Fibre
Channel
SAN.

Notice the two ESX hosts, each with two host bus adapters (HBAs) connected to two Fibre Channel switches. Switches form the fabric for the network.

The fabric connects to two storage processors (SP) that typically have some sort of high-speed cache. The SPs control the disk enclosure as well as data reads and writes.

Your disk enclosure houses the raw hard drives used to create LUNs of storage. The LUNs show up as raw disk space to your servers.

Every device that connects to a Fibre Channel SAN has a unique address called a *World Wide Name (WWN)*. This is similar to a Media Access Control (MAC) address.

As of version 3.5, iSCSI SANs are fully supported. Read more about this in the section "Considering Whether to Use iSCSI," later in this chapter.

What's nice about the setup in Figure 3-5 is that even if several parts fail, your system can still run. You might lose an HBA in a server, a switch, a storage processor, or a disk — and still run. In fact, if you're running a VMware cluster (two or more ESX hosts that can access the same virtual machines), you can lose an entire server, and all the virtual machines will move to one of the remaining servers. Clusters are covered in Chapter 12.

For your production environment, always build for fault tolerance. This simple philosophy has saved my users and me hours of pain many times over.

When it comes to one of your SCSI initiators finding one of your targets, a typical SCSI addressing scheme is used in Fibre Channel. In my example, the address for the second partition on the third LUN of my first storage processor looks like this: VMHBA1:0:2:1.

Here is a breakdown of the path:

- ✔ **VMHBA1:** The first true HBA in my system.

  VMHBA0 is my local SCSI adapter and isn't really a Fibre Channel or an iSCSI HBA.

- ✔ **0:** The first storage processor.

  Computer engineers like to start counting from 0 instead of 1. (This is because — and I say this lovingly — scientists, in general, tend to be a bit eccentric and bizarre!)

- ✔ **2:** The third LUN

- ✔ **1:** The second partition on the LUN

Weighing the advantages and disadvantages of Fibre Channel SANs

You gain many advantages if you decide to use a Fibre Channel SAN:

- **Mature:** It is a mature technology, meaning most of the bugs have already been worked out.
- **Fault tolerance:** It can be set up for extreme fault tolerance.
- **Speed:** It is typically faster than iSCSI.
- **Efficiency:** Frame for frame, Fibre Channel is more efficient than iSCSI. If you put as much data as you can into each type of frame, an Ethernet frame has 184 bits of overhead for 368 bits of data. That's 50 percent overhead. On the other hand, a Fibre Channel frame has 288 bits of overhead for 2112 bits of data: only 13 percent overhead.
- **Security:** Using *zoning* and *LUN masking* (methods of limiting which devices can see each other), you can hide parts of the SAN from different servers for security and to prevent accidental overwriting of data.

Here are the disadvantages:

- **Expense:** Using Fibre Channel can be a great deal more expensive than using iSCSI. However, when I was comparing prices, iSCSI was almost as expensive as Fibre Channel. However, you have a lot more options for the price point. Fibre Channel options are typically sold á la carte, whereas iSCSI typically includes them.
- **Gateways:** You need gateways to route Fibre Channel traffic over IP networks, which requires more hardware and software to buy and support.
- **More to learn:** Aside from requiring new hardware, you need to learn a new technology instead of using the one you already know — Ethernet.

Considering Whether to Use iSCSI

Some of you are likely thinking, "What's he talking about? iSCSI is much cheaper than Fibre Channel." Yes, it certainly can be. You can build an iSCSI SAN for 60 to 70 percent of the price of a Fibre Channel system — that is, as long as performance and fault tolerance aren't high on your priority list.

When I priced a system, I was looking at building a separate IP network just for disk traffic. That required two high-end switches, two TCP/IP Offload Engine (TOE) cards for each server to prevent a performance hit on the CPU, and a high-end disk enclosure. iSCSI cost about 20 percent less. Unfortunately, when I wanted to virtualize, Virtual Consolidated Backup (VCB) from iSCSI storage was not supported.

Version 3.5 provides support for VCB from your iSCSI SANs.

The new SAN on the block

iSCSI is a newer technology. However, like Fibre Channel, iSCSI puts SCSI commands and data blocks into network frames. The difference is that iSCSI uses TCP/IP instead of Fibre Channel Protocol (FCP). To frame data, iSCSI needs a protocol initiator. This can be

- ✔ **Software based:** Think Microsoft's iSCSI Software Initiator.
- ✔ **Hardware based:** Think TOE card.

If you're using a network TOE card as a hardware initiator, the card is referred to as an *iSCSI HBA*.

You can't use both software and hardware initiators at the same time.

Figure 3-6 shows a fault-tolerant VMware Infrastructure with an iSCSI SAN. Just like the Fibre Channel SAN, you can lose various parts of your SAN, and your system will still continue to run.

It's not a question of "if" something will fail, but "when" something will fail. I can't stress enough how important redundancy is!

Because iSCSI uses a TCP/IP network to transport your disk data, security is now a concern. VMware Infrastructure 3 (VI3) supports CHAP (Challenge-Handshake Authentication Protocol) authentication. Although CHAP works with both software and hardware iSCSI initiators, it is disabled by default. When enabled, the target authenticates the initiator.

To enable CHAP, you need to look at the properties of your iSCSI initiator and click configure. Choose a CHAP initiator name and enter the shared secret.

Just because you enable CHAP doesn't mean that your data stream is encrypted. CHAP forces authentication only between target and initiator without transmitting a password. It doesn't provide a way to encrypt your data stream.

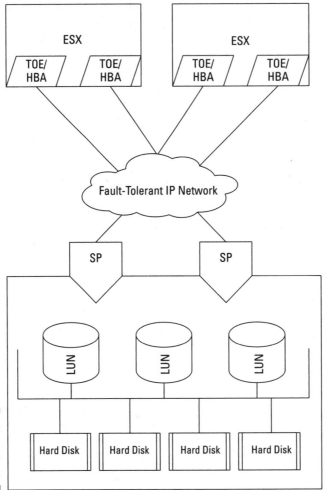

Figure 3-6:
iSCSI SAN
compo-
nents.

Communications in an iSCSI SAN

iSCSI nodes are iSCSI devices. They can be initiators, targets, or both. Regardless, they need names and IP addresses. An iSCSI qualified name (IQN) name looks like this

```
iqn.2001-05.com.rmdom:storage1
```

The name has several parts, separated by periods:

✔ iqn.

✔ The year and month the domain was registered: 2001-05.

✔ A valid, reversed domain name: com.rmdom.

✔ An iSCSI alias: storage1

You might wonder how an initiator on a server finds a target somewhere in an IP network. In order for initiators to find iSCSI targets, you must go through an iSCSI discovery process. This process can be a static configuration or a query method called SendTargets.

✔ **Static configuration method:** Target IP address, port number, and target name are kept in a list available to your initiator. In essence, all targets are prediscovered. This is like using an LMhosts table for IP address lookup instead of a DNS server. If you've ever maintained IP addresses and names manually, you know that this is not the way to do it. This method requires you to manually update the list every time you make a change.

✔ **Query method:** Your initiator uses an iSCSI device's IP address and port number to establish an IP session. Your initiator then sends the SCSI SendTargets command. The device, in turn, replies with its target information as well as any other target information it is aware of.

Software initiators support only SendTargets discovery. iSCSI HBAs support both static and query methods.

Here is one other caveat to using iSCSI. If you're using the software initiator, both the VMkernel (which managed hardware access) and the Service Console (which provides the management interface) need to be able to reach your iSCSI storage. This is because the Service Console talks to the iSCSI daemon called vmkiscsid, and the VMkernel authenticates and transfers data to iSCSI devices.The kernel and Service Console are covered in Chapter 4.

You can allow both to see your iSCSI devices in one of two ways:

✔ Have the proper IP routing in place so that a VMkernel on one virtual switch (Covered in Chapter 7) and a Service Console on another virtual switch can both see your iSCSI storage. This is shown in Figure 3-7.

✔ Create a virtual switch on the same subnet as your iSCSI storage with both a Service Console and VMkernel port on it. This is shown in Figure 3-8.

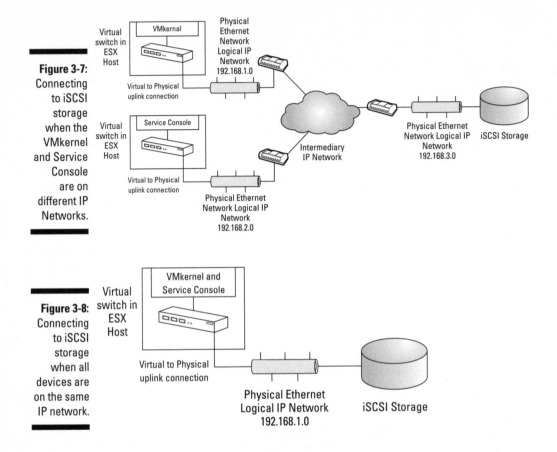

Figure 3-7: Connecting to iSCSI storage when the VMkernel and Service Console are on different IP Networks.

Figure 3-8: Connecting to iSCSI storage when all devices are on the same IP network.

Weighing the advantages and disadvantages of iSCSI

As of version 3.5, iSCSI is probably a better fit for most deployments because of the cost savings. The only time it is worth spending the extra money on fibre channel technology is if you anticipate sustained high disk throughput. Fibre channel is a lot more efficient in that situation. However, using iSCSI has the following advantages over using Fibre Channel:

✔ **Cost:** iSCSI can cost anywhere from 20 to 70 percent less than Fibre Channel, depending on the equipment and configuration. For high-end equipment in a fault-tolerant setup, you save a great deal less.

✔ **Fault tolerance:** iSCSI can be set up to be extremely fault tolerant by using redundant Ethernet switches and disk enclosures.

- ✔ **Routing:** Because it's based on TCP/IP, iSCSI is already routable over IP networks without requiring an additional gateway.

- ✔ **Familiarity:** iSCSI uses the standard TCP/IP protocol you already know and love, used over the equipment you're already familiar with.

Here are some disadvantages to using iSCSI:

- ✔ **Speed:** iSCSI speed is dependent on the underlying network's speed. Depending on traffic, it can be a great deal slower than Fibre Channel.

- ✔ **Efficiency:** iSCSI has a higher percentage of overhead for data transmissions than Fibre Channel. This is because the percentage of data to the size of the frame is much smaller with TCP/IP vs. FCP so you have to transmit more bits to move the same amount of data.

- ✔ **Stolen CPU cycles:** If you're using a software initiator, it will steal some CPU performance. How much performance is stolen depends on your setup and how many packets you're transmitting. The only way to remove this incalculable variable is to use a hardware initiator.

- ✔ **Security:** It's easier to hack iSCSI than Fibre Channel, especially if your regular data network doubles as your SAN transport (not recommended). The safest setup is to create a separate physical and logical IP network for your iSCSI traffic.

Network Attached Storage: The Good and the Bad

Up until this point, I've discussed only block-level storage equipment. Comparatively, *Network Attached Storage (NAS)* is a file-level protocol. Instead of looking at all data as fixed length blocks, data is viewed as variable length files.

Understanding NAS

A NAS device is typically a plug-and-play storage device that supports one or both of two protocols:

- ✔ **Network File System (NFS):** Open source
- ✔ **Server Message Block (SMB):** SMB is Windows Networking.

VMware uses the NFS protocol because it's more of an open standard than SMB. Most of VMware's datacenter features, such as VMotion and DRS, work with NAS. However, VCB does not.

The history of CIFS

SMB is often called *Common Internet File System (CIFS)*. How do you get CIFS from SMB? Well, SMB was originally invented by IBM to use the DOS Interrupt 33 for networked file systems. Microsoft merged SMB with its LAN Manager product in 1990. Although it was originally designed to run on top of NetBIOS, SMB was later adapted to use TCP (port 445) in Windows 2000. In 1996, Microsoft launched a campaign to rename SMB to CIFS. They submitted partial drafts to the IETF but have since let them expire. However, the name CIFS stuck around even though Vista officially uses SMB 2.0.

While I'm on the topic, the Samba project was created to reverse-engineer the SMB protocol to provide a free implementation of SMB on non-Windows based machines. You can have an awful lot of fun trying to make a Samba client talk to a Windows machine. My home network uses OS X and Samba to offer file shares to my Windows clients. A Mac serving Windows: How's that for ironic?

NAS devices have their own built-in operating system that handles networking and converts files to blocks for local storage. NAS is generally considered a much slower way to store and retrieve data. This lack of speed happens for these two primary reasons:

- ✔ **Inherent delays:** You're usually using your production network to transfer the data, so it's subject to load-induced delays.
- ✔ **Conversion overhead:** SCSI speaks in blocks, and NAS speaks in files. You have to convert between the two, which introduces overhead. In fact, if NAS dealt with data in blocks, you could argue that it would be iSCSI!

In order for VMware to use NAS, you need the following:

- ✔ A **VMKernel port** on the virtual switch that connects to the NAS.
- ✔ A **NAS share** with the following:
  - • *Read/write access*
  - • *The ability for VMware to run as root user*

    Use the `no_root_squash` parameter when creating the share.
  - • *The restraint of writing all files before telling the client the file write has completed*

    Use the `sync` parameter when creating the share.

Setting this up will vary from platform to platform. Consult your hardware's documentation for further information.

Comparing advantages and disadvantages of NAS

As I've suggested, you can use NAS for several things. Yes, you can host virtual machines on NAS, but if they are high I/O machines, you will likely have problems. Here are some of the more appropriate and advantageous uses for NAS:

✔ **Relatively inexpensive storage:** NAS is great for anything that doesn't require high throughput. You can store your ISO files on NAS, and it also makes great archive or tier-three storage.

✔ **Ease of use:** NAS is extremely easy to deploy and connect to.

Here are the two main disadvantages to using NAS:

✔ **Limited throughput:** NAS doesn't have as high of throughput as iSCSI or Fibre Channel although some newer NAS devices are breaking that stereotype. These devices are called *high performance NAS.* While no standardized definition exists, high performance NAS generally offers more Ethernet ports, cache, and processing power. BlueArc has some amazingly fast NAS devices (www.bluearc.com).

✔ **Backups:** NAS doesn't work with VCBs.

SAN and NAS Best Practices

The following is a list of SAN and NAS best practices:

✔ Use fault-tolerant HBA cards in each server.

✔ Use fault-tolerant Fibre or Ethernet switches in your SANs.

✔ Use fault-tolerant RAID configurations for all LUNs.

✔ Use hardware iSCSI initiators for better CPU performance.

✔ Set up iSCSI on a separate physical network.

✔ Use Fibre Channel SANs when high throughput is your primary concern.

✔ Use iSCSI if cost concerns trump throughput concerns.

✔ Only use NAS for purposes that require lower throughput.

✔ Only use SAN hardware that has been certified by VMware. (Consult the VMware Hardware Compatibility List [HCL].)

✔ Put higher I/O machines on different LUNs and even different cluster nodes for optimal performance.

✔ Provide different active paths to storage for higher I/O machines to maximize performance if your SAN supports it.

✔ Enable ISL trunking on fabric SAN switches to aggregate bandwidth.

✔ Assign a unique zone between the ESX initiator and the storage processor ports to isolate initiators from Fibre Channel SAN Register State Change Notification disruptions.

Part II

Setting Up ESX Hosts

The 5th Wave   By Rich Tennant

"I guess you could say this is the hub of our network."

In this part . . .

This part covers the next layer of your virtual onion —
the ESX Server itself. Chapter 4 walks you through the
ESX architecture. Chapter 5 assists you with a full-blown
installation.

Chapter 4

ESX: The Brawn Behind the Brains

*A*t the heart of your VMware Infrastructure 3 is your ESX. *ESX servers,* referred to as *ESX hosts,* manage the sharing of resources between your virtual machines. Every option that VMware offers builds on your ESX host foundation.

This chapter covers the parts that make up ESX and how they work together to provide you with a stable and scalable virtual environment. This includes everything from the design of an ESX host and building for fault-tolerance to picking the right hardware to meet your needs.

Checking Out ESX Host Anatomy

ESX is one of the best written pieces of software I have seen. Before going further, a quick distinction needs to be made: *ESX* is an operating system (two actually) and *ESX hosts* are server hardware that is running the ESX operating systems. ESX offers rock-solid reliability and can truly drive down your computing costs. It does this through a combination of well-written software and thoroughly tested hardware. And VMware is the industry leader, setting the trends and direction for virtualization while the rest of the players play catch up. Figure 4-1 shows the relationship between ESX hosts and virtual machines.

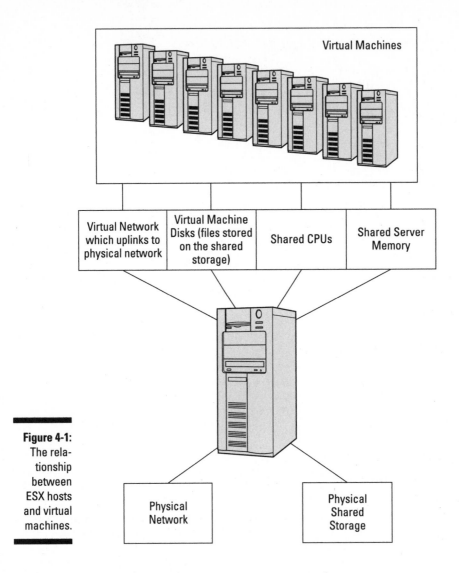

Figure 4-1:
The rela-
tionship
between
ESX hosts
and virtual
machines.

One host is never enough

I can not stress this enough: Hardware failure is not a matter of *if* it will
happen: It is a matter of *when* it will happen. The only way to compensate
for it is through a fault-tolerance system design, which is really a layered
combination of fault-tolerant subsystems.

Read about creating a fault-tolerant system design in Chapter 12.

Think of if this way: Your disks are in a RAID configuration in case one disk dies. And you have more than one NIC and power supply in your servers in case either die. VMware allows you to use a concept similar to RAID, which I call a Redundant Array of Moderately Expensive Servers (RAMES).

When you combine VirtualCenter, a SAN, and two or more ESX hosts, you can create an extremely fault-tolerant environment. However, the servers themselves don't have to be as fault tolerant as a standalone server, which means that they cost less. You can even get away configuring a server with a single power supply and no disks if you wanted to. However, I recommend using a minimum fault-tolerant network cards and host bus adapters (HBAs) because they give you a lot more flexibility for load-leveling and hardware failures.

When you have ESX hosts set up as a RAMES and then one host fails, all the virtual machines on it will move to another host. Depending on the severity of the failure, this can be done with no interruption to the virtual machines. The worst-case scenario is a brief interruption of service. The mechanisms VMware uses when a host dies are VMotion and HA. VMotion moves running machines from one ESX host to another when it detects a communications problem without interruption. HA restarts virtual machines on a new ESX host if the one they are running on suddenly dies. HA does cause a brief outage, but it is under a few minutes — rebuilding a server and restoring data can take hours. VMotion and HA are covered in more detail in Chapter 12.

So, when planning your VMware Infrastructure 3, one server will not be enough. Although you certainly could use an extremely fault-tolerant single server to run your virtual machines on, you would lose flexibility in two ways:

- ✔ **You won't have a fault-tolerant motherboard.** If something goes wrong there, all your virtual machines will stop working.

- ✔ **You lose your ability to load-balance virtual machines across physical machines.** If you have VirtualCenter and two or more ESX hosts, VMware can automatically move virtual machines between hosts so that no one host is over-utilized. To do this, VMware utilizes Distributed Resource Scheduler (DRS). Setting up DRS is covered in Chapter 12.

The minimum number of servers I would recommend for a virtual infrastructure is three: two servers for ESX hosts, and one server for VirtualCenter.

Figure 4-2 shows a simple VMware system. Although you can run VirtualCenter on a virtual machine if you want to, I feel that it's better to keep it on a separate physical machine. If you have problems with your virtual infrastructure and your VirtualCenter is running on a virtual machine, you might have a more difficult time isolating and solving the problem. The good news is most VMware problems are attributable to hardware or the system configuration, and not bugs in the software.

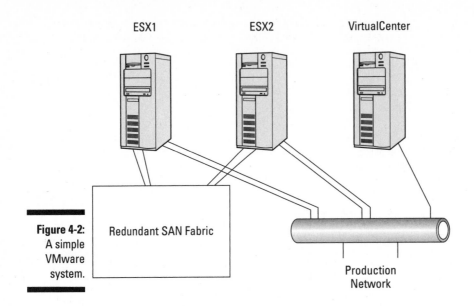

ESX1   ESX2   VirtualCenter

Figure 4-2:
A simple
VMware
system.

Redundant SAN Fabric

Production
Network

Big host or small host: It all depends

From your capacity planning (see Chapter 2), you know how much power you need to virtualize your machines. The question becomes whether you want to provide that power with fewer, beefier servers; or, use many less-powerful servers. I lean toward using more servers.

✔ **Pros**

- The more servers you have, the lower the percentage of overall processing power you lose if one server dies.

- You can spread out the cost of hardware purchasing over a longer period of time by building your system modularly as you need more power.

- You can easily use rack mount or blade systems with the "more servers" approach.

    If you go with a blade-based system, you might not have as many I/O ports as you want. Just make sure that if you need dual HBAs and four NICs per server, your blade system will allow it.

✔ **Cons**

- One potential downside to the "more server" approach is technological obsolescence. For virtual machines to move from one host to another without any service interruption, each host needs to use the same processor instruction set. At some point in time, the first servers you buy are going to have CPUs that are no longer produced, and you will only be able to buy ones with different instruction sets.

• You have more hardware, which requires more hardware service contracts.

• You have more servers to manage.

The other option is to purchase fewer, extremely powerful servers (I call them "super servers") and run more virtual machines on them. Here are the pros and cons of this approach.

✔ Pros

• This option lowers the total number of servers you need to maintain hardware contracts for.

• You have less servers to manage.

✔ Cons

• If you lose a server, you lose a much higher percentage of your total processing power.

• You can potentially run into bottlenecks for network and disk traffic because of a limited number of slots for NICs and HBAs if you put as many virtual machines on a super server as the CPU and RAM can use. This will force you to buy another server and leave the existing one underused as far as processing power goes.

Each virtualization project is different. You need to decide which option gives you the best fit and the most bang for your buck. As far as VMware licensing goes, you are paying a fee *per CPU,* not *per CPU core.* Thus, two systems with two dual-core processors will cost the same as a single system with four dual-core processors or a system with four single-core processors. Some of the factors for you to consider for server sizes are

✔ **Equipment reuse:** Can you reuse some of what you already have?

✔ **Physical space:** Can you fit many smaller servers in your space constraints or only a few?

✔ **Power:** Do you have enough power for many smaller servers or can you only accommodate a few large ones?

✔ **Number of cards:** How many NICs and HBAs do you need per server and will the hardware you plan on using meet your needs?

✔ **Cost:** A large amount of RAM for a beefy server can even cost as much as an entire small server!

Getting Two Operating Systems in One

ESX actually loads two operating systems: the VMkernel in high memory, and the Service Console in low memory. VMkernel is used for sharing resources, and the Service Console is for management functions.

VMkernel

The VMkernel loads in high memory and controls all your hardware. It is an *abstraction layer* (hiding the implementation details of hardware sharing) that virtualizes hardware, as shown in Figure 4-3. The VMkernel assumes that all the hardware in your system is functioning properly. Any faulty hardware can cause it to crash, yielding the Purple Screen of Death (PSOD). Additionally, the VMkernel controls all scheduling for the ESX machine. This includes virtual machines and the Service Console (covered in the next section).

The VMkernel was built from the ground up to be a lean, mean, scheduling machine. This means it runs extremely fast and efficiently. Of course, trade-offs had to be made for speed. This is one of the reasons the VMkernel just assumes all the hardware is working instead of using resources to monitor and check the hardware.

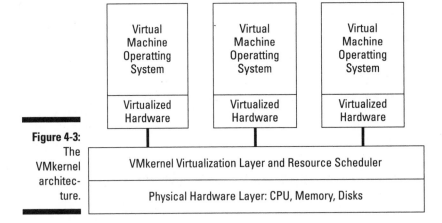

Figure 4-3: The VMkernel architecture.

Service Console

Your ESX host's Service Console provides an environment to monitor and administer your ESX host. The Service Console is based on Red Hat Enterprise Linux but is highly modified. All services that are unnecessary for management are stripped off, and all client communications are secured through *SSL* (secure sockets layer).

Your Service Console has its own firewall, and all unnecessary ports are initially closed. This is a security consideration because compromising the Service Console compromises your server's and virtual machine's security as well. The Service Console's architecture is shown in Figure 4-4.

ESXi does not have a Service Console and VMware plans to remove the Service Console from ESX down the road.

Service Console	
Firewall	Web Server
Other Services Via API	SNMP

VMkernel Virtualization Layer and Resource Scheduler
Physical Hardware Layer: CPU, Memory, Disks

Figure 4-4: The Service Console components.

ESX is Like an Octopus

ESX touches many different areas of your infrastructure, including your servers (which are now virtualized), network, and storage systems. You need to give careful consideration to integrating ESX into your existing environment.

How ESX touches your network

ESX *abstracts* — creates a software only switch that allows multiple VMs to use a single physical NIC — the network cards in your physical server. You need to create at least one virtual switch in each ESX host. The virtual switch gets assigned one or more of your host's network adapters so that it can communicate with your physical network. Virtual machines plug into virtual switches so that they, too, can communicate with the physical world. You can also add Service Console ports to a virtual switch, as well as VMkernel ports. Virtual switches and networking are covered in Chapter 7. The networking model is shown in Figure 4-5.

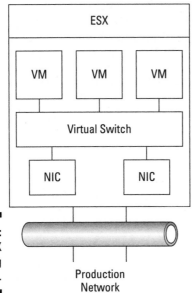

Figure 4-5:
The ESX
networking
model.

ESX controls your storage

ESX will run on local SCSI, but if you want to cluster servers for fault tolerance, you need to use some sort of shared storage. Fibre Channel or iSCSI SANs are your best bet. (You can read about those in Chapter 3.)

ESX formats share storage with the Virtual Machine File System (VMFS). This file system allows multiple ESX hosts to access it at the same time. However, the files that make up a virtual machine itself are locked by the server that opens them so only one server can run a virtual machine at any time. Storage is covered in greater detail in Chapter 3.

Disk Partitions: Please No More Than Four

Because Linux is an x86-based OS, so are the ESX operating systems. And there is a disk limitation that is a function of the x86 partition table: You can have only four primary partitions which means four drives on a disk. Fortunately, here's a workaround with which you can create more than four drives if you need them.

Primary partitions

Primary partitions cannot be subdivided. They are the partitions on which you install your operating system. For an operating system to boot, the primary partition that it's installed on must be marked as *active*. An x86 machine can have either

- ✔ Between one and four primary partitions
- ✔ As many as three primary partitions and one extended partition

Extended partitions

Unlike primary partitions, extended partitions can be divided into logical chunks of space called *logical drives*. Often, they are assigned drive letters, but not always. With Red Hat Linux, an x86-based IDE drive can have up to 63 partitions, and a SCSI disk can have up to 15. Figure 4-6 shows a fully partitioned hard disk.

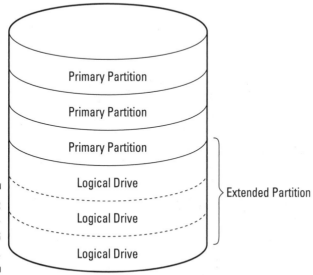

Figure 4-6:
A fully partitioned x86 IDE drive.

Chapter 5

ESX Installation — Now the Fun Begins

*E*SX hosts are a critical piece of VMware Infrastructure 3. They manage and provide all the hardware that your virtual machines use. Long-term VMware users might tell you the best way to get things done is through the command line, but the latest version of the system (3 and on) is designed to be managed by a GUI interface. VI Client provides that interface. So without further ado, it is time to install — and connect to — your ESX.

What You Need to Know Before You Install

By themselves, ESX host installations are extremely easy. You'll have to invest only about 15 minutes from the time you pop in the CD to when the installation is finished. (I wish all installations were like this!) However, you'll have to put in some time upfront to get to the point of installation.

Before you're ready to install your ESX host, you need to have completed your capacity planning (Chapter 2), SAN design (this is dependent on your individual situation), and your VMware design (Part IV of this book). Additionally, you should have a fully functional IP network infrastructure (this is also dependent on your individual situation). The preinstall steps are what really take up a lot of time!

You also need to know that after you have completed the installation, you will have a server that is running two distinct operating systems:

- ✔ **VMkernel:** The VMkernel loads in high memory and controls all the hardware. Furthermore, it assumes that all the hardware in the system is functioning properly. *Be advised:* Any faulty hardware can crash the VMkernel! The VMkernel also controls all scheduling for the ESX machine. This includes virtual machines and the service console.

- ✔ **Service Console:** The Service Console provides the administrative interface to your ESX. Your Service Console is a modified Linux distribution

ESX shares memory and CPU resources

Your ESX hosts are full of trickery! They fool all the virtual machines running on them into thinking they have their own hardware. The VMkernel intercepts hardware calls and schedules the resources for them. The virtual machines never even know they don't have exclusive use of the hardware. Heck, they don't even know that they are virtual!

ESX wears a different red hat

Your ESX's Service Console provides an environment in which you monitor and administer your ESX host. The Service Console is based on Red Hat Enterprise Linux 3, but is highly modified. All services that are unnecessary for management are stripped off, and all client communications are secured through SSL (secure sockets layer).

Your Service Console has its own firewall, and all unnecessary ports are initially closed. This is a security consideration because compromising the service console compromises your server's and virtual machine's security as well, since it controls the management of your virtual machines

Installing ESX is very similar to a Linux install. You can pick a text-based or graphics-based installation. If you go with the graphics-based install, that's the first and last time you'll need a mouse on the server.

Never put Red Hat patches on your ESX. Use only those patches that come directly from VMware.

Play nice with your HCL

If you read nothing else today, heed this:

If it's not on the Hardware Compatibility List (HCL), do not put it in production!

Although ESX will indeed run on many platforms that aren't on the HCL, these platforms have not been fully tested for stability. Using untested hardware can present you with three problems:

- **Unexpected server behaviors:** Not good. This can lead to instability.

- **Lack of support:** If you use uncertified hardware, technical support might not be able to help you solve a problem. While they are a very helpful bunch in general, they are under no obligation to support hardware that has not been certified. While you may find a technician who will help for a while, they are under pressure to spend their time helping those that bought certified hardware.

- **Out in the cold:** VMware makes programming decisions based on certified hardware. If you use uncertified hardware and code is changed in an update, something that works today might not work after you apply the update.

VMware is very good about updating its hardware compatibility lists. In fact, they're updated every Wednesday. Here is the URL to all the compatibility guides:

    www.vmware.com/resources/techresources/cat/119

At this site, you can find separate compatibility lists

- By VMware product
- By version of VMware product
- For server and SAN hardware

For test systems, use whatever hardware you like. However, never roll out a production system with hardware that's not on a VMware HCL.

Using mount points versus drive letters

All your operating systems need a way to find their available file systems. It doesn't matter whether the file systems are on a hard disk, CD, or USB drive. And inherently, Windows- and Unix-based systems have different ways of addressing these file systems:

- **Windows:** A Windows-based machine assigns a drive letter to each separate file system. For example, your boot partition is likely your C:\ drive, and your CD drive is likely your D:\ drive. If you add a USB drive, it might become your E:\ drive. In Windows, file systems from different partitions are noncontiguous, and each starts with a drive letter.

✔ **Unix:** A Unix-based machine uses mount points. Each separate file system is seamlessly added as a subdirectory off your root directory. The root directory is notated with a /. Instead of being addressed as your D:\ drive (as in the Windows world), your CD drive is addressed as /mnt/cdrom. File systems from different partitions are contiguous, and all files are found by following a path from / instead of using drive letters.

Because your ESX is a Unix-based system, it uses mount points instead of drive letters.

Default partitions

You are required to use five mandatory partitions when you install ESX. Additionally, there is one optional partition: /var/logs. To keep your root from being filled by log files, VMware recommends using a separate partition of 2 GB for log files. The default partitions are detailed in Table 5-1.

Table 5-1			Default Partitions		
Mount Point	*Disk*	*Type*	*Used For*	*Used By*	*Approximate Size*
/	Boot	ext3	root	Service Console	5GB
/boot	Boot	ext3	boot	Service Console	100MB
/vmfs/ volumes	Local	VMFS3	VMs and ISO Images*	VMkernel	Varies
None	Any	vmkcore	Core dump	VMkernel	100MB
None	Boot	Swap	Swap files	Service Console	544MB
/var/ logs	Boot	ext3	Log files	Service Console	2GB

VM: Virtual Machines; ISO: International Standards Organization Formatted CD Images.

Unless you have a very good reason to do otherwise, keep the default partition recommendations during the install procedure since they are what VMware has deemed acceptable.

Stepping Through the Install

This section covers your prerequisites and walks you through a typical ESX install.

Hardware preparation

You can install ESX on an Intel processor that is Xeon and later; or an AMD Opteron processor in 32-bit mode. You also need at least 2GB of RAM and 560MB of disk space. Of course, the more CPUs, RAM, and disk storage you have, the more virtual machines you can support.

Check the latest hardware compatibility guides to see the current requirements.

Before you install your ESX, you need to choose whether you want to boot from a SAN. Since version 2.5 of ESX, VMware has given you the option to boot the server from a SAN volume. This might come in handy if you want to copy the boot partition to another disk enclosure using SAN utilities.

I prefer booting each server locally instead of from SAN for the following reasons:

✔ You have a local hard drive if you ever need one for any reason. Adding a Microsoft cluster would be an example of a reason to need a local hard drive.

✔ I prefer keeping the operating system files mirrored on the local server.

✔ If your SAN goes offline, your server will still be running because it can boot locally.this may aid in troubleshooting your SAN problem.

✔ You don't have to use any expensive SAN storage capacity for your ESX operating system.

If you do decide to boot from local storage, unplug the server from the SAN before you run the install to avoid accidentally formatting any logical unit numbers (LUNs) or installing the operating system on the SAN.

There are a couple of new features regarding SATA disks in version 3.5:

✔ Support for local installation on serial ATA (SATA) drives.

✔ SATA drives can host Virtual Machine File System (VMFS) volumes.

Installing ESX

The following procedure assumes that you're installing the server on local storage and using the graphical install. Follow these steps to install the server:

1. **Disconnect your SAN cables from the server's host bus adapters (HBAs).**

2. **Load the Install CD-ROM into your server.**

3. **Boot your server to the installation CD.**

   You might have to set this option in BIOS.

4. **When you're presented with the choice of launching the install in text-based or graphical mode, press Enter to launch the graphical mode.**

   Linux loads and launches the graphical install. You can see device drivers being loaded.

   Text-based mode is handy for remote installs over a slow connection. To launch the install in text-based mode, type **esx text** and then press Enter.

5. **When the CD Media test launches, test the media if you haven't used it before (just to make sure the installation CD is in pristine condition). Then press Enter after the test if the media is okay.**

   You see an installer splash screen similar to Figure 5-1.

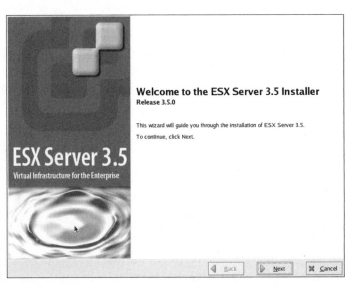

Figure 5-1: You're on the right track when you see this screen.

6. **Click Next.**

7. **Choose your language and then click Next.**

8. **Choose your mouse configuration and then click Next.**

9. **Read and accept the license; then click Next.**

10. **Choose the default partition setup.**

    A partition removal warning window pops up.

11. **As long as you don't have any data on this server, click Yes.**

12. **Verify the partition settings and then click Next.**

    The Advanced Options Screen appears.

    Like the text on this screen reads, these options usually don't need to be changed. However, if you want to boot from SAN, this is where you can select that option. Click Next.

13. **Enter your IP and DNS (domain name system) information; then click Next.**

14. **Pick your Time Zone and then click Next.**

15. **Put in the root password and then click Next.**

16. **Review the summary information screen and then click Next.**

    The install bar scrolls by.

17. **Click Finish to complete the installation.**

Installing ESXi

I haven't used ESXi, but my understanding is that the installation is so easy that, um, a "non-technical person" can perform it. To install ESXi, just connect the machine, boot it up, and then run through the menus. VMware Distributed Resource Scheduler (DRS) can start moving virtual machines to the new server immediately.

VMware High Availability (HA) is supported only experimentally in ESXi. If it does not work, you will need to manually start virtual machines on another ESX or ESXi host if the one they were running on fails.

Installing VI Client Sure Beats Typing

When you install ESX, you automatically install a management Web site with limited functionality. After the installation is complete, you want to install VI Client to fully manage your server. VI Client is a Windows program that provides an intuitive GUI interface for managing your ESX hosts.

Installing VI Client

To install VI Client, download and install the latest version of the Microsoft .NET Framework. After that, install VI Client:

1. **Open a Web browser.**
2. **Put the DNS name or IP address you gave your ESX host during the install in the address bar.**
3. **Click the Download VMware Infrastructure Client link.**
4. **Run the VI Client installation package.**

The ESX Web page is shown in Figure 5-2. At this site, you can also

- ✔ Download a Quick Start Guide.
- ✔ Log in to Web Access to perform some simple administrative functions.
- ✔ Log in to the scripted installer to automate installations.
- ✔ Download the Software Developer Kit (SDK).
- ✔ Browse objects managed by the ESX.

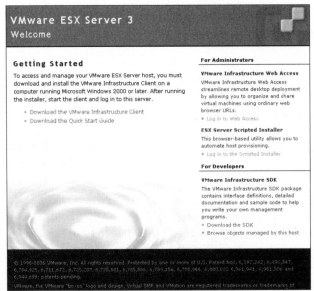

Figure 5-2:
The ESX
Web page.

Connecting to the server's Service Console

The majority of your server management will be done through your server's Service Console. Here's how to connect to the Service Console:

1. **Open VI Client.**

2. **Enter the following:**

    • The server's DNS name or IP address

    • The server's root account name

    • The password for the root account

3. **Click OK.**

The VI Client management interface is shown in Figure 5-3. The screen is divided into three sections:

- ✓ **Inventory:** (Upper left) This area shows you what virtual machines are on your server as well as their current status.

- ✓ **Configuration:** (To the right of the Inventory section) This is where you perform all your virtual machine and server configuration tasks.

- ✓ **Recent Tasks:** (Bottom) This section shows the status of current and recently completed tasks. As you can see, it took me a few tries to log in to this server as root! To avoid this, know your password and try to type it right the first time.

A few other handy ways to connect to your server

VI Client is an extremely powerful tool, but there are two other tools you will need. To ease administration tasks, you want to download these two open-source programs:

- ✓ **PUTTY:** This program allows you to connect to the command line of your server by using Secure Shell (SSH). By default, the root account is not allowed to log in remotely. I cover this in Chapter 13.

- ✓ **WinSCP:** This secure FTP client enables you to upload and download files to your ESX host. This is very handy for putting installation ISO disk images into your data store.

Inventory section   Configuration section

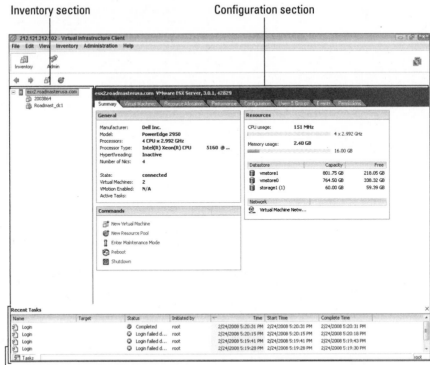

Figure 5-3:
VI Client
connection
to the serv-
er's Service
Console.

Recent Tasks Section

Even though I don't follow my own advice all the time, making a secondary user that's allowed to remotely connect to your server is far more secure than allowing root remote access.

To connect via PUTTY, do the following:

1. **Download PUTTY from this URL:**

   `www.putty.org`

2. **Open PUTTY.**

   You see a screen like the one shown in Figure 5-4.

3. **Enter your server's DNS name or IP address. Also, make sure that SSH is selected.**

4. **Click Open.**

5. **Log in as a user who has been given remote login capabilities, as outlined in Chapter 13.**

Figure 5-5 shows a PUTTY remote login session after you are connected and logged in.

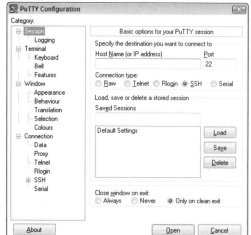

Figure 5-4:
The PUTTY
connection
setup.

Figure 5-5: A
live PUTTY
session.

Installing virtual machines or software on virtual machines is much faster
and easier from ISO disk image files. In order to use disk image files, you have
to store them in a place where your ESX host can see them.

ISO disk images can take up a significant amount of space. I once made the
mistake of storing a few on my boot drive and almost ran out of space. ***Do not
do that.*** Instead, store the ISO images on a SAN volume or an NFS store.

To get your ISO images into a data store, you need a secure FTP client, such
as WinSCP. Then, to connect to your server via WinSCP, do the following:

1. **Download and install WinSCP from here:**

```
www.winscp.net
```

2. **Open WinSCP.**

   You see a screen like Figure 5-6.

3. **Enter your server's DNS name or IP address. Also, make sure that SFTP is selected as the file protocol.**

4. **Enter the username and password of a user with the right to log in remotely, as outlined in Chapter 13.**

5. **Click the Login button.**

   You'll likely see a warning like the one shown in Figure 5-7.

6. **After you determine that you're connecting to the correct server, click Yes.**

Figure 5-8 shows an active WinSCP session. You can see I have an ISO images folder stored on a VMFS-3–formatted SAN volume. It's likely faster to run an install from an ISO image on a SAN volume than it is from an NFS volume. However, as space gets tighter, I will probably move the ISO images to an NFS volume.

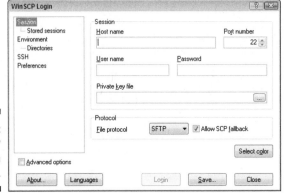

Figure 5-6: The WinSCP connection page.

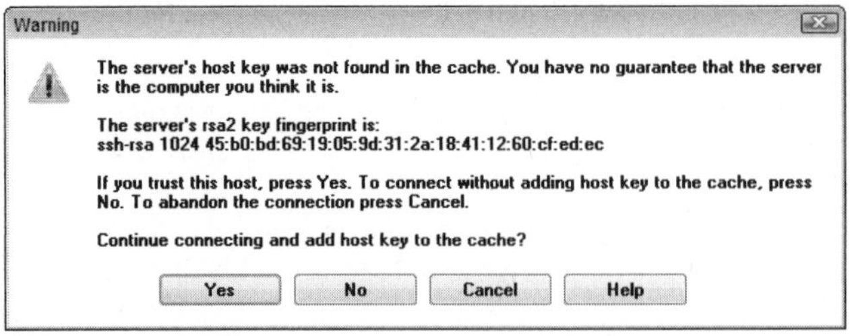

Figure 5-7: A WinSCP security warning.

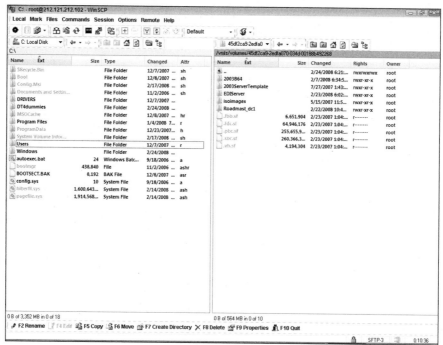

Figure 5-8:
An active
WinSCP
session.

Part III

Connecting the Physical to Your Virtual Environment

The 5th Wave   By Rich Tennant

©RICHTENNANT

"You the guy having trouble staying connected to the server?"

In this part . . .

You bridge the gap between virtual and physical environments in this part. Chapter 6 covers how VMware Infrastructure looks and feels so you can get a handle on how the management software is laid out. Chapter 7 is all about networking. This chapter helps you to configure your virtual network and then connect it to a physical network. Finally, Chapter 8 shows you how to connect to storage.

Chapter 6

Embracing the Look and Feel of VMware Infrastructure Client

In This Chapter

▶ Getting familiar with VMware Infrastructure Client

▶ Installing VMware Infrastructure Client

▶ Understanding how VMware Infrastructure Client groups things

*T*he most common way for you to manage, view, and modify your VMware Infrastructure 3 is through the VMware Infrastructure Client (also called the Virtual Infrastructure Client). The *VMware Infrastructure Client (VIC)* runs on your local Windows machine and logs in to your ESX hosts or your VirtualCenter (a centralized management framework for virtual infrastructures; see Chapter 9 for more on VirtualCenter). VIC is arranged in a very logical fashion and is an easy and intuitive interface after you get used to it. To use it, though, you first need to install it.

In this chapter, we discuss the ins and outs of VIC. We look at how to install it and how it organizes your virtual and physical infrastructure components. By the end of the chapter, you should feel pretty comfortable using VIC.

Introducing the VMware Infrastructure Client

VMware Infrastructure Client (VIC) is your one-stop-shopping for all your VMware Infrastructure 3 needs. VIC can log in to and manage ESX hosts directly, or as a proxy through VirtualCenter.

Using VirtualCenter is the better way to go because it allows you to manage your entire infrastructure from a single point instead of logging in to each server separately. Additionally, VirtualCenter provides server fault-tolerant add-ons, such as VMware clusters, VMotion, VMware Distributed Resource Scheduling (DRS), and VMware High Availability (HA) (all of which are discussed in Chapter 12).

All the advanced features and everything else in your virtual infrastructure are managed through VIC. VIC allows you to configure all your hardware and software, assign rights, and create and manage virtual machines. VIC is the entry point to VMware Infrastructure 3 . . . and you'll use it a lot.

Installing VMware Infrastructure Client

Each ESX and VirtualCenter has a Web page. This Web page allows you to perform many common management functions, but more importantly, it provides a link to install VIC. You can install VIC from either source. To use an ESX to install VIC, follow these easy steps:

1. **On your network, boot your ESX.**

2. **Update your Microsoft .NET Framework to the latest version on your local Windows machine.**

   This local machine is the machine you install VIC on.

3. **Connect to the ESX Web page by openening a browser and entering the host's DNS name or IP address.**

   This is the IP information you entered when installing your host.

4. **Click the Download the VMware Infrastructure Client link shown in Figure 6-1.**

5. **Run the client installation, which launches a wizard.**

   You only need to accept the license agreement and installation location. Just install VIC with the defaults and you should be fine.

You can also download the client from the VirtualCenter machine's Web page, if you want. Whether you download VIC using the ESX or the VirtualCenter doesn't matter — you're downloading the same client. Once installed, you can use VIC to connect to and manage either your ESX host or VirtualCenter. I suggest using of VirtualCenter for managing production environments, so everything shown in this chapter will be through VirtualCenter.

After you have VIC installed, start it and connect to your VirtualCenter machine. Figure 6-2 shows the initial logon screen. You need to provide the DNS name or IP address of your VirtualCenter as well as the logon credentials — you will assign these when you install VirtualCenter (covered in detail in Chapter 9).

Click this link.

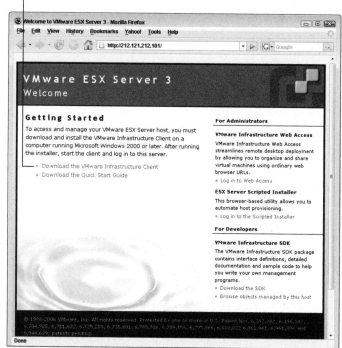

Figure 6-1:
Click the
link on the
ESX host
home page
to download
VIC.

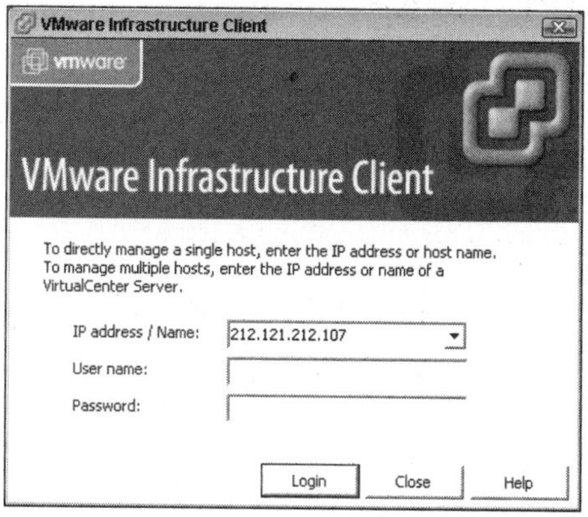

Figure 6-2:
Begin by
logging on
from here.

Here's where to find the valid logon credentials:

> ✔ **If the VirtualCenter machine is a member of the domain:** Credentials
> are pulled from the Active Directory (AD) Administrators' group.

 ✔ **If the machine is a standalone:** Credentials are pulled from the local Administrators' group.

 I prefer leaving the VirtualCenter server as a standalone server instead of joining an AD domain. To me, this is more secure because you need to explicitly define a user before they can connect to your VirtualCenter and manage your virtual infrastructure. The downside is losing the define a user once in AD for a single sign-on. This is my preference, not a necessity.

Understanding the VIC Interface

The VIC is composed of five window options, all located at the top of the screen beneath the menu bar. The two primary windows are

 ✔ **The Inventory window:** From the Inventory window, you can deal with your virtual machines and server hardware. If you're connected to VirtualCenter, you can also manage clusters, resource pools, and all your fault-tolerant features (covered in Chapters 12 and 14).

 ✔ **The Admin window:** From the Admin window, you can manage users, rights, logs, and licensing.

Using the Inventory window

Use the Inventory window (as shown in Figure 6-3) to manage your machines, both physical ESX hosts and virtual machines. The window is divided into the three main panes:

 ✔ **Inventory pane:** This pane appears on the left side of the window and lists the following:

  • *Logical items:* Logical items can include clusters, data centers, templates, and resource pools.

  • *Virtual items:* Virtual items are your virtual machines.

  • *Physical items:* Physical items include your ESX hosts.

 Change the view of the Inventory pane by clicking the Inventory window button and choosing the view that suits your needs from the drop-down list. You can choose from Hosts and Clusters, Virtual Machines and Templates, Networks, or Data Stores.

✓ **Details pane:** This pane is located to the right of the Inventory pane. The Details pane lets you view metrics and perform tasks on the object you select in the Inventory pane. Functionality is grouped in tabs across the top of the Details pane.

As of version 3.5, a new tab — Getting Started — provides an almost wizard-like interface to creating data centers, clusters, and virtual machines.

✓ **Recent Tasks pane:** Anything that has recently happened is shown in the Recent Tasks pane, located along the bottom of the screen. This can be handy to see the status of any recent request you have made like taking a snapshot (making an image of a virtual machine) or suspending a virtual machine (putting it to sleep).

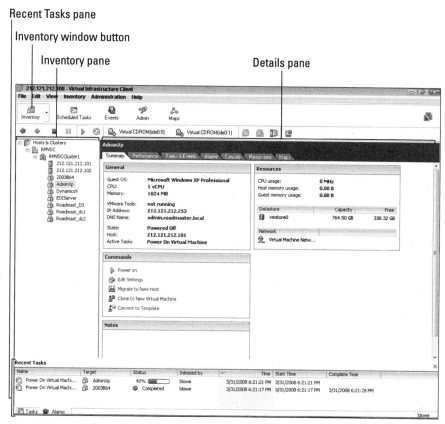

Figure 6-3: The Inventory window of VMware Infrastructure Client.

Understanding the Admin window

The security model in VMware works by permissions. A *permission* consists of a user and a role that is assigned to an object in inventory. The Admin window (as shown in Figure 6-4) allows you to create and edit various roles. Each role has tasks associated with it that anyone linked to that role can perform. Several default roles are created during the installation of VirtualCenter, such as No Access, Read Only, Administrator, and a few others. These are covered in more detail in Chapter 13.

There are four management tabs in the Admin window:

- ✔ **Roles:** Used to list any roles that have been defined. This includes the built in roles and any other roles you create.

- ✔ **Sessions:** Lists the current connections to VirtualCenter.

- ✔ **Licenses:** Lists the products you are licensed to use.

- ✔ **System Logs:** Allows you to read the system logs for the VirtualCenter server.

Admin window button

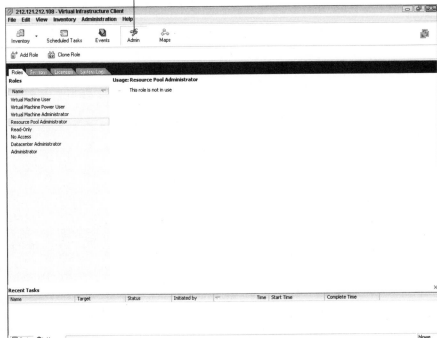

Figure 6-4:
The Admin
window of
VMware
Infra-
structure
Client.

A glimpse at the other sections

You likely won't use the three other windows in VIC as often as the Inventory and Admin windows. The other three windows are Scheduled Tasks, Events, and Maps. The following sections cover each in detail.

Scheduled Tasks window

From the Scheduled Tasks window (see Figure 6-5), you can automate common virtual machine tasks. You can perform such tasks as powering machines on and off, taking snapshots, and making new virtual machines. A host of other tasks such as creating a virtual machine and adding a new host are also available from this window, as shown in Figure 6-5.

Click here to schedule a new task.

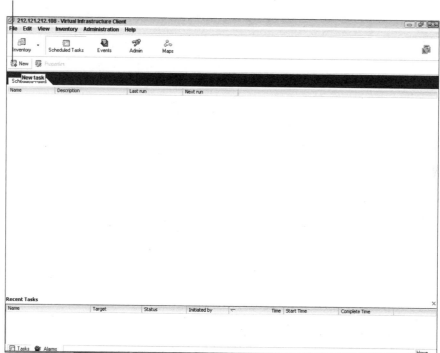

Figure 6-5:
Automate
common
tasks here.

To schedule a new task, follow these steps:

1. **Click on the Scheduled Tasks button.**

2. **Click the New button (refer to Figure 6-5).**

3. **Select the type of task to schedule from the drop-down list shown in Figure 6-6, then click Next.**

   In this example we are selecting Change the Power State of a Virtual Machine.

4. **Pick the virtual machine you want to apply the task to as shown in Figure 6-7 and then click Next.**

5. **Select the option(s) regarding your task and click Next.**

   Since the example task is changing the power state, we can choose from the options listed in Figure 6-8. The options will vary by task.

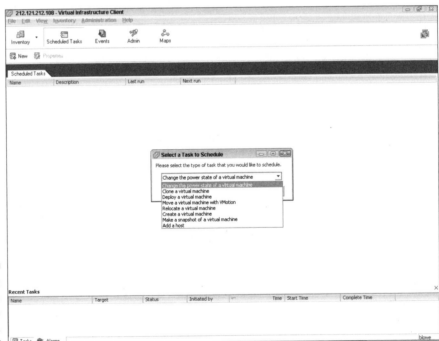

Figure 6-6: Pick the task to automate.

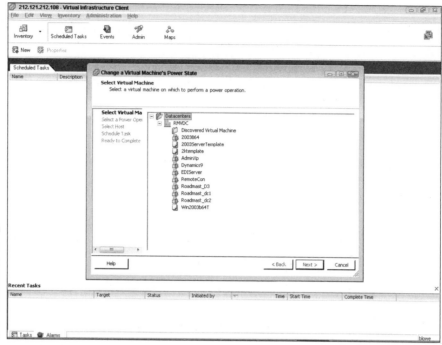

Figure 6-7:
Select
the virtual
machine to
apply the
task to.

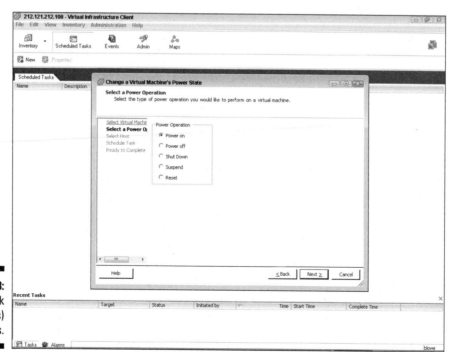

Figure 6-8:
Making task
option(s)
selections.

6. **Pick the host this action applies to.**

7. **Provide a task name, description, frequency, and time as shown in Figure 6-9 and click Next.**

8. **Review the summary screen and click Finish.**

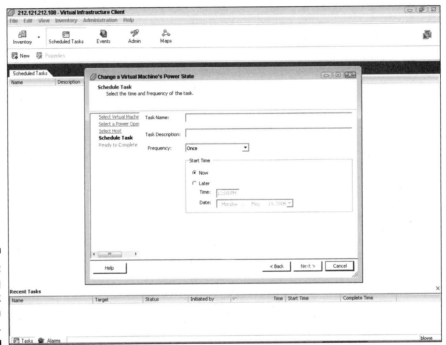

Figure 6-9:
Entering
task
information
and details.

Events window

The Events window (as shown in Figure 6-12) lists everything that has happened in your virtual infrastructure in detail. When your Recent Tasks disappear, they wind up here. You can sort by any column of information you want by clicking on the column title. Additionally, you can search by data in any column to filter your results.

This is the place to go to look at a detailed history of what happened. For example, I had one machine that flipped the yellow or red CPU alarm on every now and again. I filtered by this server alone and monitored the behavior over time. I saw that at least once a day, at varying times, the CPU alarm state switched from green to yellow and sometimes yellow to red. A minute or two later, it switched back to the previous state. Since it only happened on the Graphics server when people were in the office, it made sense that a graphics user was kicking off some process at random intervals. I eventually traced this back to graphics users manually updating their local Version Queue cache at random intervals.

Export Events button

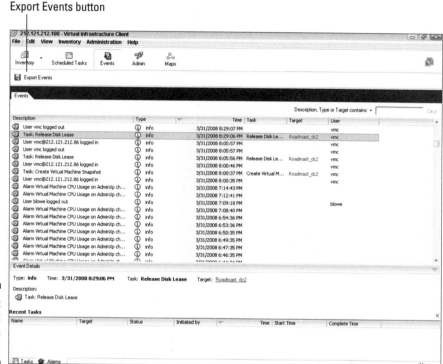

Figure 6-10:
The VIC
Events
window.

Another thing you can do in this window is exporting events. By clicking Export Events button (refer to Figure 6-10), you launch the Export Events window shown in Figure 6-11. Notice you can filter events by system or user initiation, severity, and time, and can limit the total number exported. The export file is a fixed width text file that you can easily import into Excel.

Maps window

The Maps window (shown in Figure 6-12) is a handy visual tool for checking VMotion *dependencies*. VMotion allows you to move a virtual machine from one ESX host to another with no down time. (VMotion is covered in Chapter 12.)

For VMotion to work, each ESX host involved must be able to see the virtual network and data store used by a virtual machine. For example, Figure 6-12 shows that my EDIServer can utilize VMotion to move between the 212.121.212.101 and 212.121.212.102 ESX hosts because each host can see vmstore1 and the virtual machine network. I know both ESX host processors use the same instruction sets, so I won't have to power-off the machine to move it from one host to the next.

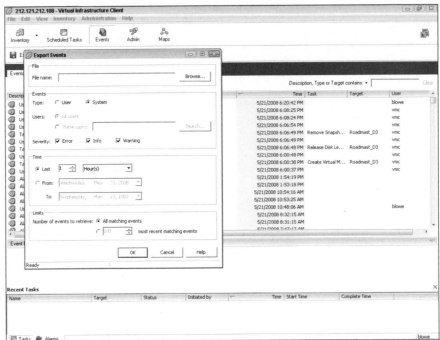

Figure 6-11:
Export
Events
options.

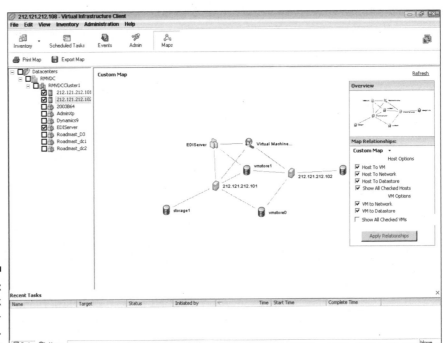

Figure 6-12:
Check
dependen-
cies here.

Chapter 7

Virtual Networking

- -

In This Chapter

▶ Creating virtual switches

▶ Introducing three port types

▶ Assigning network policies

▶ Following best practices

- -

More often than not, you want virtual machines to be able to reach the physical world, and the only way they can accomplish that is through virtual switches. *Virtual switches* are software-only devices and exist solely in the VMkernel on your ESX host. Think of them as the bridge that your virtual machines cross to get to your physical network.

In this chapter, we examine how to setup virtual switches, connect virtual machines to them, how to make virtual switches fault tolerant, and how to assign various policies to ports on a virtual switch.

Virtual Switch Options

Many configuration options exist for virtual switches. You can assign virtual local area networks (VLANs) and security as well as limit the amount of traffic that virtual machines can generate. Additionally, you can assign many NICs to a virtual switch for load balancing and fault tolerance. NICs are called *uplink adapters.* Multiple uplink adapters are a wise choice for production environments.

If you want an isolated virtual network — for testing or any other reason — you can set up a virtual switch without an uplink adapter. Any virtual machines plugged in to a disconnected switch can see only each other: They can never see the outside world or virtual machines connected to any other virtual switch. This lets you create a great isolated test environment.

However, if you want your test environment to access the outside world, you certainly can. Virtual machines can be set up with two network cards to act as a firewall and a router. The router, which connects to both the disconnected and physically connected switches, can be used to determine what network traffic flows in to and out of your test network.

Hardware Out of Nowhere: Virtual Switches

Your virtual machines connect to virtual switches. Virtual switches, in turn, connect to NICs in your ESX host. (Read all about ESX hosts in Chapters 4 and 5.) And the NICs connect to your physical network.

Virtual switches have many similarities with physical switches:

- ✔ They sport varying number of ports to connect to machines.
- ✔ Each frame's destination Media Access Control (MAC) address is looked up on arrival.
- ✔ Each frame is forwarded to one or more ports for transmission.
- ✔ They offer support for VLANs.
- ✔ They have varying port speeds.
- ✔ They offer security policies.

And despite their similarities, virtual switches and physical switches also have quite a few differences:

- ✔ You can change the number of ports on a virtual switch.
- ✔ Several physical NICs can be assigned to a single virtual switch to combine throughput or for fault tolerance.
- ✔ Virtual switches are software-only and exist in the confines of the VMkernel. (Read about the VMkernel in Chapter 4.)
- ✔ Virtual switches don't have to learn their MAC address tables. They already know them because the switches and virtual network adapters are both software-only devices.
- ✔ Virtual switches know the configuration of the virtual network adapters connected to them.
- ✔ You cannot cascade virtual switches like you can physical switches (see Figure 7-1).

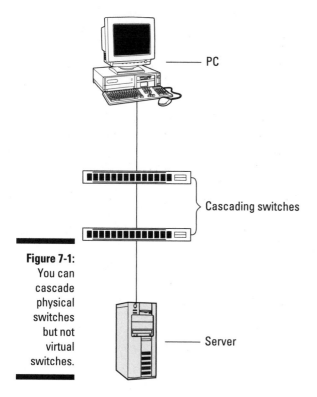

PC

Cascading switches

Figure 7-1:
You can
cascade
physical
switches
but not
virtual
switches.

Server

Functions of virtual switches

Virtual switches perform three different functions for an ESX host. Each function is considered a different connection type or port:

- ✔ **Virtual machine:** As the name suggests, *virtual machine ports* are where you connect your virtual machines.

- ✔ **VMkernel:** VMkernel connections access IP-based services, such as networking, IP storage, and VMotion. *VMotion* enables you to move virtual machines from one ESX host to another. You can even do this while they're on. I have pinged a virtual machine while moving it with VMotion and lost only a single packet. Think about that for a moment. You have moved your applications and operating system from one physical machine to another with no loss of service!

- ✔ **Service Console:** This connection type provides access to ESX management services. They are also called *host management services*.

The following sections describe each of these in more detail.

Virtual machine ports

Virtual machine ports connect your virtual machines with each other and the outside world. Every virtual machine plugs in to a port on one or more virtual switches. Any uplink adapters that you assign to the virtual switch provide a bridge to your physical network.

The networking functions of an ESX virtually extend the physical network into the server itself. In larger environments, for example, network people and server people are usually in different groups. If these groups don't have a good working relationship, rolling out VI3 may have political ramifications, such as project delays due to negative cross-group dynamics.

VMkernel

Virtual switches provide IP connectivity to the VMkernel. This enables you to remotely connect to the command line on your server. It also allows the VMkernel to access IP-based storage, such as network attached storage (NAS) and Internet Small Computer System Interface (iSCSI). Storage is covered in Chapter 3.

Service Console

Virtual switches access host management services. The Service Console connects to a virtual switch port. Virtual Infrastructure Clients (VIC) connect to the Service Console so you can configure and manage your server. I recommend having a spare Service Console port in case you lose one due to hardware failures.

Without the Service Console, you can access your ESX only from the physical server's command line, which looks just like Linux.

Figure 7-2 shows the networking model in more detail. You can view it as three different layers. The top layer is the services layer; your Service Console and virtual machines live here. The services in the services layer connect to virtual switches.

The virtual switches exist in the VMkernel layer. In fact, the kernel itself connects to one or more switches. Since the kernel also controls hardware access, it provides the means of assigning uplink adapters to virtual switches. The uplink adapters connect to your physical network.

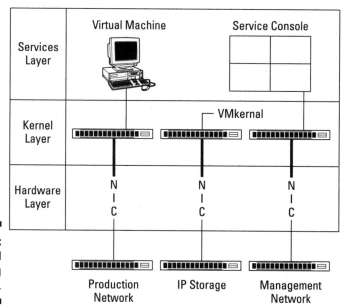

Figure 7-2:
The virtual
networking
model.

Multiple uplink adapters are important for virtual switches. In more than 15 years of professionally working with computers and networks, I have seen only two network cards die. If a NIC in a single machine dies, you lose access to that machine. A bad situation, but at least the outage is limited. However, if you have only a single uplink NIC connected to a virtual switch and that NIC dies, all the virtual machines connected to that switch become inaccessible — a much worse situation. However, things can further go downhill if the switch was also used for your only Service Console. Suddenly, you no longer have access to server configuration and management features. Although the chances of a NIC dying are low, don't tempt fate and take the risk of using only a single uplink adapter.

Also, multiple uplink adapters enable you to combine outgoing network capacity and load-level your outgoing network traffic. This can be extremely handy if you have any high-traffic servers. VI3 provides three different load-leveling models, which I discuss shortly.

Creating a virtual switch

During the server install (see Chapter 5 for information on ESX installation), a default switch with a Service Console is created. Note that all Service Console ports are named with the following convention: vSwif#:IP_Address. Best practices dictate creating a new switch for your virtual machines. To create a virtual switch, you need to log on to your server through the VIC. After you're logged in, follow these steps:

1. **Click your ESX host to select it.**

2. **Click the Configuration tab.**

   The Networking section of the Configuration tab (shown in Figure 7-3) shows switches, port groups, and the virtual machines connected to each.

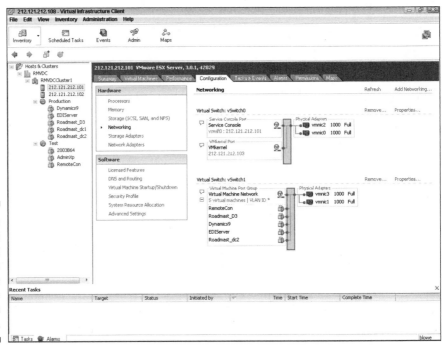

Figure 7-3:
The
Networking
section
of the
Con-
figuration
tab.

3. **In the Hardware section, click the Networking link.**

4. **Click Add Networking (upper-right corner).**

The Add Network Wizard (as shown in Figure 7-4) opens. The first step
is choosing what kind of connection the switch will provide. You can
add other connection types and additional NICs later by modifying the
switches properties.

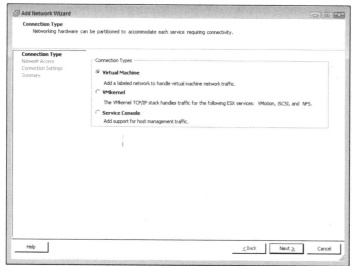

Figure 7-4:
Create a
virtual
switch here.

5. **Choose the appropriate connection type and then click Next.**

   In this case, select Virtual Machine.

6. **Select the physical adapter you want this switch to use by checking
   the appropriate check box.**

7. **Select Create a Virtual Switch and then click Next.**

8. **Accept the default network label and then click Next.**

9. **Click Finish.**

After you finish, you should see a virtual switch similar to the one shown in
Figure 7-5. Providing that this is the first switch you manually added, your
switch's name will be vSwitch1 (default naming convention). You will also
see a switch named vSwitch0, which is the default switch created during your
ESX install. By default, a new switch has 56 ports. All these ports are put into
a single port group. In this case, the port group is labeled Virtual Machine
Network. You can add additional port groups later by editing the virtual
switch's properties.

Your new virtual switch

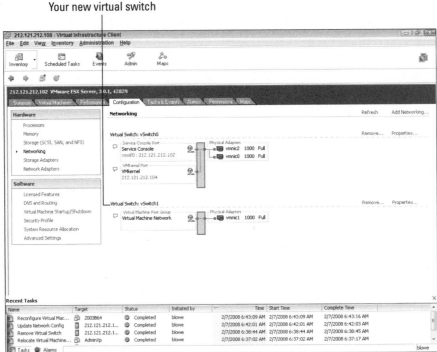

Figure 7-5:
The new
vSwitch1.

Now explore the properties of the new switch by clicking the Properties link closest to the switch's name. The Properties window that appears has two tabs:

✓ **Ports:** The Ports summary tab (see Figure 7-6) is shown by default. Here, you can view the switch and port group policies. You can also add new port groups as well as edit existing ones. For more on working with ports, see the next section.

A summary of networking topics is required for the port groups section:

• *VLANs are a way to segregate network traffic.* All hosts connected to the same VLAN act as though they are on the same network segment, regardless of physical or virtual location. They were originally created to shrink the size of collision domains and have an added security benefit of segregating network traffic. For example, VLAN1 cannot see traffic on VLAN2. In order for a machine on VLAN1 to connect to a machine on VLAN2, they must connect to a port that is aware of all VLANs in a switch. This is a *trunk port.* The VLAN standard used in VMware is IEEE 802.1q.

- *MAC addresses are unique physical addresses assigned to Ethernet cards.* They contain a manufacturer number combined with a unique identification number.

- *Ethernet frames are Open Systems Interconnection (OSI) Layer 2 communication mechanisms.* They contain a source MAC address and a destination MAC address, along with flags and data. Some of the data will likely be an encapsulated IP frame.

- *NICs can be set to promiscuous mode.* Although fun, promiscuous mode isn't as naughty as it sounds. When an Ethernet adapter is in promiscuous mode, it can intercept all frames on the virtual or physical wire it connects to instead of just the ones with the adapter's MAC address as the destination. Network sniffers are a good example of an application that needs a NIC set to promiscuous mode since they need to see all traffic on a network segment.

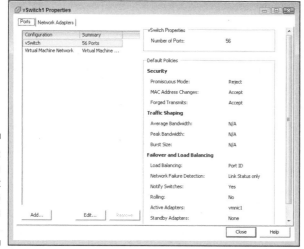

Figure 7-6:
View switch
and port
group
policies
here.

✔ **Network Adapters:** From the Network Adapters tab (see Figure 7-7), you can add, edit, and remove uplink adapters from the virtual switch.

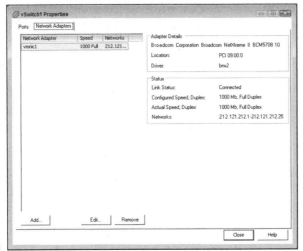

Figure 7-7:
Manage
uplink
adapters
from the
virtual
switch here.

If you need to add additional network adapters to a virtual switch, follow
these steps:

1. **Click your ESX host to select it.**

2. **Click the Configuration tab.**

3. **In the Hardware section, click the Networking link.**

4. **Click the Properties link closest to your switch.**

5. **Click the Network Adapters tab.**

6. **Click the Add button to launch the Add Adapter Wizard.**

7. **Select the check box next to the adapter you want to add (see Figure
   7-8) and click Next.**

   Notice that any unused NICs appear under the Unclaimed Adapters
   section.

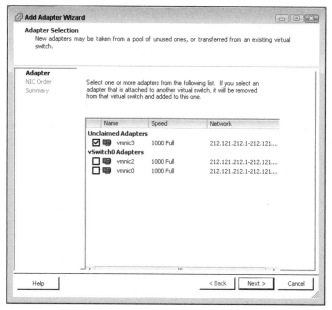

Figure 7-8:
Add your
adapter to
the switch.

8. **Accept the default NIC Order and then click Next.**

9. **Review the Summary page and then click Finish.**

   You see a screen similar to Figure 7-9. Notice that two adapters are now listed.

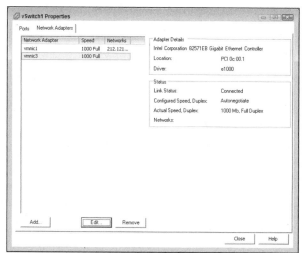

Figure 7-9:
Reviewing
your new
adapters.

Depending on your network configuration, you may want to adjust the NIC settings. If you click the Edit button, you can configure the port speed of the uplink adapter (see Figure 7-10). If you're using 1 Gbsp (recommended), leave this setting to Autonegotiate. If you're using any other network speed, you want to manually set the speed and duplex to match.

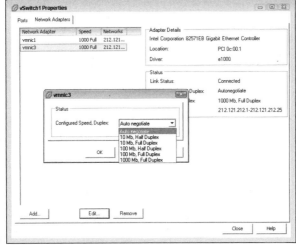

Figure 7-10:
Configuring
the port
speed of
your uplink
adapter.

Many networking problems can be avoided by manually setting the speed and duplex of your network connections if they use anything less than 1 Gbps . If you use a 1 Gbps connection, auto negotiation should be set.

Configuring Port Groups and Their Properties

Port groups unite several virtual switch ports under common settings. Every one of your port groups has a label that virtual machines can connect to. By default, all ports on a new switch are in a single port group. This group is called the Virtual Machine Network, as shown in Figure 7-11. You can add port groups in a switch by clicking the switch's Properties link and then clicking the Add button. In essence, you are adding a configuration subdivision the virtual switch. Port groups can come in handy if you want to have a switch with different network settings for different virtual machines. You can assign different security, traffic shaping, and load balancing settings to each port group (all of which are covered in the next few sections). ESX hosts can support a maximum of 512 port groups each, which is likely more than anyone will ever need.

The Virtual Machine Network

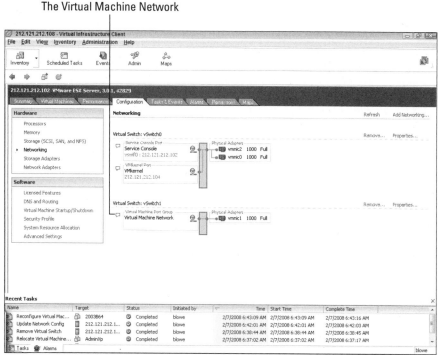

Figure 7-11:
Begin
configuring
your Virtual
Machine
Network.

When you subdivide a switch into port groups, they show up as labels in the switch properties. There are no fixed number of ports assigned to a port group. Instead, virtual machines chose which port group to connect to in their network configuration screen. You can connect up to the number of unused ports on a switch in any combination of port groups.

Various networking policies covering network traffic, VLANs, and security can be assigned at the switch or port group level. A port group setting that differs from the switch's setting will override the switch's setting.

Setting the network polices for a switch is much the same as setting the network policies for a port group. The only difference is that you can change the number of ports on a switch. To access the policies, open your switch's properties, highlight your switch, and click the Edit button.

Changing the number of switch ports

If you want to change the number of ports on a virtual switch, you certainly can. The number of ports you need is a function of the number of virtual machines you have and your switch philosophy.

At one extreme is several switches with a small number of ports. The other extreme is fewer switches with a large number of ports. I lean toward the fewer larger switches end because less objects are easier to manager for you and the VMkernel. However, several smaller switches may come in handy if you have a few different physical network segments in order to segregate traffic without using VLANs.

This change requires a reboot, so change the ports only when you can afford for your system to be offline briefly.

To change the number of ports on a virtual switch, do the following:

1. **Log in to your server using your VIC.**

2. **Highlight your server.**

3. **Click the Configuration tab.**

4. **Click the Networking link in the Hardware section on the left-hand side of the screen.**

5. **Click the Properties link near your virtual switch.**

6. **In the Properties window, highlight the switch's label.**

7. **Click the Edit button.**

   The switch's Properties window opens, as shown in Figure 7-12.

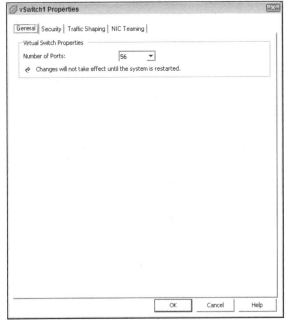

Figure 7-12: Configure switch policy here.

8. **On the General tab of the Properties window that opens, select the number of ports you want from the drop-down list.**

9. **Click OK.**

10. **Click the Close button.**

11. **Reboot your server.**

Modifying security

From your switch's Properties window, click the Security tab to configure various security options. Switches and port groups both have the same options. The options affect how frames are handled. As shown in Figure 7-13, you can set Promiscuous Mode, MAC Address Changes, and Forged Transmits. These policies are all about preventing someone from seeing all network traffic or pretending to be someone they're not to perform a man-in-the-middle attack.

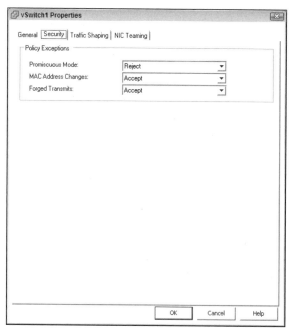

Figure 7-13: Set security policies here.

✔ **Promiscuous Mode** determines what frames a virtual machine's network adapter can see.

- *Reject:* If you set this to Reject (the default), only frames destined for that virtual machine's MAC address will be passed to it. You might want to do this for security. No one will be able to run a network sniffer on a virtual machine if this policy is set to Reject.

- *Accept:* If the policy is set to Accept, the virtual machine sees all frames that pass through the virtual switch subject to the VLAN restrictions.

✔ **MAC Address Changes** control inbound traffic.

- *Reject:* If you set this policy to Reject and someone changes the MAC address of his virtual machine, all inbound frames will be dropped. Don't worry, though: If the MAC address is changed back, the frames will come through again. This policy can be used to prevent someone from pretending to be a machine he is not.

- *Accept:* If the policy is set to Accept, frames are passed to the virtual machine with the changed MAC address. The default setting is Accept.

✔ **Forged Transmits** affect outbound traffic only.

- *Reject:* If you set this policy to Reject, any outbound frames with a different MAC address other than the MAC address assigned in the virtual machine's configuration file will be dropped.

- *Accept:* If you set this to Accept, the default setting, a virtual machine can send a frame with a different MAC address.

At the port group level, you get to choose whether you want to enable the security policies on a port group-by-port group basis. When you edit the properties of the Virtual Machine Network port group, for example, notice the check box that appears to control this in Figure 7-14. The policies are already filled in based upon the policies you set for the switch. Placing a check mark in the box allows you to change the policy for that specific port group.

If the switch and a port group have conflicting policies enabled, the port group's setting overrides the switch's setting.

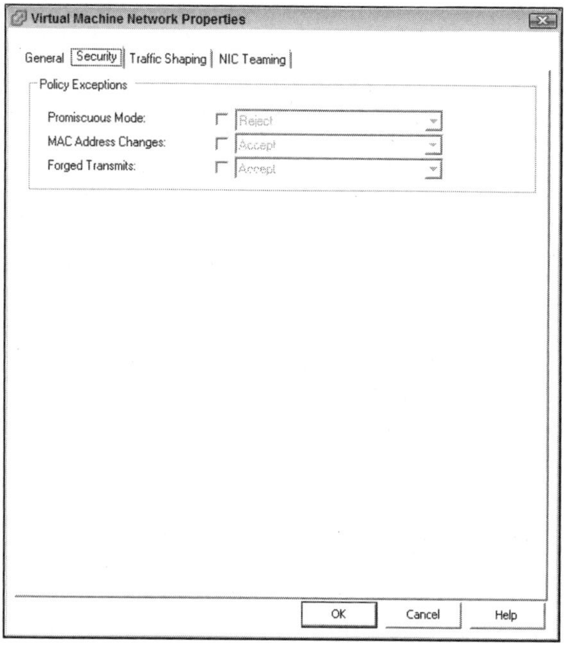

Virtual Machine Network Properties

General | Security | Traffic Shaping | NIC Teaming |

Policy Exceptions

Promiscuous Mode: ☐ Reject

MAC Address Changes: ☐ Accept

Forged Transmits: ☐ Accept

OK   Cancel   Help

Figure 7-14:
The Security
policy tab
after adding
port groups.

Traffic-shaping policies

You can control the outbound traffic on a switch by using traffic shaping.
Thinking about how machines communicate sheds some light on the settings.
Say you have a Web server running on a virtual machine. Until someone goes
to the Web site, the server just sits there, doing nothing.

After a person connects, the server sends the data (that represents a Web
page) in a quick burst of traffic. After the page is sent, the server just sits
there again doing nothing. When more people connect, more bursts of traffic
are sent.

Using *traffic shaping* enables you to control the average bandwidth used, the
maximum bandwidth allowed, and the size of the bursts.

Playing (or not playing) traffic cop

Personally, I'm against using traffic shaping outside of a test environment because I don't want to place a limit on how much data a machine can output. If a virtual machine is generating more traffic than my system can handle, I am either using more capacity than I planned for or there is a problem with the virtual machine. Either way, the issue will show up more quickly

if I don't mask it with a traffic shaping policy. Since action needs to be taken in either scenario, I want to know about it sooner than later. I did see one Web site where a person used traffic shaping to mimic slow wide area network (WAN) links to test their global network in a virtual environment. Pretty slick.

Other than when testing, you shouldn't need to enable this policy to limit machine's output.

Enabling traffic shaping can lead to dropped frames. However, if you planned your capacity correctly (see Chapter 2), this should not be an issue.

The Traffic Shaping tab of the switch Properties screen is shown in Figure 7-15.

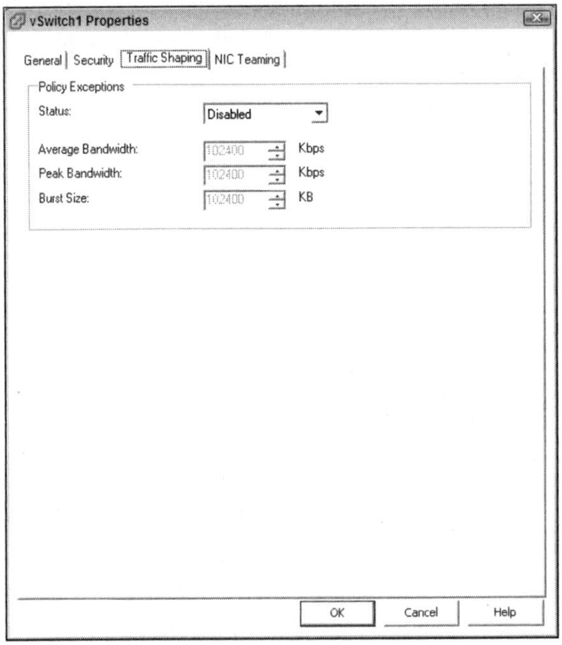

Figure 7-15:
Set traffic
shaping
here.

✔ **Status:** Use the Status drop-down list to toggle the policy on and off.

  • *Disable:* No traffic shaping takes place.

  • *Enabled:* Traffic shaping takes place.

✔ **Average Bandwidth:** This controls the long-term, allowable average of traffic bursts. This is the number of bits per second allowed to cross the virtual switch, averaged over time.

✔ **Peak Bandwidth:** This is a limit on the short-term average traffic. After this limit is exceeded, packets are queued for later transmission. If the packet queue gets full, packets are dropped.

Think of peak bandwidth as a bucket for which you pick the size. After a few virtual machines are transmitting above peak bandwidth, packets are put into the bucket for later transmission. When that bucket becomes full,new packets will not fit in the bucket and are lost. The bucket is emptied when there is spare capacity.

✔ **Burst Size:** This is the maximum size, in kilobytes, allowed for a traffic burst. This works like a bucket as well. If a virtual machine exceeds this limit, the bucket starts filling. When the bucket is filled, new packets are dropped. Then the bucket is emptied when less data is being transmitted and spare capacity is available once again.

NIC teaming

You can set a great many options on the NIC Teaming tab (see Figure 7-16). I generally go with the default settings unless I have a good reason not to. So, if you don't want to get into all the gritty details, you can skip this section. However, if you want to know what all your options are, you should read on.

From the NIC Teaming tab, you can configure load balancing and failover behaviors for multiple NICs assigned to a virtual switch. In a production environment, you will always assign at least two NICs to a virtual switch that connects to a physical network, right?

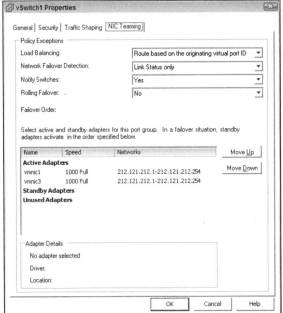

Figure 7-16:
Set NIC
teaming
policies
here.

The NIC Teaming tab is divided into three sections:

- ✔ **Policy Exceptions:** Here is where you configure your policies.
- ✔ **Adapters:** Here, specify the state of each NIC assigned to the switch.
- ✔ **Adapter Details:** In this section, you can see the driver and PCI slot for each adapter you highlight.

Policy Exceptions: Load Balancing

Load balancing offers three different ways to pick which uplink adapter to use for outgoing traffic. You can choose from a virtual port–based algorithm, a MAC address–based algorithm, an IP address–based algorithm, and an explicit failover order. Each has its tradeoffs.

Here are the routing methods to choose from:

- ✔ **A route based on originating virtual port ID** is the default algorithm. This method is fast and doesn't require any ongoing calculations by the VMkernel. The kernel is busy enough, so keep the default unless you have a good reason to change it.

  This algorithm assigns a network card based on the virtual switch port number that a virtual machine is plugged in to. The assignment is made when the virtual machine is powered-on and all packets use the same path until the machine is powered-off or a until network failure is detected. Because the path never changes, the VMkernel can concentrate on doing other things. This method is compatible with all physical switches.

Tradeoff: This is a mock load leveling algorithm. Traffic isn't actually analyzed with the goal of even distribution over physical NICs. The path traffic takes does not change over time unless a virtual machine is powered off or a network failure occurs.

✔ **A route based on IP hash** picks an uplink adapter for each packet based on a hash of the source and destination IP addresses. This method evenly distributes traffic loads over uplink adapters, which allows a machine to use the aggregate bandwidth of all physical adapters better. This choice works well for high-traffic machines.

Tradeoff: You didn't expect something for nothing, did you? This method has a higher CPU overhead and isn't compatible with all physical switches. Physical switches need to support link aggregation (IEE 802.3ad standard) to work with this distribution method.

✔ **A route based on source MAC hash** maps traffic to a physical NIC based on the virtual machine's MAC address. On the upside, this method has very little overhead and is compatible with all physical switches.

Tradeoff: This algorithm might not distribute traffic as evenly as a route based on IP hash.

Routing by the MAC address can place all traffic on the same uplink adapter if you are very unlucky with the MAC addresses assigned to your virtual machines. If this unlikely event occurs, consider using a different algoritm.

✔ **Explicit failover order** can also be called no load balancing! When you set the policy to explicit failover, all traffic goes through the first active adapter in the active adapter's list.If that adapter fails, all traffic goes through the next adapter in the list.

Tradeoff: You have no load leveling and can saturate a single NIC with too much traffic cause dropped packets.

Policy Exceptions: Network Failover Detection

The two methods to test for a network failure are Link Status Only and Beacon Probing. Again, stick with the defaults unless you're troubleshooting.

✔ **Link Status Only** relies solely on the link state reported by the NIC. If a cable gets unplugged between the NIC and a physical switch, or if a physical switch loses its power, the link status will switch, and the network failure will be detected. But what if your NIC is on the wrong VLAN? What if a cable is unplugged on the other side of the physical switch? The NIC will still show that it has a link, but you also have a network failure. Your ESX host will never know.

✔ **Beacon Probing** addresses this by sending out a network probe and listening for it on all adapters. If an adapter doesn't receive the probe, it is considered a network failure even if the NIC says it still has a link to the physical network. Of course, this method is a bit more resource intensive. Use the default Link Status Only unless you have a reason to turn on the beacons.

Policy Exceptions: Notify Switches

Notify Switches is a Yes or No choice. The default is Yes.

✔ **Yes:** If you set this option to Yes, an Address Resolution Protocol (ARP) notification is transmitted to the physical switch so that it can update its MAC address lookup table. The notification is sent whenever a failover occurs or a virtual machine is powered-on and connects to a virtual switch.

✔ **No:** Set Notify Switches to No if you're using Microsoft Network Load Balancing in *unicast mode* (single IP address to MAC address mapping).

Policy Exceptions: Rolling Failover

Rolling Failover determines what happens to a failed adapter after it's back online. The default is No:

✔ **Yes:** When set to Yes, the recently fixed adapter goes into standby mode and leaves the active adapter alone.

✔ **No:** If you leave this set to No, after an adapter comes back online, it takes over the duties of the standby adapter that took its place. The standby adapter goes back into standby mode.

Policy Exceptions: Failover Order

This area lets you assign how you want to break up your network adapters. You use all your adapters all the time, or save some in reserve for failures. You can also have a great deal of fun here with port groups because a single adapter can be active for one port group yet serve as standby for another.

These are the three adapter classifications:

✔ **Active Adapters:** Actively used as uplinks to the physical network

✔ **Standby Adapters:** Remain inactive until an active adapter fails

✔ **Unused Adapters:** Assigned to the switch or port group but not in use as active or standby

Now it's time to have some fun. Say you have two port groups with five virtual machines on each of them. Also say that you have four uplink adapters. Call the port groups P1 and P2. Call the uplink adapters U1 through U4. See Figure 7-17 to understand the following setup:

✔ **For P1:** Assign

 • U1 and U2 as active uplinks

 • U3 and U4 as standby adapters

✔ **For P2:** Assign

 • U3 and U4 as active uplinks

 • U1 and U2 as standby adapters

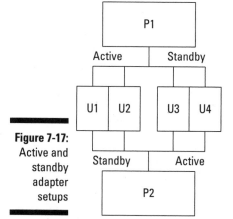

Figure 7-17:
Active and
standby
adapter
setups

If any one card goes, both port groups will share one active card, and each will have its own dedicated card.

In Figure 7-18, U2 fails. However, one downed NIC results in a fractional loss of capacity. Now try to picture that with four port groups and eight uplink adapters!

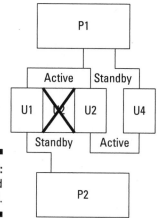

Figure 7-18:
One failed
NIC.

At this point, you might wonder what happens if you have two active adapters in a switch with no standby adapters and one adapter dies. When I tested it with a single virtual machine, the switch was smart enough to re-route traffic over the good card. So, again, always keep at least two uplink adapters in a production switch.

Following Networking Best Practices

Many of these networking best practices come directly from VMware, others just make sense:

- ✔ **Keep your service console on a separate network for security.** If someone can take control of the Service Console, he can take control of your server.

- ✔ **Keep your VMkernel ports on a separate network for throughput.** Remember that a virtual machine's memory is copied over this network link when you use VMotion.

- ✔ **Always use multiple uplink adapters for failover capabilities.**

- ✔ **Always use multiple uplink adapters for load-balancing capabilities.**

- ✔ **Separate virtual machines from each other for higher performance or better security.** You can do this with port groups or separate virtual switches.

- ✔ **Use fewer, larger switches unless you have a reason not to.** Simple systems have fewer problems to begin with and are easier to trouble-shoot.

- ✔ **Use the default settings for policies unless you have a reason not to.**

- ✔ **Use a virtual firewall if you need to protect your most sacred machines.** You can do this by using a virtual switch with no uplink adapters and a virtual switch with uplink adapters connected to a virtual machine that is a firewall.

- ✔ **Make use of VLANs and security policies if you need extra security.**

- ✔ **Everything is a tradeoff between cost and capacity or features and efficiency.** Carefully weigh the tradeoffs of doing something versus your needs and goals.

Chapter 8

Connecting to Storage

· ·

In This Chapter

▶ Viewing and connecting to storage

▶ Setting up multipathing

▶ Understanding and manipulating the VMFS file system

· ·

*E*SX hosts connect to a wide variety of storage subsystems. The majority of them use block-level Small Computer System Interface (SCSI) protocols, but some use file-level protocols as well. The choice of what type of storage to use to meet which goal is up to you. The tradeoffs between the various types of storage are discussed in Chapter 3.

In this chapter, we discuss the VMware storage model. Next, we create fault-tolerant disk configurations. We then look at connecting to and the appropriate uses of various SCSI and Network Attached Storage (NAS) subsystems. Finally, the VMware File System (VMFS) is covered. So without further ado, it is time to configure and get connected to your storage.

The VMware Infrastructure 3 Layered Storage Model

VMware Infrastructure 3 (VI3) uses a layered storage model (shown in Figure 8-1) comprising your virtual machine files, a unique and robust file system called VMFS to manage access to the virtual machine files, and raw storage subsystems. The three layer storage model is as follows:

▶ **Virtual machine layer:** This top layer consists of virtual machine disk files. There is one disk file for each hard drive in a virtual machine.

▶ **ESX host layer:** The middle layer consists of VMFS-formatted logical unit numbers (LUNs). This allows multiple ESX hosts to access the virtual machine files.

Only one ESX host can have any virtual machine's files open at a time.

✔ **Raw storage layer:** The bottom layer consists of your storage arrays, local disks, and network attached storage (NAS). Here, your disks are grouped to provide some form of fault tolerance. The disk groups are presented to the middle layer as LUNs — or in the case of NAS, as a Network File System (NFS) share.

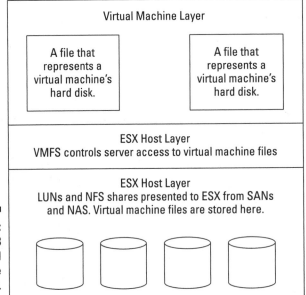

Figure 8-1:
The VI3 layered storage model.

How ESX Sees Disk Partitions

Your raw storage layer presents your ESX with LUNs that can be used as data stores. Whether you're using a SAN or local SCSI storage on your production system, you will use some type of Redundant Array of Inexpensive Disks (RAID) to achieve fault tolerance. Most RAID sets use either parity blocks or direct data copies that allow information on a failed disk to be reconstructed from the remaining functional disks. This way, you can lose a single disk but still keep running.

When you're planning for the potential for disk failure, remember that disk failures aren't completely random. Instead, disk failure rates follow a bathtub-shaped curve: like a U-shaped curve, with a much longer bottom (see Figure 8-2).

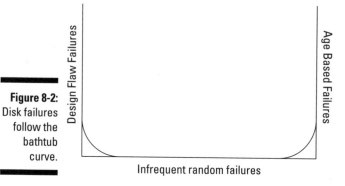

Figure 8-2: Disk failures follow the bathtub curve.

Failure rates tend to be high in the beginning and end of life. The first part of the curve represents decreasing probability of failure. A failure early in life is usually attributable to a manufacturing defect; most disks suffering from that defect will fail. If the disks survive to the bottom of the curve, that represents a low and completely random failure rate. The last part of the curve indicates increasing failures attributable to age. After all, unless you're using solid-state disks, you have a mechanical device that is always on and always spinning — and it has to die sooner or later.

Advanced RAID levels allow you to lose more than one disk as well. You need to decide the tradeoff between price and redundancy. Your RAID level determines how disks are grouped for different levels of redundancy. Here are some common levels:

✔ **RAID 0,** or disk striping, simply writes your data across two or more physical disks.

The good: The advantages of this method are speedy disk reads and writes as well as full use of your raw storage (because no storage is used to keep redundant parity information).

The bad: Of course, nothing is free, so you have to pay for RAID 0 by not having any fault tolerance. When — not if — one of your disks dies, you lose all your data!

The possibly ugly: RAID 0 is appropriate only for test systems, storage of data that can be lost without a creating a problem, or any other system that needs to be fast and has some other type of redundancy built in. The more disks you add, the more the overall reliability of a RAID 0 set goes down.

To calculate the reliability of RAID 0, simply take the average mean time between failure (MTBF) of all the disks and divide by the number of disks in the set.

✔ **RAID 1,** or mirroring, is writing all your data twice to two identically sized disks or groups of disks.

The good: RAID 1 is far more fault tolerant than RAID 0 and is fast to read data because each disk can seek blocks independently.

The bad: The price you pay for using RAID 1 is slower writes because the data needs to be written twice and also because you lose half of your storage capacity (for redundancy). RAID 1 is appropriate for system partitions and log files.

You can calculate the general probability of both drives failing (at the bottom of your bathtub curve) by squaring the probability of one disk failing. Say that you have two disks with a MTBF of 1:1000. To find the probability of both failing, square $\frac{1}{1000}$ — which gives you $\frac{1}{1000000}$, or a 0.0001 percent chance of both disks dying at the same time. There are more complex statistical models that take the full bathtub curve into account, but the point is multiple redundant disks make a complete failure less likely than a single disk.

✔ **RAID 5,** or striping with parity, is one of the most commonly used RAID levels.

The good: RAID 5 provides relatively inexpensive redundancy because the total amount of disk space used for redundancy is the number of disks in the group minus one (N–1). This is because each time data is written, it is written onto N–1 disks, and the parity information is written to the remaining (1) disk.

Also, RAID 5 is extremely reliable because you can lose one disk and keep all your information as long as a second disk doesn't die in the time it takes to replace and rebuild the first failed drive. This is why you always want to use a *global hot spare.* If one disk dies, the global hot spare is used to replace it instantly. The only window of danger is while the RAID data is getting recalculated and written to the global hot spare-turned-replacement disk.

The bad: The cost of RAID 5 is lower write performance because of calculating parity information.

✔ **RAID 1+0,** called RAID 10, is a combination of mirroring and striping where you stripe data across mirrored sets of disks. To implement this, you split your disks into groups and then mirror the groups. After your mirrors are established, you stripe your data across the mirrors.

The good: You can lose one disk from every mirrored group and still run.

The bad: If you lose a mirrored set, you also lose your data. Of course, the price for this high level of redundancy is using many disks to store redundant information.

When you mirror striped sets, it is called RAID 0+1.

✔ **RAID 1+5** mirrors disk sets and then stripes data across them with parity, achieving extreme fault tolerance at the expense of everything else.

The good: You can lose one disk out of each mirrored set as well as an entire mirrored set and still run.

The bad: You achieve extreme fault tolerance at the expense of everything else.

If you stripe data and parity across mirrored sets, it is called RAID 5+1. If you need this level of fault tolerance, you should probably look into mirroring two SAN disk enclosures in two different physical locations and use RAID 5 in each enclosure. You can then withstand the loss of an entire site as well as one disk from each RAID 5 set in the remaining enclosure. This is an extremely high grade of fault tolerance but an expensive way to go.

Addressing LUNs and partitions

At the raw storage level, after you group one or more disks in some RAID configuration, the grouping is given a LUN. The LUNs are then presented to the ESX host layer. You can then partition the logical units to put a file system on. LUNs are grouped under SCSI target IDs. ESX hosts see partitions by referencing the host card; the adapter ID; the SCSI target ID; the LUN number; and finally, the partition number.

You can see in Figure 8-3 that the boot partition on the local ESX host is referenced as `vmhba0:0:0 partition 0`. The local RAID controller is always called `vmhba0`. Because there is only one SCSI target on this controller, the second number is 0. Furthermore, there is only one LUN on that target, so you see that number as 0 as well. And finally, because there is only one partition, you see yet another 00 to identify it.

Computer scientists always like to start numbering things with 0 instead of 1.

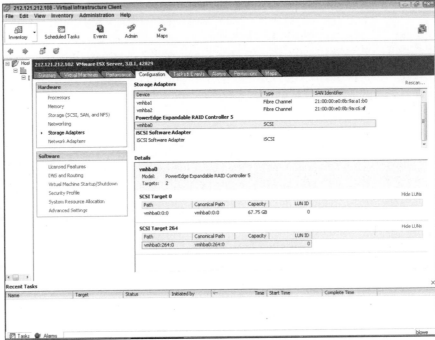

You should also notice three other items in Figure 8-3: namely, the
`vmhba0:264:0 partition 0`, the Hide LUNS link, and the Rescan link:

- ✔ **`vmhba0:264:0 partition 0`:** This is the SCSI target for PERC 5 RAID
  controller in my Dell PowerEdge server. It is not configurable and can be
  safely ignored.

- ✔ **Hide LUNs:** Clicking the Hide LUNs link conceals the details of the LUNs
  under a SCSI target.

- ✔ **Rescan:** Clicking the Rescan link (upper-right corner) searches the entire
  SCSI chain for new or changed LUNs.

  Use this link if your storage configuration has changed in any way or you
  won't see your changes.

You can see in Figure 8-4 that Fibre Channel adapters are addressed the same
way as the local RAID controller. The only difference is the SAN Identifier, or
the World Wide Name (WWN), for the controller. Also notice that the Fibre
Channel cards have multiple SCSI targets, one for each storage processor.

- ✔ `vmhba1.0.0` and `vmhba1.1.0` provide a fault-tolerant path to reach
  LUN 0 on the SAN.

- ✔ `vmhba1.0.1` and `vmhba1.1.1` provide a fault-tolerant path to two LUN 1.

If one of the two SAN storage processors dies, ESX can still see the SAN disk files on each LUN through the other processor. Similarly, if one host bus adapter (HBA) dies, the other can take over. I cover this in greater detail in the multipathing section of this chapter.

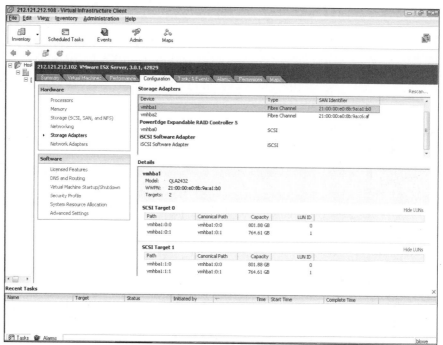

Figure 8-4:
Addressing
Fibre
Channel
LUNs.

Scanning for LUNs

Your ESX installer program can see only 128 LUNs. However, when your VMkernel boots up after a completed install, it scans up to 256 LUNs, numbering from 0–255. If anything changes on the storage side, you need to rescan. To rescan storage, do the following:

1. **Log into your server using your Virtual Infrastructure Client (VIC).**

2. **Highlight your server.**

3. **Click the Configuration tab.**

4. **Click the Storage Adapters link in the Hardware section on the left side of the screen.**

   You see a screen similar to Figure 8-4.

5. **Click the Rescan link in the upper right of the screen.**

   You should now see any storage changes that took place.

Understanding Multipathing

Multipathing provides fault-tolerant access to LUNs. If you lose access to a storage processor in your SAN, your system can access LUNs through a path to another storage processor. If you lose an HBA card, a secondary card can take over so that you maintain the critical connectivity from your ESX host to your storage.

Figure 8-5 shows four possible paths the server can use to get to LUN 0 (only one path is active at a time).

- ✔ HBA 1 to Storage Processor A to LUN 0.
- ✔ HBA 1 to Storage Processor B to LUN 0.
- ✔ HBA 2 to Storage Processor A to LUN 0.
- ✔ HBA 2 to Storage Processor B to LUN 0.

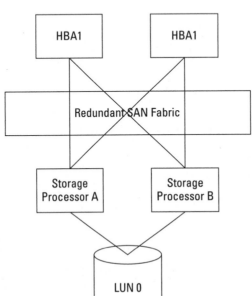

Figure 8-5:
Four
possible
paths to
reach
LUN 0.

Multipathing with Fibre Channel

You need two HBAs in each ESX host that you want to be able to multipath. ESX automatically configures multipathing, depending on the type of array that's detected on your SAN. This is another very good reason to choose only SAN hardware on your hardware compatibility list (HCL). You need to know the following:

- ✔ **Multipathing automatically fails-over from one HBA to another in case of a hardware failure so you do not have an outage.**

- ✔ **Only a single path to any LUN is active at any time.**

- ✔ **The two multipathing polices are Most Recently Used (MRU) and Fixed Path (also called Preferred Path).**

  - *MRU* continues using whatever path is currently working. If path 1 fails and path 2 takes over, the system continues to use path 2 after path 1 becomes available again. In other words, MRU does not fail-back to the last-used path. This is the default policy for active/passive storage arrays.

  - *Fixed Path* is just the opposite of MRU. It uses a preferred path whenever that path is available. If the preferred path stops working, another path is used. After the preferred path is functional again, it becomes the active path. This is the default setting for active/active disk enclosures.

    You should not manually change the defaults since VMware sets them based on the type of storage array you have. However, if you want to tempt fate, you can change the multipathing policies clicking the manage paths button on your data store's properties (covered below).

Version 3.5 offers experimental support for a Fibre Channel–HBA load-balancing algorithm. However, the HBA round-robin algorithm isn't yet supported for production environments.

Figure 8-6 shows the properties for a data store. Notice you can change the store's name if you want. You can also add *extents* to increase the size. Extents are covered in the "Extending VMFS data stores" section later in this chapter. Additionally, you can see file system format and path information.

Figure 8-6:
Data store
properties.

To get to the properties screen in Figure 8-6, do the following:

1. **Log in to your server using your VIC.**

2. **Highlight your server.**

3. **Click the Configuration tab.**

4. **Click the Storage (SCSI, SAN, and NFS) link in the Hardware section on the left-hand side of the screen.**

5. **Click the storage group you that interests you.**

6. **Click the Properties link.**

Multipathing with iSCSI

TCP/IP provides multipathing through IP routing. iSCSI makes use of a request — called `SendTargets` — that communicates storage processor IP addresses and ports that allow access to different paths to LUNs. Optionally, you can manually define iSCSI paths. You need to know the following:

✔ **The iSCSI initiator can sit on top of multiple NICs.**

   The NICs and IP routing provide multipathing.

✔ **Fixed and MRU algorithms are the same for iSCSI.**

✔ **Paths are discovered with the iSCSI SendTargetsSendTargets request.**

✔ **Only active/passive configurations are supported.**

✔ **Pointing both iSCSI and a Fibre Channel HBA to the same LUN is not supported.**

Understanding VMware File System

VMware File System (VMFS) is an advanced, multimaster, distributed lock file system. (More on that in a minute. For now, just try saying that three times fast.) VMFS is designed to be a high-throughput, clustered file system The best way to understand it is to compare it with a more-typical file system. A typical file system allows only a single server to have read/write access. Comparatively, VMFS allows multiple servers read/write access simultaneously. Don't worry, though: Your data isn't at risk. VMFS makes use of distributed journaling to provide rapid recovery as well as on-disk locking to prevent two servers from writing to the same files.

When you format a data store with VMFS, you're creating a SCSI-based file system. This means that any protocol that supports SCSI commands can access it. This includes Fibre Channel SCSI, iSCSI, and locally connected SCSI.

As shown in Figure 8-7, all your virtual machines are just a set of files stored in a common directory that lives on a VMFS data store. You have virtual machine configuration files and virtual machine hard disk files for each of your virtual machines. Notice that every hard disk a virtual machine has is a separate file.

Watch your plugs and locks

When I first built my system, I ran a test. I unplugged all the networking cables of one server at roughly the same time, expecting the virtual machines to immediately start on the other server in the cluster. When they did not, I tried to manually start them but got an error, saying the virtual machine files were locked. This happened because the server didn't crash — it just lost all its network and management communications.

The moral of the story: Don't unplug all your network cables at once and expect the on-disk locks to be freed!

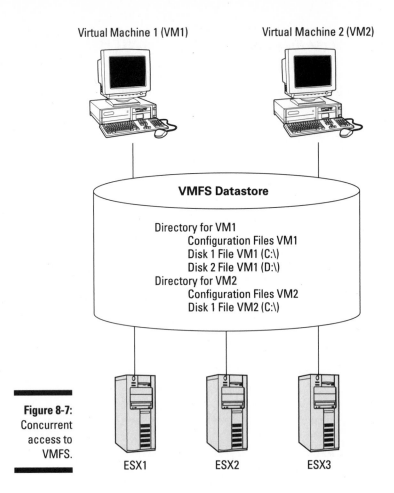

Figure 8-7:
Concurrent
access to
VMFS.

You can call VMFS a multimaster, distributed file system because up to 32 ESX hosts can access a single VMFS volume at the same time. This allows you to run any virtual machine on any ESX that can see the files. However, only one ESX can access a virtual machine's files at a time. Your VMFS data store controls access to files with on-disk locking. The locks are distributed because any server can lock any virtual machine file that is currently unlocked. If a server dies, the locks that it has are released so that the virtual machine can be restarted on a different server.

Designing your VMFS

Here are the three schools of thought for VMFS design:

✔ **Consolidation:** Uses large data stores with many virtual machines on each of them

- *Pro:* Fewer data stores to manage and better resource utilization

- *Con:* A higher potential for I/O (input/output) contentions that can decimate performance

✔ **Isolation:** A single data store for each virtual machine

- *Pro:* Lack of I/O contentions for high-throughput systems

- *Con:* Potential for lower hardware utilization and the management overhead of many data stores

✔ **Hybrid:** This approach is the most common and it is a combination of strict consolidation and strict isolation. Good capacity planning is essential for the hybrid method. Basically, you aggregate the disk throughput of all your servers that will be on a single data store and then make sure that it's less than the throughput of that data store.

- *Pro:* Very good resource utilization and lower potential for some I/O contention (but your capacity planning should protect against this).

- *Con:* Resource utilization is not as good as the consolidation model and the potential for I/O contention is higher than the Isolation model.

For an example of each approach, say that you have two domain controllers, two database servers, an e-mail server, a Web server, and a file server. Also assume that you have a 2-Gbps SAN with two storage processors. Here is the average disk throughput by server:

✔ Domain Controller 1: 10 Mbps

✔ Domain Controller 2: 10 Mbps

✔ Database Server 1: 50 Mbps

✔ Database Server 2: 100 Mbps

✔ E-mail Server: 500 Mbps

✔ Web Server: 50 Mbps

✔ File Server: 25 Mbps

If you used the consolidation approach, you would put all machines on one massive data store. And this approach would be fine as long as it worked with the SAN-vendor recommendations for the number of spindles per LUN. The average throughput would be 0.745 Gbps, of an available 2 Gbps. You'd have plenty of room to spare and only one data store to manage.However, if you're an isolationist at heart, you could make a separate data store for each machine. The overall throughput would be the same, but you'd have seven data stores to manage. That means seven LUNs, each with their own RAID setups to support the seven data stores. This approach would waste disk space and really make life far more difficult than it need be. Sorry!

Say you choose the hybrid approach. One way would be to try to split I/O down the middle and make the following two data stores:

- **Data store 1:** Uses the first HBA and the first storage processor to get to the first LUN. Store both domain controllers, both database servers, the Web server, and the file server for an average throughput of 0.245 Gbps.

- **Data store 2:** Uses the second HBA and the second storage processor to get to the second LUN. Store the e-mail server for an average throughput of 0.500 Gbps.

With this setup, you have only two data stores to manage. One large data store can be used for the multiple servers, and one smaller data store can be used for e-mail. Because your SAN has a data throughput of 2 Gbps, you're covered if a storage processor, an HBA, or one of each fails, forcing all disk traffic to take the same path. Worst case scenario, the throughput would still average only 0.745 Gbps on a 2-Gbps path. You're left with plenty of breathing room for throughput!

- Always look at the worst-case scenario to make sure that you have enough capacity when employing the hybrid approach.

- KISS (Keep it simple, silly). Always choose a simpler system design over a more complex one. Simpler systems break less and are easier to troubleshoot, which is always nice if a system breaks.

- Always check your SAN vendor's documentation to make sure that it can adequately support the number of spindles you want to use per LUN and the throughput you need.

Using Raw Device Mapping

You also have the choice to use VMFS or a Raw Device Mapping (RDM), also often called a *Raw Disk Mapping*. An RDM allows a machine to access the LUN directly instead of storing its disk data in a file. For most applications you want to use VMFS, but some exceptions are noted with the compatibility modes.

A virtual machine still accesses a file to see an RDM. The file just points to the actual LUN and lets your virtual machine know which mode the RDM is in. The two modes are

- **Physical Compatibility Mode:** This mode allows the virtual machine direct access to the hardware. In other words, the guest operating system has direct access to the SCSI device. This mode is typically used for Microsoft clustering or if you're running a utility on a virtual machine that's aware of the SAN.

✔ **Virtual Compatibility Mode:** In this mode, the physical LUN acts like a virtual disk, allowing snapshots, virtual machine clones, and virtual machine templates. Use this mode if you want your virtual machine to have raw disc access, but not complete SCSI control.

Regardless of the mode, VMotion, DRS, and HA all work with RDMs. Now that sentence is an acronym salad!

Creating VMFS data stores

Creating a VMFS data store is done through the Add Storage Wizard. To add storage, do the following:

1. **Log into your server using your VIC.**

2. **Highlight your server.**

3. **Click the Configuration tab.**

4. **Click the Storage Adapters link in the Hardware section on the left side of the screen.**

5. **Click the Rescan link in the upper-right corner of the screen.**

6. **Click the Storage (SCSI, SAN, and NFS) link in the Hardware section on the left side of the screen.**

7. **Click the Add Storage link in the upper-right corner of the screen.**

   The Add Storage Wizard opens, as shown in Figure 8-8.

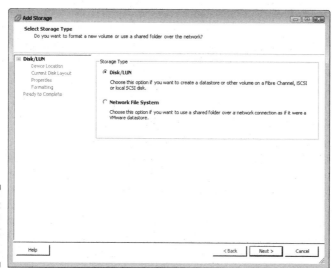

Figure 8-8: The Add Storage Wizard.

8. **Choose DISK/LUN as the storage type.**

9. **Click the LUN you want to add from the list and then click Next.**

10. **Review the Disk Layout and then click Next.**

11. **Enter the Data Store name and then click Next.**

12. **Pick the Maximum File Size that you want to be able to support and then click Next.**

13. **Review the information. If it's correct, click Finish.**

    Your new VMFS data store will now show up with the rest of your storage.

Browsing VMFS data stores

Browsing through the files on a data store is easy. Just follow these steps:

1. **Log into your server using your VIC.**

2. **Highlight your server.**

3. **Click the Configuration tab.**

4. **Click the Storage (SCSI, SAN, and NFS) link in the Hardware section on the left side of the screen.**

5. **Double-click the data store that you want to browse.**

    You see a window similar to Figure 8-9.

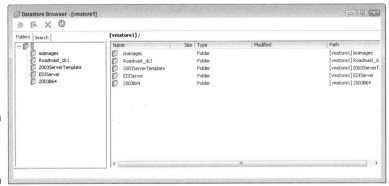

Figure 8-9:
Browsing a
data store.

Extending VMFS data stores

When you extend a VMFS data store, you wind up storing data on two or more VMFS data stores. The multiple data stores appear as one large VMFS volume. Use an *extent* — a way to span two VMFS volumes— if you want a VMFS data store that is larger than the maximum size of 2TB. You can extend a volume on the fly without rebooting.

✔ **The maximum number of LUNs allowed in an extent is 32.**

✔ **The first volume that you are extending loses no data.** Any other volume used in the extension loses all its data.

✔ **If you remove an extent, all data on all volumes is destroyed.**

✔ **The first volume contains the metadata for the entire extent.** If you lose this volume, you can potentially lose data on other volumes.

If you want to extend a VMFS volume, pick the volume you want to use and follow these steps:

1. **Log into your server using your VIC.**

2. **Highlight your server.**

3. **Click the Configuration tab.**

4. **Click the Storage (SCSI, SAN, and NFS) link in the Hardware section on the left side of the screen.**

5. **Click the LUN you want to extend.**

6. **Click the Properties link.**

7. **Click Add Extent button to launch the Add Extent Wizard.**

8. **Pick the LUN you want to use in the extent.**

9. **Review the disk layout, making sure you have no data you mind losing on it the LUN you are extending on to. Then click Next.**

10. **Set how much capacity you want to use for the new extent (usually Maximize) and then click Next.**

11. **Review the information. If it's correct, click Finish.**

Connecting to NAS

As I mention in Chapter 3, NAS is a good choice for anything that doesn't require fast storage. Among other things, you can use NAS for test systems, tiered storage, and storing ISO (disk) images. Here's how to connect to NAS:

1. **Log into your server using your VIC.**

2. **Highlight your server.**

3. **Click the Configuration tab.**

4. **Click the Storage Adapters link in the Hardware section on the left side of the screen.**

5. **Click the Rescan link in the upper-right corner of the screen.**

6. **Click the Storage (SCSI, SAN, and NFS) link in the Hardware section on the left side of the screen.**

7. **Click the Add Storage link in the upper-right corner of the screen.**

   The Add Storage Wizard opens.

8. **Choose the Network File System radio button and click Next.**

9. **Enter the Server address and folder name, provide a Data Store name, and then click Next.**

10. **Review the information. If it's correct, click Finish.**

Part IV
Fault Tolerance and Data Centers

The 5th Wave   By Rich Tennant

"Sure, at first it sounded great — an intuitive virtual network that helps people write memos by finishing their thoughts for them."

In this part . . .

This part shows you how to build and manage a rock-solid virtual foundation upon which you build your virtual machines. Chapter 9 covers installing and configuring your central management interface — VirtualCenter. Chapters 10 and 11 cover creating and managing your virtual machines, respectively. Creating and managing active/active hardware clusters for extreme fault tolerance is addressed in Chapter 12.

Chapter 9

Getting VMware VirtualCenter Running

. . . .

In This Chapter

▶ Seeing what VirtualCenter can do for you

▶ Understanding the parts and pieces of VirtualCenter

▶ Installing and using VirtualCenter

. . . .

*V*Mware VirtualCenter is your single management interface for fault-tolerant virtual infrastructures. Although you can manage each ESX separately, VirtualCenter gives you a single place to go for all your virtual infrastructure–management tasks, such as creating virtual machines and monitoring how everything is running. (You can read about ESX in Chapters 4 and 5, and fault-tolerance in Part IV.)

Sorry, but some quick nomenclature is needed before delving into VirtualCenter. When using the proper name of the product, I write this name as *VMware VirtualCenter* (or just *VirtualCenter*). When I refer to any virtual center, or the concept of a virtual center, I write it as lowercase letters.

With that said, This chapter covers the information you need to know to install VirtualCenter and add ESX machines to it.

VMware VirtualCenter: The Brains Behind the System

After you add an ESX to a virtual center, you never have to connect to that server directly again. VirtualCenter installs a remote management agent on any ESX that you add to its inventory. Your virtual center becomes a proxy manager. However, centralized management is just the beginning. Using VirtualCenter gives you many other benefits.

Figure 9-1 shows the initial page when you connect to VirtualCenter using you VIC. You can see virtual clusters (a way to make your VMs fault-tolerant is covered in Chapter 12) and the ESX hosts in them. Below that you can see any resource pools (a way to limit CPU and memory resource allocation when resources are low; resource pools are covered in Chapter 14) and the virtual machines in them.

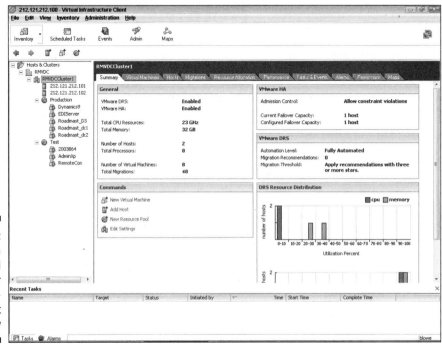

Figure 9-1:
The
Virtual
Center
manage-
ment
window

What VirtualCenter can do for you

VirtualCenter provides you with a great deal of functionality that can all be managed from a single place. You can break the functionality of VirtualCenter into three areas: core services, distributed services, and interface services.

Core services

Core services provide your management functionality to inventory and quickly create your VMs. It also allows you to set warning alarms that proactively alert you about problems. You can schedule tasks like rolling out a new virtual machine. Lastly, this is where you can access logs that provide information on your entire virtual system.

✔ **Resource and virtual machine inventory management:** Use to keep track of your resource utilization and your virtual machines.

✔ **Alarms and events management:** You can set alarms for various events in your system. These services keep track of any alarms and also log every event that occurs in your system, as shown in Figure 9-2. *Events* can include creating a new virtual machine, making a snapshot, rebooting a virtual machine, and releasing a disk lock — basically, anything that happens on an ESX.

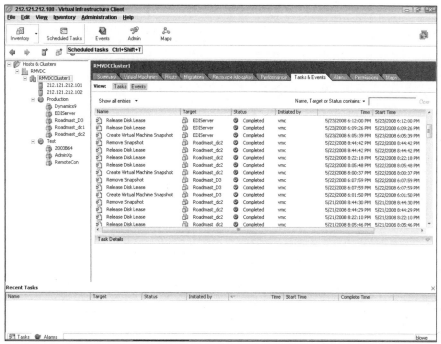

Figure 9-2:
Various
events that
have been
logged.

✔ **VM provisioning:** This service guides and automates the provisioning of virtual machines.

✔ **Statistics logging:** This service tracks performance and resource utilization across your virtual infrastructure, as shown in Figure 9-3.

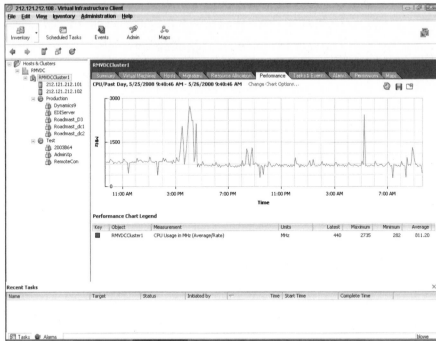

Figure 9-3:
CPU
statistics
over time.

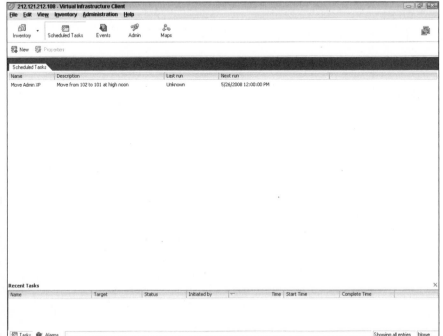

Figure 9-4:
A
scheduled
task to
automati-
cally move a
machine via
Vmotion.

✔ **Task scheduler:** You can schedule various tasks, such as shutting down or powering-on virtual machines. Additionally, this service (see Figure 9-4) schedules movement of machines from one ESX to another via VMotion.

✔ **Host and virtual machine configuration:** This service enables you to centrally configure ESX hosts and virtual machines.

Distributed services

This group provides add-on functionality outside the core services. These services include ways to restart virtual machines if the ESX host they are running on fails. You have the ability to move running machines from one ESX host to another with no loss of service. The system can even move machines automatically to load level CPU and memory resource utilization across several ESX hosts.

✔ **High Availability (HA):** Using High Availability restarts a virtual machine on a new host server if its original host has failed.

✔ **VMotion:** Use this service (see Figure 9-5) to move virtual machines from one host server to another (called migrating), while running, without losing connectivity.

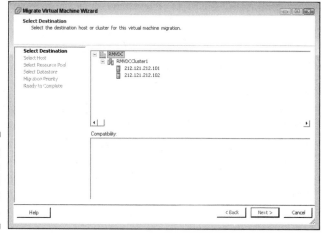

Figure 9-5:
The Migrate
Virtual
Machine
Wizard.

✔ **DRS:** Distributed Resource Scheduler (see Figure 9-6) always watches host servers to see whether they become overloaded. If they do, DRS can be set to automatically utilizing VMotion to move some of your virtual machines from highly utilized hosts to those with lower utilization rates. This is basically a way to load balance your virtual machines across multiple ESX host servers.

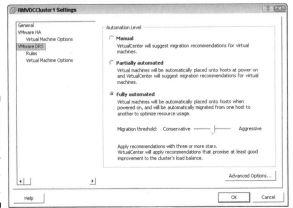

Figure 9-6:
Ditributed
Resource
Scheduler
configura-
tion page.

Version 3.5 introduces two additional distributed services:

✔ **Storage VMotion:** Using this service enables you to change the storage location of a virtual machine's files while the machine is running.

✔ **Distributed Power Management:** Although supported only experimentally, this service enables you to attempt to consolidate all your virtual machines on as few hosts as possible so that any extra hosts can go into a low-power state.

Interface services

These interfaces allow your virtual center to talk to other service providers.

✔ **Database Interface:** This interface (shown in Figure 9-7) provides connectivity to your virtual center database. The database stores all your virtual center information. It can be an Oracle or SQL Server database.

✔ **Active Directory Interface:** This interface allows your virtual center to talk to Active Directory to get a list of accounts to use with access control lists. Your Windows accounts become the base accounts for your virtual infrastructure. Security in Windows and VMware Infrastructure 3 are similar, yet also very different. I cover this in Chapter 13.

✔ **ESX Server Management:** This interface relays your commands to your ESX hosts via the VirtualCenter Agent that gets installed on each ESX host when you add it to your virtual center.

✔ **VI API:** The VMware Infrastructure API allows additional functionality to be plugged into your infrastructure. One example is *VMware Converter:* This product clones a physical machine into a virtual machine through the VI API. Another example is VI Client (VIC).

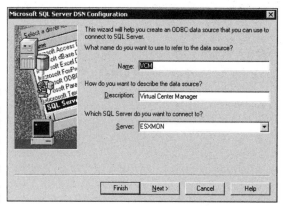

Figure 9-7:
ODBC
configuration
screen for
database
connectivity.

If your virtual center server is not part of a Windows Domain, it uses the local security accounts as the Access Contol List (ACL) accounts for your virtual infrastructure. This allows you to separate your virtual infrastructure security from your Windows Domain accounts if you want. In some situations this might be the way to go.

If, for example, you did not want your Domain or Enterprise administrators to have full access to your VirtualCenter and everything in it, you can use a machine that is not a member of the domain to run VirtualCenter on. You can also look at this from a security perspective: If the VirtualCenter machine is not running on a server that is part of the domain, no domain users have any access to VirtualCenter. Each user must be defined separately. Of course the downside is losing single sign-on and being forced to create new accounts and groups for anyone you want to have access.

Making your VirtualCenter server a member of a domain or not does not matter to VMware. Whichever way works better in your situation is the correct way to go.

Understanding your virtual center's components

VMware VirtualCenter is made up of six separate software components. They are as follows:

- ✔ **VirtualCenter Server:** This service centrally administers ESX hosts and virtual machines.

- ✔ **VMware License Server:** This server-based licensing framework enables you to centrally manage your licenses.

✔ **Web Access:** This Web-based interface can be used to manage virtual machines.

✔ **VI Client:** This is the same client that you use to connect to your ESX hosts.

Different versions of VI3 servers require different versions of VIC. The newest version is backward compatible, and older versions prompt you to update. I have run into one small problem with the new client for v. 3.5: It would not run on my 64-bit Vista machine. The older 3.0.x version did, however.

✔ **VirtualCenter Database:** Use this database server to store configuration and performance metrics. You can keep the database on the local machine or a separate database server. The more machines you have to virtualize, the stronger the argument is for separating your VirtualCenter server and database server. You can always start with one box and move the database later.

✔ **VirtualCenter Agents:** This software runs on ESX hosts. Your agents take commands from the virtual center and enact them on the host server.

Windows services you see

Your virtual center consists of four Windows services (shown in Figure 9-8). You need to know them in case you ever want to stop or restart one of them:

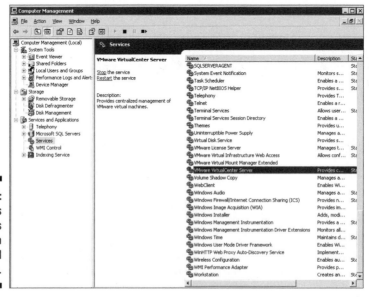

Figure 9-8:
Windows
services
that run
Virtual
Center.

- ✔ **VMware VirtualCenter Server:** Should always be on; is set to start automatically.

- ✔ **VMware License Server:** Should always be on; is set to start automatically.

- ✔ **VMware Virtual Infrastructure Web Access:** Should always be running; automatically started.

  In Version 3.5, VMware Virtual Infrastructure Web Access is now called VMware Infrastructure Web Access.

- ✔ **VMware Virtual Mount Manager Extended:** Should be on only when you are cloning or deploying a virtual machine from a template; set to manual start.

  These processes are covered in Chapter 11.

  In Version 3.5, VMware Virtual Mount Manager Extended is now called VMware Mount Service for VirtualCenter.

In Version 3.5, you can choose to install a few other services when you install VirtualCenter. These services are designed to help you virtualize physical machines and ease patch management:

- ✔ **VMware Capacity Planner Service:** Optionally installed; set to start automatically.

- ✔ **VMware Converter Enterprise Service**: Optionally installed; set to start automatically.

- ✔ **VMware Update Manager Service:** Optionally installed; set to start automatically.

VirtualCenter Housekeeping: You Need a Database

VirtualCenter tracks an awful lot of configuration, security, and event information. It tracks so much information, in fact, that it only makes sense to store it in a database for organization and fast retrieval.

A tale of two databases

You have two choices when it comes to what database to use: Microsoft SQL Server or an Oracle database. Of course, you can pick from several flavors of each database. The following are supported for VirtualCenter v. 2.5:

✔ **SQL Server 2000 Standard and Enterprise editions with Service Pack (SP) 4:** You need MDAC 2.8 SP1 on Windows 2000 and XP clients.

✔ **SQL Server 2005 Enterprise SP1 or SP2 with the native client:** You need MDAC 2.8 SP1 on Windows 2000 and XP clients.

✔ **SQL Server 2005 Express SP2 with the native client:** You need MDAC 2.8 SP1 on Windows 2000 and XP clients. This comes bundled with VirtualCenter v. 2.5 and can support up to 5 hosts and 50 virtual machines.

✔ **Oracle 9i Standard or Enterprise with patch 9.2.0.8.0 applied on both client and server**

✔ **Oracle 10g Standard or Enterprise Release 1**

✔ **Oracle 10g Standard or Enterprise Release 2 with the following:**

  • Patch 10.2.0.3.0 applied to both server and client.

  • Patch 5699495 applied to the client.

Here are some general caveats:

Always check the requirements on the VMware site before installing.

✔ For all Microsoft operating systems other than Windows Server 2003 SP1, you need to download and install Windows Installer 3.1.

✔ VirtualCenter v. 2.5 runs only on 32-bit operating systems.

✔ You need Internet Explorer 5.5 or higher to run VirtualCenter.

Finding a home for your database

You need to decide whether you want your database to run on the same server as your virtual center. If you're running VirtualCenter on a virtual machine (yes, you can do that, but it is not the VMware recommended setup), VMware strongly recommends running the database on a physical server. If you choose to ignore VMware's sage advice, you can run the database on a virtual machine but it should be a different VM that the one VirtualCenter is running on.

In general, the larger your deployment, the greater the need to separate the database server from the VirtualCenter server. On physical machines, performance is also a function of your hardware.

The bare minimum requirements for VirtualCenter are

✔ 2.0 GHz or higher Intel or AMD x86 processor

✔ 2GB RAM

✔ A Gigabit network interface card (NIC) is recommended

✔ 560MB of free disk space, but it is recommended that you have a minimum of 2GB

You need more hardware if you're also running your database on the VirtualCenter server. A faster processor, more RAM, and more disk space are all required.

If you have only 2GB of disk space left on your server, you're installing VirtualCenter on the wrong machine. The last thing you want to do is run out of space for your database.

For anything but a small virtual infrastructure deployment — say, up to 5 hosts with up to a total of 50 virtual machines — you're better off keeping your database on a separate server. This is also the limit of SQL Server 2005 Express. Therefore, if you can run SQL Server 2005 Express, you can keep your database on the same server provided that you're above the minimum hardware requirements for VirtualCenter.

To give you a very rough idea of the database size, VMware estimates that after one year, a system with 25 hosts that each running 8–16 virtual machines will swell your SQL Server database roughly 2GB in size. Comparatively, an Oracle database will take up approximately 1GB of disk space under the same conditions. To get a more concrete idea of database size, read the next section.

Calculating your database size

Your database size is a function of your statistics gathering level and the number of hosts and virtual machines in your infrastructure. You can change the settings for gathering your statistics and you know how many hosts and virtual machines you will have over time from your capacity planning (see Chapter 2).

To adjust the statistics settings, do the following:

1. **Login to VirtualCenter using VIC.**

2. **Click the Administration drop-down list.**

3. **Click VirtualCenter Management Server Configuration.**

4. **Click on Statistics, as shown in Figure 9-9.**

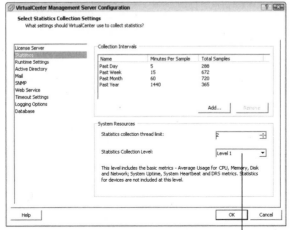

Figure 9-9:
Checking
your
statistics
settings.

The Statistics Collection Level

Changing the Statistics Collection Level (found in the lower-right corner of the dialog box; refer to Figure 9-9) will affect the size of your database. The higher the level, the more information gathered, and the bigger the database.

Now download the Database size calculator from the URL that follows. Bear in mind the link points to the calculator for VirtualCenter 2.0. This will give you a worst case scenario because VirtualCenter 2.5 uses less database space.

```
www.vmware.com/support/vi3/doc/vc_db_calculator.xls
```

Installing the database

Follow your vendor recommendations for server sizing, database connectivity, and database installation. This section assumes a small rollout with VirtualCenter on the same machine as the database. SQL Server 2005 Express SP2 is bundled with VirtualCenter v. 2.5.

To install it, do the following:

1. **From the VirtualCenter 2.5 CD, double-click the Redist folder.**

2. **Open the Dotnet folder.**

3. **Open the x86 folder.**

4. **Run Dotnetfx.exe to begin the Dot Net Framework installer.**

5. **Click Next.**

6. **Read and accept the license agreement; then click Install.**

7. **Watch the install bar for a while.**

   While you're watching the installation bar scroll across your screen, remember that when the first 90 percent is finished, you have the other 90 percent to go! These bars never seem all that accurate.

8. **Reboot if necessary.**

   You don't have to reboot with Windows 2003 SP2. Your mileage might vary with other OS versions.

Now install SQL Server Express SP2 by following these steps:

1. **Navigate back to the install CD and open the `\redist\sqlexpr32` folder.**

2. **Run `SQLEXPR32.EXE` to launch the SQL Server Express SP2 installation.**

3. **Read and accept the license agreement; then click Next.**

4. **Click Install.**

5. **Watch the install bar while Micrososft SQL Native Client and Microsoft SQL Server 2005 Setup Support Files are installed (these are installation prerequisites); then click Next to launch the actual SQL installation.**

6. **When you're presented with a SQL Server installation Welcome screen, click Next.**

   A system configuration check runs.

7. **When the check completes successfully, click Next.**

8. **Fill out your name and organization; then click Next.**

9. **Click Next to perform a default install.**

10. **Click Next to use Windows Authentication mode.**

    The other choice is mixed mode, which allows users to connect using Windows or SQL authentication. Microsoft recommends Windows Authentication.

11. **Click Next to enable User Instances (part of the default installation).**

    This setting allows users without administrative permissions to run a separate instance of the SQL Server Express DB engine.

12. **You can set SQL to report errors to Microsoft. Select the checkbox if you want to do this otherewise, leave it blank. Click Next to continue.**

13. **Click Install to begin the installation.**

14. **After the installer finishes, click Next.**

    The default installation of SQL Server 2005 Express is properly configured for VirtualCenter after a default installation.

15. **Click Finish.**

Licensing Your Virtual Infrastructure

VirtualCenter has a licensing server component that you need. While you can download VMware Infrastructure v. 3.5, install it, and run it for 60 (same with v. 3.0.x) days without a license, you will eventually need one. The 60 days allow you to test and run a proof of concept (to show the design meets your goals).

Never use unlicensed virtual machines in production. If the machine shuts down, you cannot restart it after the grace license expires. Other VMware Infrastructure features become unavailable when the grace license expires, as well. If you're in the midst of testing, VMware will usually give you an extension of 30–60 days if you call them.

Two ways to handle licenses

ESX hosts can use host-based or server-based licenses:

✔ **Host-based licenses** are installed in the ESX hosts themselves and are used exclusively by the server. This option is better if you have only a single ESX host or are not using VirtualCenter.

✔ **Server-based licenses** simplify the licensing process by keeping all licenses in a centralized server. If a host needs a license, it checks one out. No other hosts can use a license while it is checked out. VMware recommends using server-based licensing. If you have VirtualCenter, this is the way to go to ease license management.

VirtualCenter comes with a license server. You can install the license server on the same machine as the virtual center. In fact, you can install it as part of the VirtualCenter installation process.

Best practices dictate using both a license server and installing it on the same machine as your VirtualCenter server.

What happens if your license server is unavailable

Your hosts regularly check in with the license server to get their licenses re-stamped. Re-stamping just re-validates your server's license. In fact, this occurs roughly every five minutes. This might make you nervous about your license server dying because of hardware or connectivity problems. Fear not, though. If your license server becomes unavailable for any reason, your hosts have a locally cached copy of their license that's good for 14 days.

However, you should monitor your licensing server service because no alert is sent if it shuts down.

Know your two types of licenses

The two types of licenses you need to be aware of for VMware infrastructure version 3.0.x are starter and standard. (I talk about licenses for v. 3.5 in a minute.)

- ✔ **Starter:** *If you have the Starter software edition,* you have a starter license.
- ✔ **Standard:** *If you have the Standard or Enterprise edition,* you have a standard license.

When you configure licensing on your hosts, you need to specify the license type. You can access the license configuration window by clicking on one of your ESX hosts in VIC and then clicking on the Configuration tab.

More licensing models are available in version 3.5. For example:

- ✔ **ESX:** This stand-alone server license includes ESX, Virtual Simple Network Management Protocol (SNMP), and Virtual Machine File System (VMFS).
- ✔ **VI Foundation:** This package includes everything in ESX plus a VirtualCenter Agent, Update Manager, and Consolidated Backup.
- ✔ **VI Standard:** This includes everything in VI Foundation plus High Availability (HA).
- ✔ **VI Enterprise:** This includes everything in VI Foundation plus VMotion, Storage VMotion, Distributed Resource Scheduler (DRS), and Distributed Power Management (DPM).

  This is the one you want for your data center.

Installing VirtualCenter Server

Installing your virtual center is relatively straightforward and easy. You just need to make sure of a few things before you launch the installation.

Installation checklist

Take care of these three things before installing VirtualCenter:

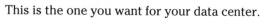

✔ **Make sure that your hardware meets (and preferably exceeds) the requirements that I list in the earlier section, "Finding a Home For Your Database."**

This host should be fault-tolerant.

✔ **Make sure that your database server has been installed.**

This server should also be fault-tolerant.

✔ **Make sure that you can connect to your database server.**

Have your connection information handy such as IP addresses and login credentials.

Installing VirtualCenter

To install VirtualCenter, do the following:

1. **Put in your VirtualCenter Installation CD.**

    If the installation wizard doesn't auto-launch, run the disc and then launch Autorun.

2. **Click Next.**

3. **(Optional) Read the recommendations and benefits.**

4. **Not optional: Click Next.**

5. **Read and accept the license agreement and then click Next.**

5. **Enter your name and organization and then click Next.**

6. **Choose Custom (see Figure 9-10) so you can select all the options and then click Next.**

Figure 9-10:
Custom install selected.

7. Make sure that all components are checked off as shown in Figure 9-11 and click Next.

This installs all the optional components so they're there if you want them later.

Figure 9-11:
Custom
install
component
selection
screen.

8. Enter your database connectivity information and then click Next.

9. Pick your license model and then click Next.

If you pick Evaluation, a warning pops up telling you that the product will work for 60 days only.

10. Review the port information for VirtualCenter and then click Next.

Notice in Figure 9-12 that port 80 is used for the default Web service. If you have another Web server on the machine, you have a conflict to resolve. You should stop or change the port of the other application that is using port 80 before continuing.

VirtualCenter uses port 902 to send information to hosts. If you have a firewall between your ESX hosts and VirtualCenter server, you need to open this port.

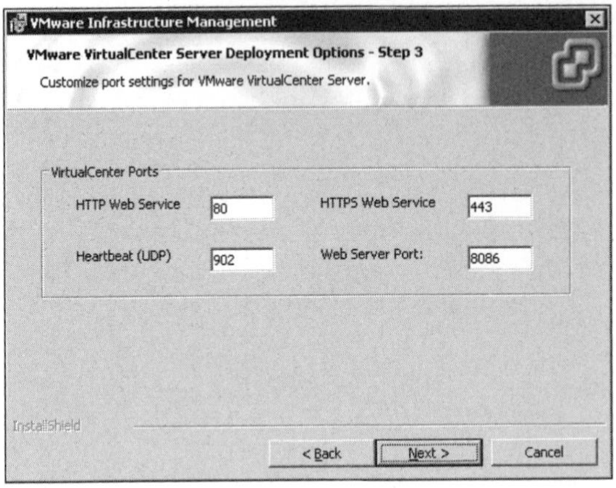

Figure 9-12:
Default
ports used
by Virtual
Center.

11. **Enter the server DNS name or IP address, and then user credentials, as shown in Figure 9-13; then click Next.**

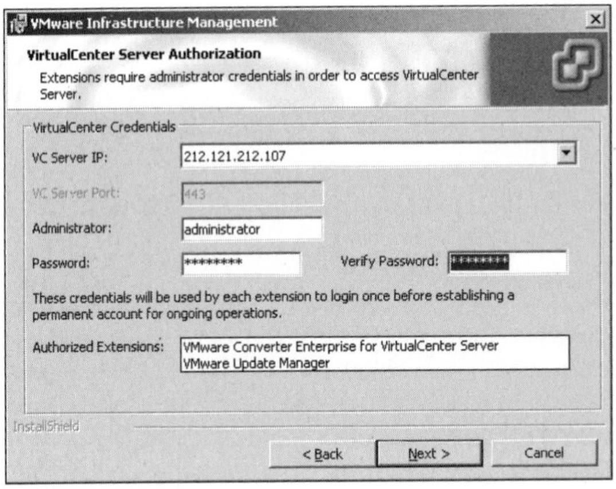

Figure 9-13:
Server
name or
IP address
entry.

12. **Select a database option for Update Manager, as shown in Figure 9-14.**

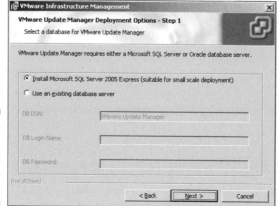

Figure 9-14:
Database
options
for Update
Manager.

13. **Review the port information for Update Manager.**

14. **Review the port information for VMware Converter Enterprise Server and then click Next.**

15. **Review the installation paths and then click Next.**

16. **Click Install.**

   All the selected components install, one at a time.

17. **Click Finish.**

   The VIC launches.

Adding Data Centers and ESX Hosts to Your Virtual Center

After you have VirtualCenter installed, you want to add ESX hosts. Before you do, though, you need to understand these two things:

- ✓ **All your management will be done from the VIC when it is connected to your VirtualCenter server.** You no longer need to connect directly to your ESX hosts for management functions.

- ✓ **You need to create a data center in your virtual center to hold all your host servers and virtual machines.** A *data center* is just a logical container object. You need at least one, but you can make more if you want. You might want two if you have two separate locations with different managers responsible for each data center. You can give each manager full access to their own data center.

To add a data center, do the following:

1. **Launch the VIC and log in to your VirtualCenter server.**

   You see a screen similar to the one in Figure 9-15.

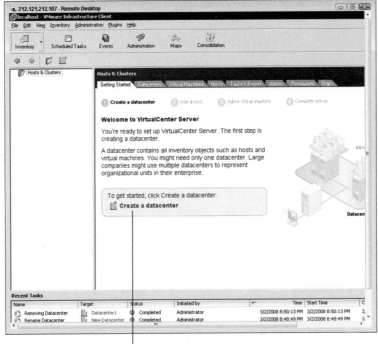

Figure 9-15:
VIC
connecting
to Virtual
Center.

The Create a Datacenter link

2. **Under the Getting Started tab, click the Create a Datacenter link (refer to Figure 9-15).**

3. **Choose an appropriate name for your data center and press the Enter key.**

Here's how to add an ESX host:

1. **Launch the VIC and log in to your VirtualCenter server.**

2. **Click your newly created data center.**

   The Getting Started tab changes to something similar to Figure 9-16.

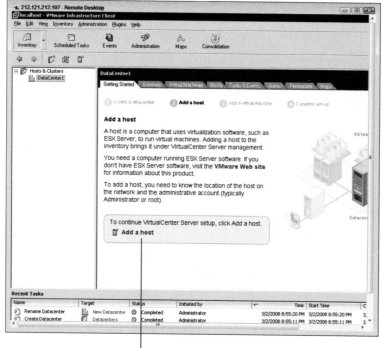

Figure 9-16:
Changes
in Getting
Started tab
after
adding a
data center.

The Add a Host link

3. **Click the Add a Host link (refer to Figure 9-16).**

   The Add Host Wizard launches.

4. **Enter the ESX host's DNS name or IP address, as well as the ESX host administrator credentials (see Figure 9-17), and then click Next.**

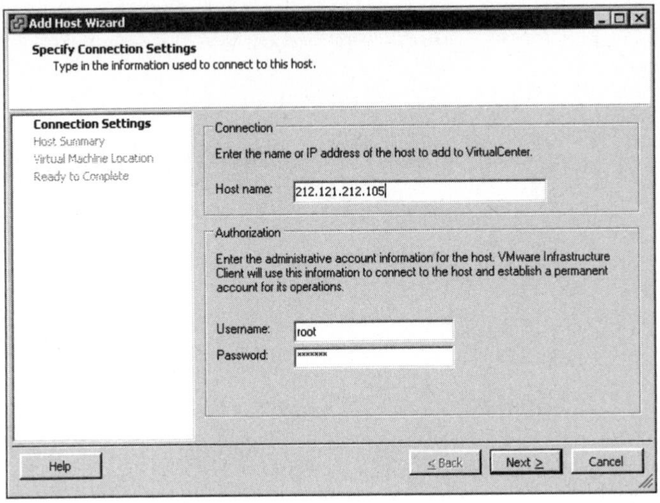

Figure 9-17:
The Add
Host
Wizard.

5. **Review the Host Summary screen and then click Next.**

6. **Pick your data center as the Virtual Machine Location and then click Next.**

7. **Review the task summary screen and then click Finish.**

   You see your ESX host appear under your data center.

Chapter 10

Making Virtual Machines

In This Chapter
▶ Understanding virtual machine makeup
▶ Creating virtual machines
▶ Connecting to virtual machines

After you build your virtual foundation, it's time to add virtual machines to the mix. Virtual machines consist of two parts: the virtual machine's hardware and the virtual machine's operating system.

In this chapter, we look at the virtual machine file structure, how VMs connect to physical hardware, and the memory management tricks that are used in VMware Infrastructure 3. Then we discuss how to deploy and connect to virtual machines.

Understanding Virtual Machine Makeup

A *virtual machine* is really just a collection of virtual hardware represented by several files. The files are typically on some type of storage area network (SAN) or network attached storage (NAS), but they can also be stored locally on an ESX host. If stored locally, options such as High Availability (HA), Vmotion, and Distributed Resource Scheduler (DRS), won't work correctly.

Virtual machine file structure

Whatever name you give your virtual machine is used in all files that define the virtual machine. Because your Service Console is Linux-based, you should avoid using spaces or special characters in the virtual machine's name. The following example is a list of files that make up a virtual machine called VM1. They are all stored in a directory called VM1. One of the first things you do when creating a virtual machine is choosing a name. As you will see, the virtual machine name gets embedded in a lot of the file names that make up the vm:

✔ `VM1.vmx`: Virtual machine configuration file that keeps track of the virtual hardware in your virtual machine. This file is created when you create the vm. It is also a text file that can be manually edited from the command line on your ESX host.

✔ `VM1.vmdk`: File describing the characteristics of the first virtual disk in the virtual machine. The file describing the second disk is called `VM1_1.vmdk`. Note that these are just files to describe the virtual disks. The actual data on virtual disks is stored in the next file type.

✔ `VM1-flat.vmdk`: The actual virtual machine disk file that contains all the data on the first virtual hard disk. The second virtual hard disk data file is named `VM1_1-flat.vmdk`. These files are preallocated (all space is given to the file at creation time) so that if your C:\ drive on VM1 is 20GB, `VM1-flat.vmdk` will take up 20GB of physical disk space.

✔ `VM1.nvram`: The virtual machine's BIOS file. This is a small binary file that contains the VMs CMOS/BIOS. For compatibility, it is based on Phoenix BIOS. If you accidentally delete this file, don't worry. It will be re-created the next time the machine is started.

✔ `vmware.log`: Current log file for your virtual machine.

✔ `vmware-#.log`: Older virtual machine log files. The # starts at 1; six files are maintained at any given time and VMware rotated through them. These are good files to look at when troubleshooting a virtual machine.

✔ `VM1.vswp`: Your virtual machine's swap file. Unlike older versions of ESX, which used a single swap file per host, v. 3.x creates a single swap file for each vm. This is the same thing as the paging file in Windows. It stores memory pages when the RAM assigned to your vm is over committed. The file is created when you turn your machine on.

✔ `VM1.vmsn`: A file that describes any snapshots for your virtual machine. This file contains the metadata relating to your snapshot. The actual data stored in the snapshot is described in the next file.

✔ `VM10000001-delta.vmdk`: When you take a snapshot of a virtual machine, all future disk writes go to this file. The file disappears when you apply a snapshot onto the original vmdk file. Snapshots are covered in Chapter 11.

✔ `VM1-some hex numbers.vmss`: If you suspend a machine, it creates this file to track the pages in memory. When you resume the machine, the file is deleted. The naming convention uses the VM Name- then a few numbers in hex.

Tricking the guest OS into thinking it has its own hardware

VMware literally tricks your guest operating system (OS) into thinking that it has its own hardware. Think of VMware as providing a box around the OS. From the outside of the box, you can tell that it's just a box. From the inside, where the OS is, it looks like raw hardware. All default virtual machines have a mouse, a keyboard, video, a CPU, RAM, a CD-ROM, a floppy drive, a NIC, a SCSI adapter, and a hard disk. You can add the following hardware to a virtual machine:

- ✔ **Serial ports:** Point to the host's serial port, an output file, or a named pipe.

- ✔ **Parallel ports:** Point to the host's parallel port or an output file.

- ✔ **Hard disks:** When added, a `.vmdk` and a `flat.vmdk` file are created.

- ✔ **Floppy drives:** Can point to either the host server, and ISO disk image file, or the local floppy drive on the machine running VMware Infrastructure Client (VIC).

- ✔ **CD-ROM drives:** Point to the host's hardware; an ISO disc image, or the machine running VIC.

Floppy drives and CD ROM drives can be redirected in the virtual machine's settings wizard. They can point to three distinct places. The first is the ESX host's own floppy and CD drive. The next choice is an ISO disk image file. The file will be mounted just like it were a physical floppy or CD. The last choice is the machine you are running VIC from to connect to your VMware infrastructure. The one you choose is a matter of convenience and lag time.

ISO images are by far the fastest way to run something using the floppy or CD-ROM. The only downside is the image has to be created. I use Magic ISO to make images. It works well. The next fastest method is using the hardware in your ESX host. The downside is you may not have easy access to the host if it's locked away in a server room in a different location. The slowest way to install anything is to point the CD-ROM or floppy to your local machine through the VIC. However, you might get by with a 1 GB network connection for a small install and it sure is convenient to use your local machine's floppy and CD-ROM.

- ✔ **Ethernet adapters:** You can add multiple virtual NICs to a virtual machine. If you have two, you can setup your virtual machine as a router or firewall.

- ✔ **RAM:** RAM settings determine how much physical memory your VM is allowed to use. The settings also regulate when VMware can borrow memory from one virtual machine for another.

- ✔ **CPUs:** Virtual machines support multiple CPUs, but that doesn't mean you should do that. More often than not, putting multiple CPUs in a virtual machine actually degrades system performance instead of enhancing it. This is because multiple CPUs limit the VMkernel's hardware scheduling abilities.

- ✔ **SCSI devices:** These devices are SCSI disk controllers only. You can add more than one.

As of version 3.0.x, you cannot have more than a total of five adapters in your virtual machine. Each SCSI card and NIC count as one adapter.

A nice side effect of virtualizing is that all your machines share a common hardware platform. This makes them portable from one environment to another allowing you to escape vendor lock-in.

VMware Tools: A must-have

VMware Tools need to be installed on any guest OS you deploy. The tools provide several benefits, as follows:

- ✔ **Device drivers for video, SCSI, mouse, and memory management**

- ✔ **Hardware acceleration for the mouse**

  This prevents mouse movement from seeming so jumpy or jittery. It also keeps virtual machines from grabbing your mouse and not giving it back easily if you drag outside of their console window.

- ✔ **Support for quiescing the file system.**

  Quiescing flushes the file system's pending writes and delays new ones for a few seconds. This is used before a snaphot is taken.

VMware Tools also allow you to synchronize your virtual machine's clock with your host server and run various scripts on the virtual machine. In fact, clicking the Power Off button on a running virtual machine without VMware Tools is akin to flipping off the power switch on a physical machine. The guest immediately goes into a powered-off state without a graceful shutdown. Comparatively, when you click the power button and VMware Tools are installed, an OS shutdown command is issued, and your virtual machine performs a graceful shutdown before powering-off.

VMware Tools are installed after you create a virtual machine and install a guest operating system; to see when exactly VMware Tools are installed, see the section "Installing a guest operating system," later in this chapter. One of the best things about VMware Tools is they are free — thye come built in to your ESX.

Memory management and your virtual machines

You need less memory on a virtual machine than you would typically put in a physical machine. I know this sounds odd, but it's true. ESX hosts and virtual machines use a few tricks to manage memory far better than a physical machine does. This is because virtual machines can, in a sense, borrow extra memory from the resource pool if they need it. The memory tricks are described in the following list:

- ✔ **Transparent memory page sharing:** If several virtual machines have the same pages in their virtual memory, all the machines point to the same single page of physical memory. This is a neat trick because if you're running many virtual machines with the same OS, you can save a lot of physical RAM. After the core OS loads, it doesn't change much. Sure, the memory a running application uses changes frequently, but the OS does not. That means that five machines running a common OS can all point to the same memory pages instead of duplicating them five times (once for each machine).

- ✔ **Balloon memory:** This is a way of taking memory from one virtual machine to use elsewhere. The balloon memory driver is installed with VMware Tools. Its sole purpose is to tell the guest OS that it needs memory. By default, it can request up to 65 percent of a virtual machine's memory. The guest just thinks that it's an application requesting more physical RAM, and swaps out pages to disk according to its own memory paging algorithm. However, the balloon application doesn't actually use the newly available physical RAM. Instead, the RAM is given back to the VMkernel. It can then be given to other virtual machines as the VMkernel sees fit. The balloon driver kicks into action only if your physical memory starts to become scarce.

- ✔ **VMkernel swap file:** When a virtual machine is first booted, it gets the VMkernel swap file. The size of the file is the difference between any guaranteed memory that a virtual machine might have (this is assigned by you) and the maximum amount of memory that a virtual machine is allocated.

  If the kernel desperately needs physical RAM, it can write a virtual machine's *non-guaranteed memory* (memory you didn't exclusively reserve for the VM) into the swap file to cull physical RAM for use elsewhere. This will obviously have a negative performance impact on the virtual machine.

  The VMkernel swap file is the last resort to reclaim physical memory. If your system is using this trick, you need more RAM. You will likely notice slow performance, which is no fun, but it's far better than randomly killing off virtual machines to reclaim RAM.

You can tell the status of your VM's memory tricks by looking at a virtual machine's performance tab in VIC. The metrics you want to look at are shown in Figure 10-1 and described here:

- **Memory Balloon:** How much memory the balloon driver is using.
- **Memory Active:** How much memory your VM is actually using.
- **Memory Swapped:** The amount of memory that is currently swapped out.

Notice that the machine in the diagram is only using active memory. Nothing is swapped out and the balloon driver is borrowing no memory.

Figure 10-1:
See which memory tricks your VM is using here.

VMware Infrastructure Client and VM Consoles: A Window into Windows

You have two ways to externally manage virtual machines. By *externally*, I mean managing the virtual machine itself, not the guest OS like Windows or Linux. Your two options for external management are the VMware Infrastructure Client (VIC) or the Web interface. The client is covered here.

The Web interface is covered in the "Using the Web Management Interface" section later in this chapter.

Creating a virtual machine

You can create a new virtual machine via

- ✔ **VMware Converter:** Use this to clone a physical machine into your virtual environment. VMware Converter is covered in Chapter 11.

- ✔ **Template:** You can also deploy machines from templates, but not before you have one machine to use as a basis for your template. Templates are covered in Chapter 11.

- ✔ **A CD or an ISO image of a CD:** Your final option is the old-fashioned way: installing from a CD or an ISO image of a CD.

To create a virtual machine using an ISO image, follow these steps:

1. **Connect to your virtual center through the VIC.**

2. **Click one of your ESX hosts.**

3. **Click Create New Virtual Machine to launch the wizard, shown in Figure 10-2.**

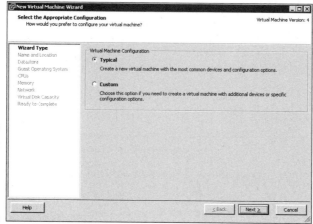

Figure 10-2:
Launch the
New Virtual
Machine
Wizard.

The virtual machine configuration type Typical is selected by default. If you had a reason to change the default SCSI bus driver, you would select Custom.

4. **Click Next.**

5. **Select your data center and then click Next.**

6. **Choose the storage location for your virtual machine files and then click Next.**

7. **Pick the operating system you want to install; then click Next.**

   Choosing the Guest OS lets VMware know what version of the VMware Tools you will install later.

   Your choices are shown in Figure 10-3:

   - *Microsoft Windows*
   - *Linux*
   - *Novell NetWare*
   - *Solaris*
   - *Other*

   If you want to try any operating system you have that isn't listed, try selecting Other. It may or may not work.

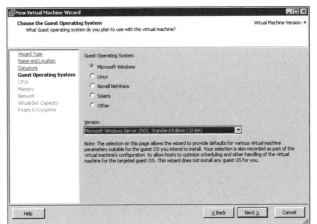

Figure 10-3: Choose your operating system here when creating a new virtual machine.

8. **Go with the default of one processor and then click Next.**

   Adding more than one Virtual CPU may actually slow your performance. This is covered in greater detail in Chapter 14.

9. **Pick the amount of memory you want for your virtual machine and then click Next.**

   As a rule, I usually start with 70 percent of what I would assign a physical machine, and then increase or decrease as needed later.

10. **In the screen shown in Figure 10-4, pick how many NICs you want, their type, and the virtual switch to connect to, and then click Next.**

Choose the defaults, but double-check that you're connecting to the virtual switch you want.

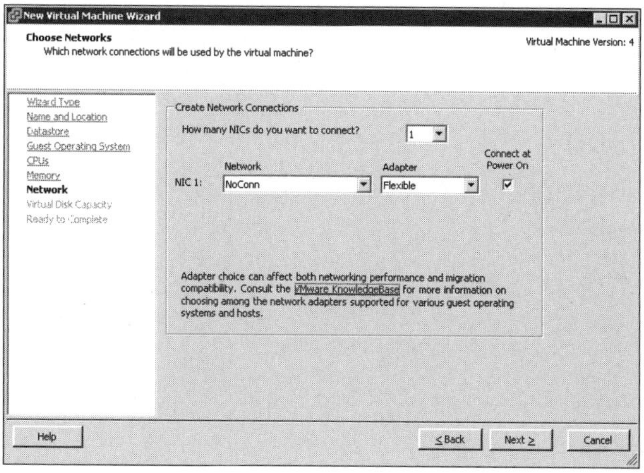

Figure 10-4:
Choose
a virtual
network
setup for a
new virtual
machine.

11. **Choose the size of your hard disk and then click Next.**

    I generally put the operating system on one disk and the data on other disks. I like the clean separation, but this is strictly my preference. I usually make the OS disk 30GB. Choose a size that works for you.

12. **Review the settings for accuracy and then click Finish.**

    You see the Create Virtual Machine task running in the Recent Tasks window. When it finishes, you have your virtual machine. This is just like a physical machine with no OS.

13. **Highlight your virtual machine and click Edit Virtual Machine settings.**

    The Virtual Machine Properties window opens, as shown in Figure 10-5.

Up, up, and away

The balloon memory driver really does act like a balloon. When there are no memory shortages on the ESX host, all virtual machines have deflated balloons. When memory gets scarce, the kernel picks a virtual machine to take memory from. The balloon is inflated, which forces the virtual machine to give up some physical RAM. That RAM is then reused elsewhere. After the shortage is over, the balloon deflates, and the virtual machine has more physical RAM available. This is a great way for virtual machines to borrow physical RAM from each other as needed.

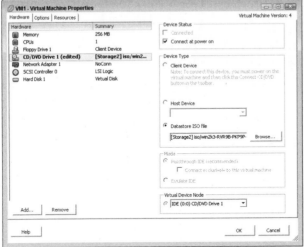

Figure 10-5:
The
Properties
window
of your
new virtual
machine.

14. Click the CD/DVD Drive in the Hardware section on the left.

15. In the Device Type section in the middle of the right side of the window, select the Datastore ISO File radio button.

You other choices are

- *Client Device:* This allows you to connect to the CD drive on the machine running the VIC.

- *Host Device:* You can connect to the CD drive that's in your ESX host.

16. Click the Browse button to find the ISO file you want to install your guest OS from.

17. In the Device Status section in the upper right of the window, select Connect at Power On (if this wasn't selected already).

Now the ISO image acts like a CD as soon as you power on the virtual machine.

18. Click OK to finish.

Installing a guest operating system

After you create a virtual machine and set it up to connect to an installation ISO file, you can install your guest OS. The ISO file acts just like a CD and is just like installing an OS on a bare-metal machine. Follow these steps:

1. Highlight your virtual machine and then click the Power on the Virtual Machine link.

2. Right-click your virtual machine and choose Open Console.

3. **Install the OS from disc like you would on a physical machine.**

   The ISO image is mounted as a CD-ROM.

4. **After you finish installing your OS, start your virtual machine and open another console to it.**

5. **From the VM drop-down menu, choose Install/Upgrade VMware Tools.**

   An ISO image is mounted, and the install launches.

6. **A notice pops up describing VMware Tools and tells you to make sure your guest OS is powered on before installing. Click OK.**

   The install wizard launches.

7. **Click Next.**

   When the installation finishes, a pop-up asks whether you want to enable hardware acceleration. As mentioned earlier, hardware acceleration will make your mouse less jittery and behave better when shifting focus from a VM console back to your machine.

8. **Click Yes.**

9. **From your Display Properties window, click Advanced.**

10. **Click the Troubleshoot tab.**

11. **Move the Hardware Acceleration slider bar to Full, as shown in Figure 10-6.**

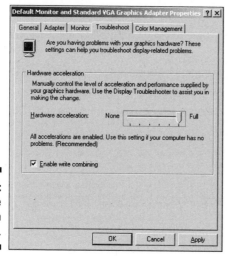

Figure 10-6:
Hardware
acceleration
settings.

12. **Click OK.**

13. **Click Finish and then select Yes to restart your virtual machine.**

Connecting to a virtual machine

After you create a virtual machine and install a guest OS on it, you can connect to it. Any way that you can connect to a physical machine, a console, or a remote connection, you can use to connect to a virtual machine. I use a lot of Remote Desktop Protocol (RDP) connections for both physical and virtual machines except for the ESX hosts. I use Putty to connect to them. Additionally, you can open a console through the VIC the same way you did during the guest OS installation. For all intents and purposes, the virtual machine acts the same as a physical machine.

Using the Web Management Interface

If you don't want to install the VIC on a machine for some reason, you can still manage your VMware infrastructure by connecting to the VirtualCenter Web page. Just open a browser and point it to the IP address or fully qualified domain name of your virtual center machine. After a self-signed certificate warning, you should see a screen similar to the one in Figure 10-7.

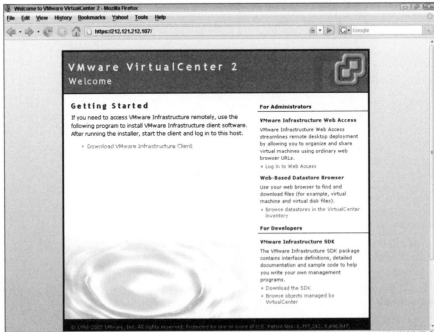

Figure 10-7:
The
Virtual
Center
Web page.

Managing things from the Web

I prefer using VIC for management functions because it's faster, but that's my preference. The Web interface works, too. To manage things from the Web, point your browser to your VirtualCenter DNS name or IP address and then follow these steps:

1. **Click the Log In to Web Access link.**
2. **Click your data center to display the virtual machines in it.**
3. **Click a virtual machine to get to its settings.**

You should see a screen similar to Figure 10-8. Notice that you can do pretty much everything you can do to a virtual machine in the VIC except create a new virtual machine. Also, the layout looks a little different, but everything is there.

To use the console from the Web interface, you need to install the browser plug-in.

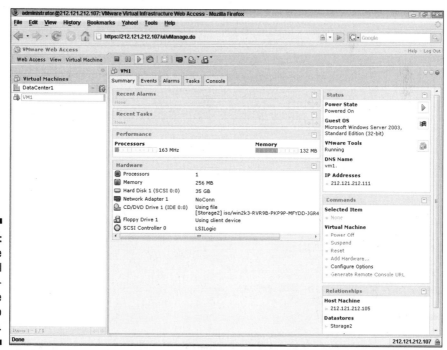

Figure 10-8: VMware Virtual Infrastructure Web Access.

Creating URLs to specific virtual machines

You can create links to e-mail–support personnel that allow them to connect to and manage virtual machines from a browser. This can be a very handy way to give someone access. To create a management URL, follow these steps:

1. **Log in to the Web Access interface from your VirtualCenters Web page by connecting to the VirtualCenter's domain name or IP address.**

2. **Navigate to a virtual machine.**

3. **Click the Generate Remote Console URL link.**

    You see a screen similar to Figure 10-9. Notice the two options that you can select:

    • *Limit View to Remote Console:* If selected, this option allows access only to the remote console of the virtual machine. It also allows the person connecting the capability to power the virtual machine on and off. Additionally, the person connecting can modify the NIC, CD-ROM, and the floppy drive connection.

    • *Limit View to Single Virtual Machine:* This option prevents the person connecting from browsing to any other virtual machines in inventory.

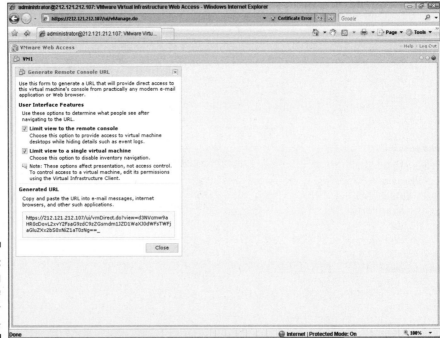

Figure 10-9:
Creating
a console
manage-
ment URL.

Chapter 11

Managing Virtual Machines

*I*f you've not gone virtual, rolling out a new machine will take you a long time. If you need a new server, you need to take several upfront steps. For example, you need to choose adequate hardware. Next, you need to order the hardware. Finally, you need to set up the hardware. These steps will take you at least one week (if not one month) to complete. That's just too long!

In this chapter, you'll discover how to rapidly deploy new virtual machines by utilizing templates. Next, we discuss a risk-free way to change or upgrade machines utilizing snapshots. Last, we'll look at just how easy it is to make a physical machine virtual.

Creating a New Server in 15 Minutes

You read that heading right: Create a new server in just 15 minutes! If you're pondering how virtualization can reduce a week- or month-long process to 15 minutes, think of it this way: What if you could take a virtual machine and make a copy (also called a *template*) of it? You could then deploy the copy. And since you are just copying files, it is really fast. In fact, it may be too fast. Your boss might expect you to roll out 32 new servers in a day!

There's only one problem to this approach: Each machine has to have its own unique identifying information. For Windows, this is the Security Identifier (SID). And, if you put two copies of the same machine on your network, your other machines would likely get confused. Fortunately, VMware has a solution to this problem.

Preparing for virtual machine templates

A *template* is simply an exact copy of a virtual machine that you can use to deploy more virtual machines. A template includes an operating system, virtual hardware, and even applications, if you want. You can even make several templates if you need to. Templates come in two flavors:

- ✔ **Normal Disk format:** This is an uncompressed copy of your virtual machine.
- ✔ **Compact Disk format:** Redundant information is removed.

Here are two pretty important things to remember about templates.

- ✔ **They can't be accidentally powered on:** This is a good thing because it prevents you from running two machines with the same SID on your network.
- ✔ **They can be stored on a VMFS data store or a NAS data store:** This is a good thing because keeping several different templates can take up a lot of disk space. You are better off storing them on low cost NAS disks and leaving the higher-cost, higher-speed SAN disks for virtual machines.

Templates are available only in VirtualCenter. If you only have ESX hosts, you can't use templates. VirtualCenter is covered in Chapter 9.

Because a template is a copy of one of your existing virtual machines, you need to decide how you're going to customize it. For Windows, you can use the sysprep utility. (I believe Linux has its own open source utilities to do this as well.) The decision you need to make is whether you want to build a *clean* virtual machine — that is, a fresh install of an operating system — and install the image deployment utility like sysprep on it to remove any unique identifiers, or whether you want to use VirtualCenter to remove the unique information.

You can install sysprep on a virtual machine and then create a template from it. After you deploy a new virtual machine, sysprep will run and launch the mini install (the same install you get with a new machine where you enter your machine name and network settings). This is likely a familiar process to you Windows administrators, but it's not the preferred method because VirtualCenter can make things even easier.

The preferred way is to put the versions of sysprep for your operating systems on your VirtualCenter server. To do this, follow these steps:

1. **Go to the Microsoft site (**www.microsoft.com**) and search for your operating system and** sysprep **to find the latest version.**

For Windows 2003, search on "Windows 2003 sysprep" for example. For Windows 2000, the most current version is sysprep 1.1. I'll use this version for the rest of this example.

2. **Download SYSprep 1.1 from Microsoft's site and double-click on the file (**Q257813_w2k_sp1_x86_en.exe**) to open it.**

3. **Extract the files to this directory on your VirtualCenter server:**

```
C:\Documents and Settings\All Users\Application Data\
       VMware\VMware VirtualCenter\sysprep\1.1
```

4. **Gather all your Windows CDs or get the latest downloads by OS version from Microsoft, then copy each** sysprep **into the appropriate subdirectory (by operating system) in this path on your VirtualCenter server:**

```
C:\Documents and Settings\All Users\Application Data\
       VMware\VMware VirtualCenter\
```

The available subdirectories for the different versions of sysprep are shown in Figure 11-1. The sysprep files are stored in the support\ tools directory of your install media in the Deploy.cab file.

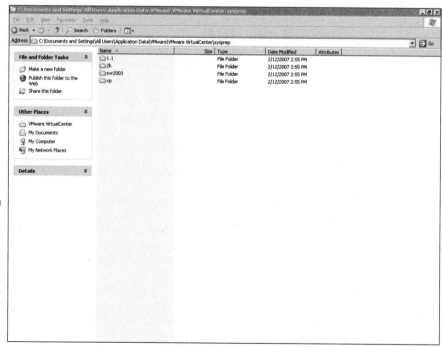

Figure 11-1: The sysprep installation directories for Virtual Center 2.0.

When using Infrastructure 3.5, you need to use VirtualCenter 2.5 instead of 2.0. More sysprep directories are available. These are shown in Figure 11-2.

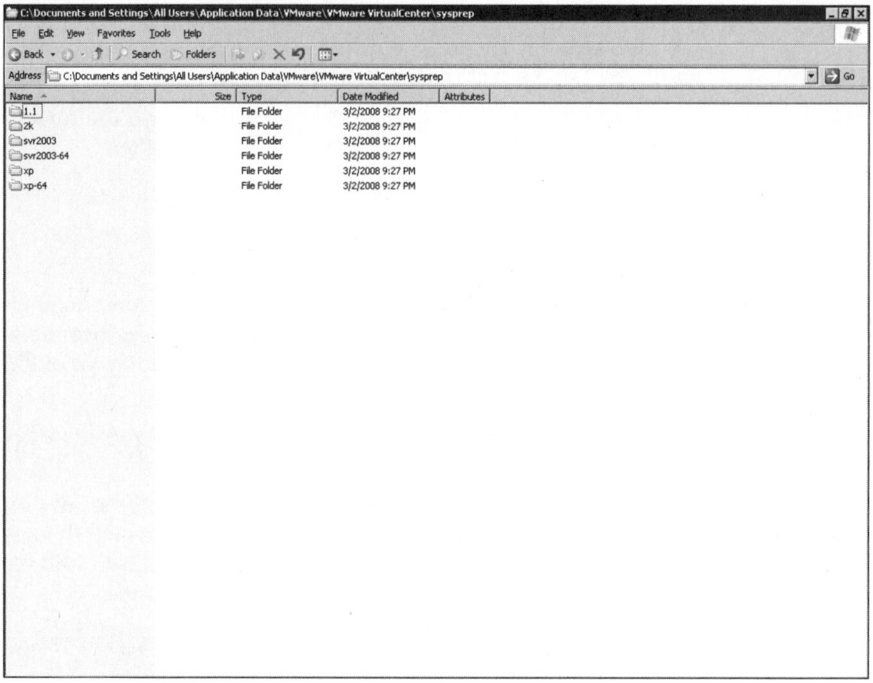

Figure 11-2:
More
`sysprep`
directories
in Virtual
Center 2.5.

5. **Open the** `Deploy.Cab` **file and extract** `sysprep.exe` **and** `setupcl.exe`.

After you have all the appropriate `sysprep` files to support the operating systems you run, you're ready to start making templates.

Creating virtual machine templates

To create a template, you can either convert a virtual machine or clone it. If you convert a virtual machine, the virtual machine is turned into a template. If you clone a virtual machine, it's copied to a template. *Convert* a virtual machine if you built the machine with specific applications for the sole purpose of using it as a template. *Clone* a virtual machine if you plan on keeping the virtual machine.

To create a template, follow these steps. The screen shots are from my nonproduction 3.5 system. Bear in mind, you need to have a running VirtualCenter Server with at least one ESX host on it.

1. **Power-off the virtual machine.**

2. **Right-click the virtual machine in the Inventory section of VirtualCenter.**

3. **Choose the appropriate action:**

   - Clone to Template
   - Copy to Template

   For this example, I'm choosing Clone to Template.

4. **The template wizard starts, as shown in Figure 11-3.**

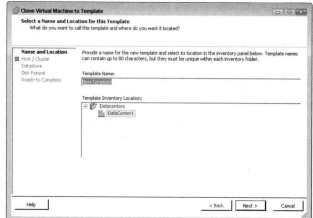

Figure 11-3:
New
template
wizard.

5. **Enter a name in the Template Name field, enter a location in the Template Inventory Location field, and then click Next.**

   It is always a good idea to have a naming standard in place that meets your needs. It may describe what is in the template of just list the OS, but either way, following a naming standard will let you know what is in your template at a glance. This is very handy if you have a lot of templates.

6. **Choose an ESX host and then click Next.**

   The host you associate a template with is much less important than the where you decide to store the template, which is the next step.

7. **Choose the data store on which you want the template to reside and then click Next.**

   As mentioned earlier, if you have a NAS share, that is the best place to store your templates. While it may be a little bit slower when you copy your template into a virtual machine, it will leave expensive high-speed storage free for what you need it for: running virtual machines.

8. **Choose whether you want to store the template normally or with duplicate data removed to save space. Then click Next.**

I usually just leave the templates as normal since it allows you the option to convert the template back to a running machine if your ever want to.

9. **Review your settings and then click Finish.**

You see the template being created in the Recent Tasks section of your VMware Infrastructure Client (VIC). When the task is complete, switch to your Inventory view by clicking Inventory and then choosing Virtual Machines and Templates from the drop-down list in the upper left of the screen. You should see your template in a screen that looks similar to Figure 11-4.

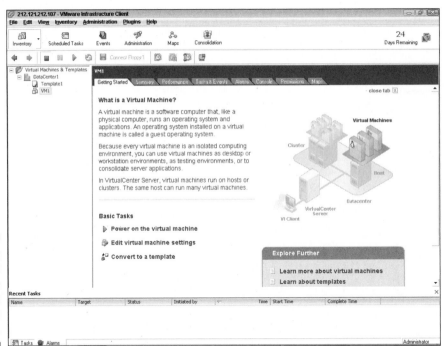

Figure 11-4:
Virtual
machines
and
templates
view.

Deploying virtual machines from templates

Now comes the fun part. Sooner or later, you'll need a new server for one reason or another. When that happens, you can go to your template and deploy a server within minutes. If your template isn't an image of a machine with `sysprep` on it, you will most likely want to customize the virtual machine so that it's not an identical copy of a production virtual machine.

The nice thing about the customization is you can save the settings and reuse them later to deploy other virtual machines.

To create a virtual machine from a template, follow these steps. The screen-shots are from VMware 3.5, and the OS deployed is Windows 2003 Server.

1. **Navigate to the Virtual Machines and Templates Inventory view in your VIC.**

2. **Right-click your template and choose Deploy Virtual Machine from This Template from the list that appears.**

   The Deploy Template Wizard launches, as shown in Figure 11-5.

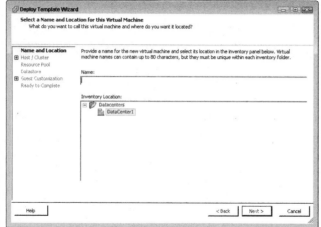

Figure 11-5:
The Deploy
Template
Wizard.

3. **Enter a name for your virtual machine in the Name field, and then click Next.**

   Again, naming conventions are important so you know what each VM does at a glance.

4. **Choose an ESX host on which to deploy your virtual machine and then click Next.**

   If you are using DRS, the host you pick doesn't really matter since DRS will move the virtual machine to another host utilizing VMotion if the current host is overloaded. DRS and VMotion are covered in Chapter 9. If you are manually load leveling your virtual machines, you will already know what host you want a new machine to run on.

5. **Choose a data store on which to store your virtual machine and then click Next.**

The data store of choice is generally a balancing act. I try to distribute servers evenly across data stores in terms of disk space usage and expected throughput. If you later decide to move a machines storage you can with storage VMotion (Chapter 9).

6. **Make the appropriate customization choice:**

   • *Do Not Customize:* Select this option if you want a virtual machine that's an identical copy of the virtual machine used to create the template.

   • *Customize Using the Customization Wizard:* Select this option to provide customization information.

   • *Customize Using an Existing Customization Specification:* Select this option if you previously chose Customize Using the Customization Wizard and saved the information to a file.

   For now, select Customize Using the Customization Wizard and then click Next. The Customization Wizard opens, as shown in Figure 11-6.

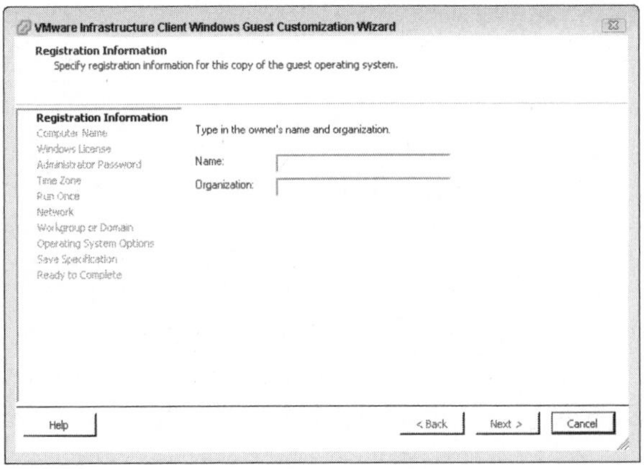

Figure 11-6:
The
Customiza-
tion Wizard.

7. **Enter your name and organization and then click Next.**

8. **Pick an option for naming the machine. Note this is the Windows Machine Name, not the virtual machine's name although they can be the same.**

   • Provide a name directly. You type in whatever name you want the machine to have.

   • Use the virtual machine name. The system automatically uses the same name as the virtual machine name. I prefer this method because it removes any naming ambiguity.

   • Prompt for a name later. This prompts the user for a name later on when the machine starts.

   For now, select Use Virtual Machine Name and then click Next.

9. **Enter your Windows Product ID (if need be), choose your licensing mode, and then click Next.**

10. **Enter the Administrator password and then click Next.**

11. **Choose your time zone and then click Next.**

12. **(Optional) You can enter a Run Once command if you choose to do so. Then click Next.**

13. **Enter your networking information and then click Next.**

14. **Pick a workgroup or domain to join and then click Next.**

15. **Leave the check box selected to generate a new SID and then click Next.**

16. **Choose whether you want to save the customization information for reuse, and then click Next.**

    If you choose to save the specification, you need to give the specification settings a name and optional description. I recommend a standardized name and detailed description so you know exactly what is in the customization file.

17. **Review your settings and then click Finish.**

I have seen some technical support articles stating that customization doesn't work after upgrading to VirtualCenter 2.5. If this happens, you likely need to copy the appropriate sysprep files to the appropriate place, which you can read about in the earlier section, "Preparing for virtual machine templates."

Freezing Time with Snapshots

I bet you would love it if you could take a snapshot of a server before making any changes to it. That way, if the changes destroy your system, you can go back to the snapshot instead of rebuilding your server. Utilities are available with which you can do this with physical machines, but it's much faster and easier with virtual machines. The mechanism that VMware uses is snaphots.

Snapshots and their uses

If you've ever installed an update that managed to crash your system, snapshots are for you! *Snapshots* are designed for short-term usage to minimize the potentially negative impacts of a system change. They capture a virtual machine's system state and memory at a point in time. You can easily go back to that point in time if need be. Think of snapshots as images of your system at a certain point in time. If something crashes your machine after the image was made, you can go back to the image and discard the damage.

When you take a snapshot, your virtual machine stops writing to its original disk file and begins writing to a differential disk file. Memory is written to a memory file. If you make a change that turns bad, you can then discard the differential file and reload the memory file. Your virtual machine is then exactly the same as it was when you took the snapshot. If the change works out, you can then apply the changes on the differential disk to the original disk. When you do this, VMware automatically deletes the differential file when the process is complete.

The following files are created when you take a snapshot:

- **Snapshot Differences file (also referred to as the *differential file*):** This new disk file for writing data is called `VM_Name-00000#-delta.vmdk`. The # starts at 1 and is incremented by 1 for each snapshot.

- **Memory State file:** This file — `VM_name-SnapshotName.vmsn` — is the size of the virtual machine's maximum amount of memory.

- **Snapshot Description file:** This file is labeled `VM_name-0000#.vmdk`.

You can make multiple snapshots if you like. Just remember that you create a different differential file for each snapshot. This can spread your data over several disk files and can slow performance. Best practices discourage you from using snapshots for long periods of time or as backups.

When you initiate a snapshot, your virtual machine attempts to calm the file system so that it stops writing. This process is *quiescing*. If you're running a database on a virtual machine, stop it before taking a snapshot or applying the differential disk back to your virtual machine. I have seen databases corrupted by applying snapshots while they were running. Corruption does not happen every time, but why take the chance?

Working with snapshots

VMware makes creating and managing snapshots easy through the Snapshot Manager program. The center of the interface is the You Are Here icon. This icon tells you where in the snapshot tree you are and is always just below the current snapshot. This is important if you have multiple snapshots and want to keep one but not another. Snapshot Manager is shown in Figure 11-7 with no snapshots. All you can see is the virtual machine itself with the You Are Here icon below it. (In a bit, I show you a screenshot that has a snapshot.)

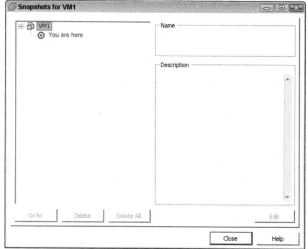

Figure 11-7:
Snapshot
Manager
with no
snapshots
present.

To open Snapshot Manager, follow these steps:

1. **Log in to your VMware Client.**

2. **Right-click your virtual machine and highlight Snapshot.**

   A menu appears with three choices: Take Snapshot, Revert toSnapshot, and Snapshot Manager.

3. **Click Snapshot Manager.**

You may have noticed the option to create a snapshot in the same list as Snapshot Manager. To create a snapshot, follow these steps:

1. **Log in to your VMware Client.**

2. **Right-click your virtual machine and highlight Snapshot.**

3. **Click Take Snapshot and the Take Virtual Machine Snapshot dialog box opens.**

4. **Add a name and description for the snapshot.**

   Once again, standardized names and detailed descriptions will make your life easier by letting you know exactly why you took the snapshot and what state the machine was in before the snapshot.

5. **Click OK.**

If you launch Snapshot Manager again, you see the virtual machine, the snapshot below it, and the You Are Here icon, as shown in Figure 11-8.

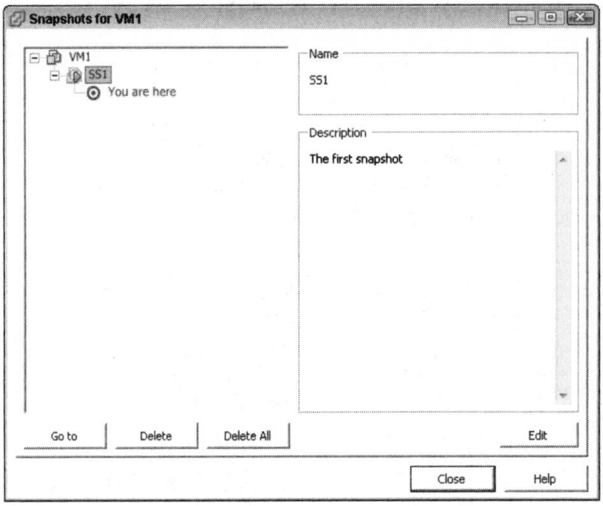

Figure 11-8:
Snapshot
Manager
with one
snapshot
present.

If you take multiple snapshots, they're all reflected in Snapshot Manager. In Figure 11-9, you can see three snapshots and the original virtual machine.

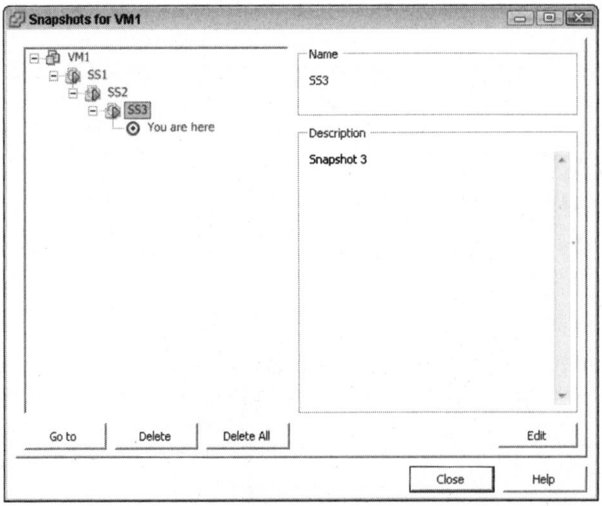

Figure 11-9:
Snapshot
Manager
with multiple
snapshots
present.

When it comes to managing snapshots, less are generally better. Unless you have a good reason to use multiple snapshots, try to keep only one at a time. If you do use multiple snapshots, you might want to jump between machine states.

Here's an example. Refer to Figure 11-9. Say your base virtual machine is working quite well, but you have an operating system patch and two application patches to apply to it.

1. You take your first snapshot to maintain your pristine machine state and call that SS1.

2. You apply the operating system patch.

   Everything seems to be working but hasn't yet withstood any test of time.

3. You take another snapshot, SS2, to maintain your theoretically working service pack level.

4. You apply the first application patch and then take a snapshot, SS3, before applying the final application patch.

5. So far, everything seems to have worked, so you apply the final application patch. This is actually getting applied to the differential file associated with SS3.

Figure 11-10 summarizes the machine states and their functions.

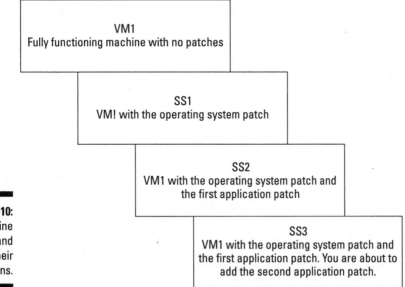

Figure 11-10:
Machine
states and
their
functions.

VM1
Fully functioning machine with no patches

SS1
VM! with the operating system patch

SS2
VM1 with the operating system patch and
the first application patch

SS3
VM1 with the operating system patch and
the first application patch. You are about to
add the second application patch.

After applying the second application patch, your machine keeps crashing. After a little troubleshooting, you realize that this is because of the last application patch. You need to go back to the stable machine state contained in SS2. To do that, follow these steps:

1. **Log in to your VMware Client.**

2. **Right-click your virtual machine and highlight Snapshot.**

3. **Click Snapshot Manager.**

4. **Click SS2.**

5. **Click the Go To button.**

   A warning pops up, saying you will lose any information since you took SS3 unless you take another snapshot.

6. **Click Yes.**

At this point, your machine state is returned to SS2, which comprises your virtual machine with the operating system patch and the first application patch. Your Snapshot Manager should look like Figure 11-11.

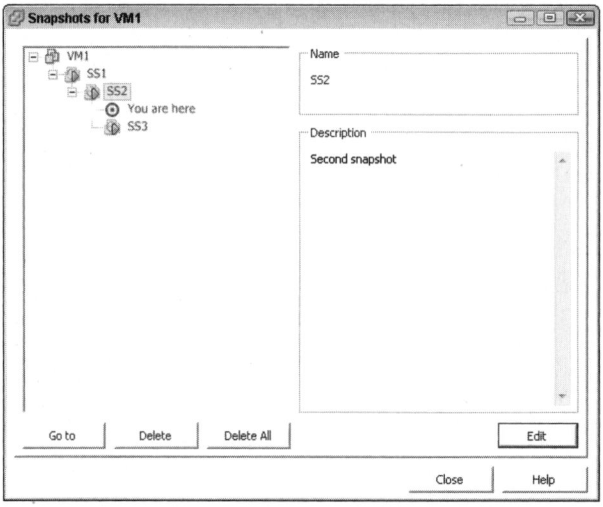

Figure 11-11: Reversion to SS2.

You can go back to SS3 by highlighting it and clicking the Go To button if you wanted to. However, you feel that the second application patch caused some problems and decide to run the program with only the first application patch for two days to feel comfortable that it's working. So now you want to get rid of SS3. To do that, follow these steps:

1. **Log in to you VMware Client.**

2. **Right-click your virtual machine and highlight Snapshot.**

3. **Click Snapshot Manager.**

4. **Click SS3.**

5. **Click the Delete button.**

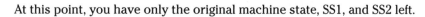

   6. **When a warning dialog box pops up asking whether you're sure you want to delete this snapshot, click Yes.**

At this point, you have only the original machine state, SS1, and SS2 left.

The Delete button has two different meanings, depending on where the You Are Here icon is:

   ✔ **When you delete anything below the icon,** you actually delete the snapshot and do not apply it to the virtual machine.

   ✔ **If you delete a snapshot that is above the icon,** VMware applies all the changes contained in that snapshot to the virtual machine before deleting the snapshot.

   In other words, deleting a snapshot above the icon *makes the changes permanent.* Comparatively, deleting a snapshot below the icon *discards the changes.*

After two days pass, you feel confident that the application is working as expected. By now, the second application patch has probably been recalled for some minor adjustments, so you want to make all the changes permanent and get rid of the snapshot differential files. To do that, follow these steps:

   1. **Log in to your VMware Client.**

   2. **Right-click your virtual machine and highlight Snapshot.**

   3. **Click Snapshot Manager.**

   4. **Click SS1.**

   5. **Click the Delete All button.**

   6. **When a warning dialog box pops up stating you are about to consolidate all the snapshots onto your virtual machine and then delete them, click Yes.**

When you finish, Snapshot Manager should only show your virtual machine with no snapshots. VMware includes a fast and easy way to drop all changes you have made since the last snapshot — Revert to Snapshot. This is a handy trick if you take a snapshot of a working machine and test something that causes a problem. You can go back to your original snapshot before the test by reverting.

To revert to a snapshot, do the following:

   1. **Log in to your VMware Client.**

   2. **Right-click your virtual machine and highlight Snapshot.**

   3. **Click Revert to Snapshot.**

A warning pops up stating you are about to lose any changes since the last snapshot.

4. **Click Yes.**

Converting Physical Machines to Virtual Machines

The fastest and easiest way to convert a physical machine to a virtual machine is to use the VMware conversion utility — *VMware Converter* — which comes in two flavors (free and pay-for versions). The free version needs to run on the physical machine you want to convert. The pay-for version runs as part of VirtualCenter and allows you to schedule conversions and run them centrally.

You can download the free version of VMware Converter from the VMware Web site (`www.vmware.com`) to get a feel for the program. After you understand how the free version works, you can decide whether buying the pay-for version is worth it to you.

To convert a physical machine to a virtual one, follow these steps:

1. **Install VMware Converter on the physical machine you want to convert.**

2. **Launch VMware Converter.**

   You see a screen similar to Figure 11-12.

3. **Click the Import Machine button.**

4. **On the Import Wizard Splash Screen, click Next.**

5. **The first step is selecting the source of your conversion. Then click Next.**

   Your choices are listed in the Step 1 splash screen, as shown in Figure 11-13.

6. **Select Physical Machine as your source and then click Next.**

7. **Choose the local machine as the source and enter your login credentials if they don't autofill. Then click Next.**

8. **Select the hard drives that you want converted and then click Next.**

9. **On the Step 2 splash screen that appears for choosing a destination for the virtual machine, click Next.**

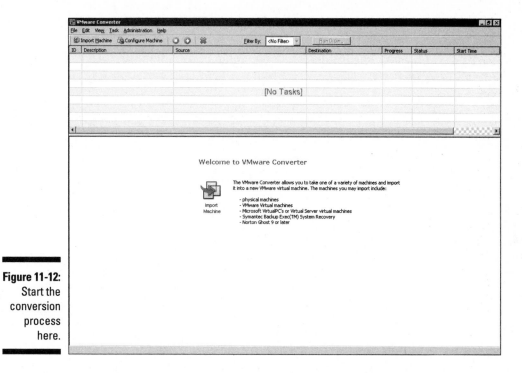

Figure 11-12:
Start the
conversion
process
here.

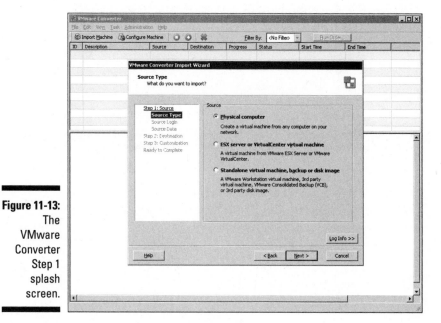

Figure 11-13:
The
VMware
Converter
Step 1
splash
screen.

10. **Choose the appropriate destination, either an ESX host or a VirtualCenter. Click Next.**

11. **Enter the destination IP and login information and then click Next.**

12. **Choose a name for the virtual machine and then click Next.**

13. **If you select a virtual center as the destination, you need to choose a host to run the virtual machine on. Select one and then click Next.**

14. **Select a shared data store and then click Next.**

15. **Select which virtual network switch the virtual machine should use and then click Next.**

16. **You can customize the machine if you need to. Then click Next.**

    You can choose to install VMware tools or change the host name or network settings if you want.

17. **Review the summary information and decide whether you want the virtual machine to power-on after conversion. Click Finish.**

    Because the virtual machine is an identical copy, I prefer the manual power-on option. That way, you can make sure the physical machine is off the network before the virtual machine comes on.

    You see a screen similar to Figure 11-14 when the conversion is complete.

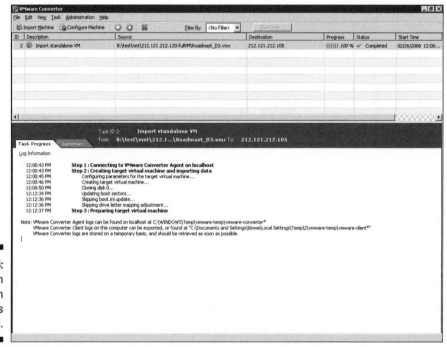

Figure 11-14: Conversion completion status screen.

Chapter 12

Keeping Things Running with Virtual Clusters

*E*very piece of your hardware will fail at some point. It might be 15 years down the road, or it might be today. Your hardware lifecycle might replace hardware before it fails, but chances are that you've experienced some sort of hardware failure since you started working with computers. Moving components fail more often than stationary ones, even if this happens less frequently. I've seen my share of hard drive and fan failures, but I have also seen RAM chips, motherboards, and network cards die.

In this chapter, we look at how to setup a fault tolerant virtual cluster to avoid any single point of failure Deciding where your single point of failure is (server, server room, site, and so on) as a function of budget is discussed, as is implementing fault tolerance at many levels. This chapter also discusses defining different types of disasters as well as their corresponding recovery time objectives (RTO). Using clusters is the most fault tolerant and redundant way to deploy VMware. I would say that again, but that would be redundant!

Reducing Single Points of Failure

If you think about it, no matter how careful you are, you always have a single point of failure. If you have a standalone server with no redundancy, the disk subsystem, the motherboard, CPU, and network cards all represent a single point of failure. Because disks fail more often than stationary components, you can remove a disk as a single point of failure by mirroring it. However, then your server is still a single point of failure.

If you cluster your servers so that if one fails and another takes over, your power source becomes a single point of failure. Toss in a UPS and a generator, and now your server room is the single point of failure.

Even if you put the nodes of your cluster in different physical locations, your building or campus can still be considered a single point of failure. Extending the example to the ridiculous, at some point, the planet becomes your single point of failure. Of course, if the planet gets destroyed, you probably won't worry too much about recovering your data!

The point is, you need to take every reasonable step to provide fault tolerance *where you can* within the confines of your budget. Higher-risk items, such as hard drives and power supplies, are usually the first choices. Servers themselves are next. The next level is typically making the site redundant. Look at SIAC for an example of this. They support the NY Stock Exchange and Amex. Do you think for a second that they don't have data co-located so if one site is lost, another can take over?

The next line of defense is to maintain reliable backups. For backups to be reliable, you need to periodically run a test restore. While I was writing this book, I used the opportunity to test my restores by taking a Virtual Consolidated Snapshot backup (covered in Chapter 16; snapshots are also covered in Chapter 11) and restoring it to the test system used for some of the screenshots in this book.

One other important note: You need to keep some backup tapes off-site in case something goes horribly wrong at your site like a fire or water leak. If your on-site tapes are destroyed and you have no off-site tapes, your data is gone.

If you work for a large public company, you'll have much stricter data retention requirements due to regulations like Sarbanes-Oxley and use a service like Iron Mountain to securely store your backup data. If you work for a small/medium business (SMB), you might use a place I call *Tinfoil Hill* — namely, your own home to keep maybe last night's and last week's backup tapes. If you think something cannot happen to your site, just ask an insurance agent for some stories about offices destroyed in one way or another.

Preparing for fault tolerance at many levels

If you design your VMware Infrastructure correctly, you'll have several levels of fault tolerance. At a minimum, you want to have fault-tolerant drive configurations in your SAN disk enclosures, redundant paths in your SAN fabrics, and clustered ESX hosts with redundant HBAs and NICs. I also like to use redundant power supplies and redundant UPS units so that when one drains, the other takes over. If you don't have a modular UPS system that lets you hot-swap components, you should double-up your UPS units in case one dies, even if you have a generator. Doubling them allows you to swap out the dead one without interrupting service.

If you have a disaster recovery site, you can use SAN utilities to replicate your entire virtual infrastructure to your recovery site. To do this, you want to boot your ESX hosts from the SAN (the SAN utilities will replicate them) and replicate your VirtualCenter database using a database replication utility.

Although real-time replication to one or more different physical sites provides extreme fault tolerance, it can be expensive. To figure out what works for your situation, you need to define what constitutes a disaster, break the answer into various levels, define recovery time objectives (RTOs) for each level, and minimize the expense to meet your needs.

In the following list, I define the potential disasters you could face and their various RTOs with the solutions. I recommend that you adapt the list to your personal situation to help you design your multiple layers of protection.

- ✔ **Complete Disaster:** This would be the loss of your computer center location, the home of your virtual infrastructure. If you didn't make the financial commitment to off-site system replication, the RTO might be something like equipment delivery plus two days. You would need to have all the information you require to order and configure new equipment off-site along with regularly updated backup tapes.

- ✔ **Mission Critical System Outage:** This category might include all mission critical systems. VMware allows you to create an RTO of 0–6 hours if your virtual machines run on clustered fault-tolerant hardware to provide safety from many potential disasters.

  Make use of RAID and global hot spare disks. If you lose a disk drive in the SAN, the global hot spare takes over and begins rebuilding parity. With RAID 5, it is possible but unlikely for a second drive to fail while parity is being rebuilt. If that happens, you would lose the entire RAID set. To further reduce this risk, store all VMs on fiber channel drives to leverage their higher mean time between failures, or use a more fault-tolerant (but costly) RAID configuration. Of course, if Murphy gets loose in the system and you lose a complete RAID set, you can always go to tape and restore an image of a virtual machine from last night's backup. As an added precaution, keep your VMs on more than one data store. If one LUN fails, you won't lose all machines.

  Keep your servers in an active/active VMware cluster with HA and DRS configured. If you have a server hardware problem, the best case is the virtual machines will move to another functioning server, utilizing VMotion, without interruption. If a cluster node just dies, HA will restart the VMs on the remaining servers with only a brief outage.

✔ **User Workstation Outage:** While many files modified throughout the day are stored on file servers, people also store things locally. Back up your local workstation files frequently. If you can keep preconfigured cold spare workstations on hand in case someone's machine suddenly decides to go south, you can maintain an RTO of less than an hour or two.

✔ **Infrastructure Outage:** Hot or cold spares can be used to replace any infrastructure equipment should it fail. The RTO can be as low as the amount of time it takes equipment to failover to a hot spare or as long as it takes you to swap in a cold spare.

After you define your potential for disaster and RTO objectives, you can design your multiple layers of protection. Then, you need to perform a cost benefit analysis and make modifications if need be.

Using clusters to provide fault tolerance

After you cluster two or more ESX hosts, you have a high level of fault tolerance. In fact, clustering ESX hosts provides you with three major advantages:

✔ **Clusters allow your system to load balance resources over each node.**

✔ **If you lose a piece of fault tolerant hardware in a server, you have no outage.** However, you now have hardware in a physical machine to replace. If your ESX hosts are clustered, you can use VMotion to move all your virtual machines from the node you need to shut down to a node you will keep running. You can do this without shutting down the virtual machines, so there is no service interruption.

✔ **If you lose an entire server, only a brief service outage occurs as HA restarts any virtual machines that were running on the dead node on one of the remaining functional nodes.** The outage is further limited by the fact that virtual machines boot much faster than physical machines because there is no hardware to check or scan on startup.

WARNING!

If you move your virtual machines off one host to fix it, the remaining hosts take over the processing load. If you have not included this scenario in your capacity planning and system design, things may run slowly until you get the damaged hardware up and running again. The moral of the story is to design your system so you can lose one ESX host and still have enough capacity to run everything normally. Capacity planning is covered in Chapter 2.

Figure 12-1 shows a simple cluster on ESX hosts. Notice that this cluster consists of two nodes in a grouping called Cluster. Each node is connected to some sort of fault-tolerant, shared storage. If you want to increase the size of the cluster, you can add more ESX hosts to it. Figure 12-2 shows a four-node cluster.

Cluster

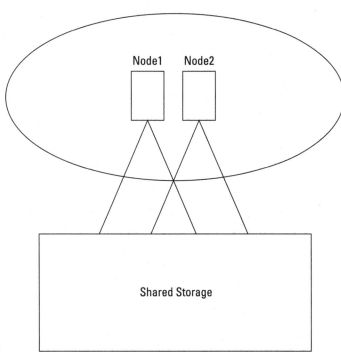

Figure 12-1:
A simple
ESX cluster.

 If all the ESX hosts in a cluster reach 100 percent utilization and one node fails, you won't be able to reallocate your virtual machines very well. As a rule, you need to figure out how many virtual machines each node can run on average (call that number V), possibly with a fudge factor to account for extremely high utilization servers if you have them. You also know how many ESX hosts you have; call that number N. The maximum number of virtual machines you want to run on any one ESX host is $V(N-1)/N$. If you can run 16 virtual machines ($V = 16$) on one ESX host (which is not at all that unusual, even higher consolidation ratios are common) and you have two ESX hosts ($N = 2$), you can safely run a maximum of 8 virtual machines on each ESX host because $16(2-1)/2 = 8$. If you have 4 ESX hosts, you can run 12 servers on each ESX host because $16(4-1)/4 = 12$.

If one of the four hosts dies, four virtual machines can go to each of the three remaining cluster nodes, bringing the total number of virtual machines on each node to their maximum of 16. Of course, if you think you might lose more than one ESX host at once (a very low probability), you can adjust the formula by subtracting the number of hosts you can lose at once from N. If you have four ESX hosts and feel that two can fail at once, the formula becomes $16(4-2)/4$, meaning that you can run 8 servers on each ESX host. Bear in mind the chances of losing 2 ESX hosts at the same time is very low.

Cluster

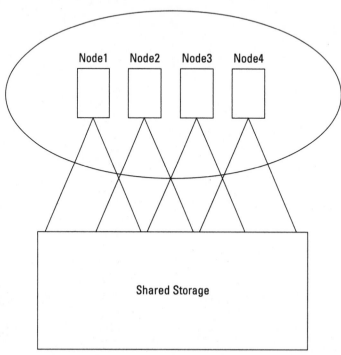

Figure 12-2:
A four-node
ESX cluster.

Creating an ESX cluster with DRS and HA

From the VMware Infrastructure Client (VIC) interface, a cluster is nothing more than a grouping object. In a lot of ways, it's similar to a folder in a PC directory — only instead of files, you add ESX hosts. You also assign various settings to a cluster for DRS and HA. To create a cluster, follow these steps:

1. **Start your VIC.**

2. **Log in to your VMware Infrastructure.**

3. **Right-click your data center.**

4. **Choose New Cluster.**

   The New Cluster Wizard opens.

5. **Provide a cluster name, and enable HA and DRS as shown in Figure 12-3. Then click Next.**

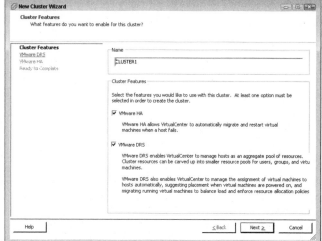

Figure 12-3:
The
cluster
setup
screen of
the New
Cluster
Wizard.

6. **Choose your DRS automation level from the three choices (as shown in Figure 12-4) and then click Next.**

 • *Manual:* VirtualCenter only makes suggestions for moving virtual machines between hosts. You actually have to move them yourself.

 • *Partially Automated:* VirtualCenter picks which host a virtual machine runs on when you turn it on. After that, VirtualCenter only suggests moving virtual machines between hosts. You have to manually move them yourself. This is a good setting to choose until you see how DRS works with your system.

 • *Fully Automated:* After you're comfortable with the suggestions DRS makes, set your system to Fully Automated. This is the setting VMware recommends. In this mode, DRS automatically implements the suggestions it makes and moves the virtual machines between hosts automatically.

 When using Fully Automated, you need to decide how aggressively you want DRS to use VMotion to move virtual machines. There is a slider bar to pick your aggressiveness. Start in the middle and decide whether you should shift to a more or less aggressive stance over time. You want to make sure DRS isn't going to play ping pong with your virtual machines by moving them from one host to another and back. If this happens, DRS is being too aggressive. This can gobble up a lot of resources and possibly slow your entire system.

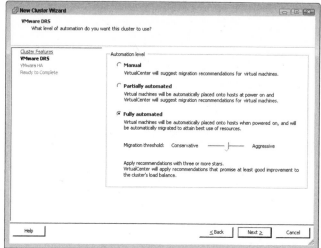

Figure 12-4:
The DRS
configura-
tion page.

7. **The HA configuration page is shown in Figure 12-5. In the Host Failures section of the VMware HA configuration screen (as shown in Figure 12-5), enter a number for the Number of Host Failures Allowed and then click Next.**

The system is asking you for the maximum number of ESX hosts you can lose before HA stops trying to restart machines on remaining hosts. Again, the probability of losing more than one at a time because of a hardware issue is low. The maximum you can choose is four.

Chapter 14 covers resource pools. They can give some machines higher priority than others and keep virtual machines from starting if not enough resources are available for them to run. The Admission Control section allows you to decide whether you want to enforce or ignore resource pools.

8. **Review your settings and then click Finish.**

At this point, you have an empty cluster. The next step is to add two or more ESX hosts to your cluster. To do that, follow these steps:

1. **Right-click your cluster and choose Add Host.**

The Add Host Wizard opens.

2. **In the Connection section of the Specify Connection Settings screen (as shown in Figure 12-6), enter the name or IP address of the host to be added in the Host Name box and the local administrative credentials on the ESX host itself in the Authorization section. Then click Next.**

This is the login for a Root or root equivalent account on the ESX host itself, not the VirtualCenter login.

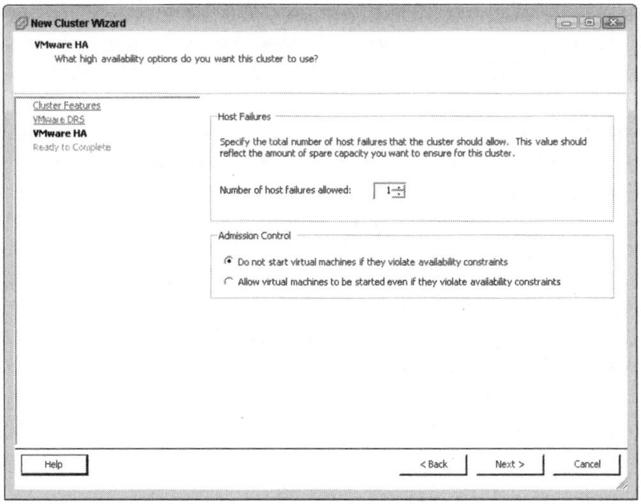

Figure 12-5:
The HA
configura-
tion page.

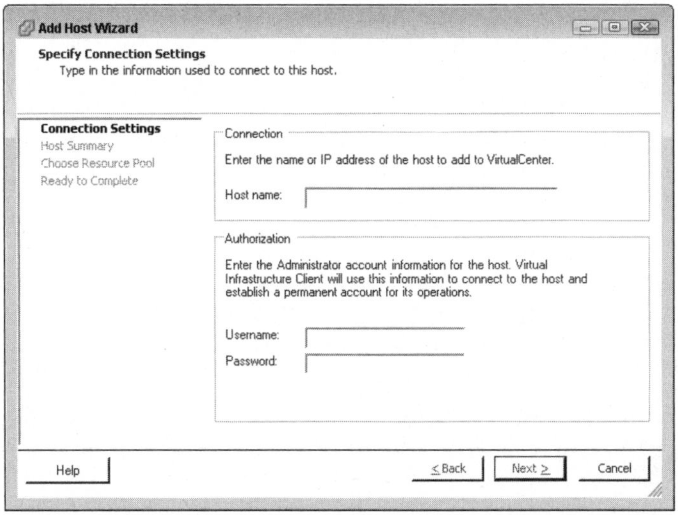

Figure12-6:
The Add
Host
Wizard.

3. **On the summary screen that shows, click Next.**

4. **You have the choice of creating a default resource pool (the entire host) or using any resource pools that exist on the host. Your choice will depend on your resource pool setup and what you are installing. Make your selection and then click Next.**

5. **Review your settings and then click Finish.**

After your cluster is created and you have some virtual machines in it, you can fine-tune three general settings. To get to these settings, right-click your cluster and choose Edit Settings. What you can do is described here:

 ✔ **HA settings:** On a machine-by-machine basis, you can tailor how HA responds to crisis. Figure 12-7 shows the HA Virtual Machine Options. Notice that you can set the restart priorities for your machines.

 Since they control authentication, domain controllers are a good choice for high-priority restarts.

 You can also choose how machines behave when the Service Console can no longer connect to the network. By default, machines are set to power-off. This actually means if the Service Console loses communication, the virtual machine is powered-off and then restarted on another host. Your other choice is to keep the virtual machine running.

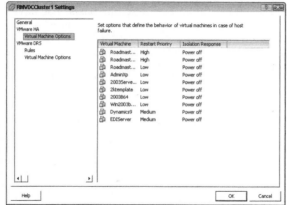

Figure 12-7:
Virtual
machine HA
settings.

 ✔ **Placement constraints:** You might always want two virtual machines together on the same host or perpetually separated on different hosts. Virtual machines that constantly send a lot of data to each other often perform better if they're on the same ESX host because their network traffic travels on the ESX host's internal bus instead of going out to the network (as long as they are on the same virtual switch).

 On the other hand, if you have two high-utilization machines, you might want to always try to keep them on separate ESX hosts. This provides a more balanced approach to load leveling. Figure 12-8 shows the placement constraints screen.

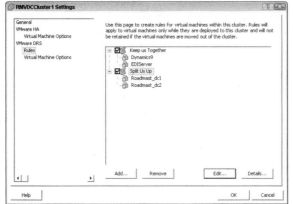

Figure 12-8:
Placement
constraints
screen.

▶ **Machine-level DRS automation settings:** You can decide DRS
automation levels on a machine-by-machine basis. You have the same
choices for each machine as you did when setting up DRS — Fully
Automated, Partially Automated, or Manual. (You can read about DRS
set up earlier in this chapter.) Additionally, you can disable DRS for a
virtual machine if you like. The virtual machine DRS configuration page
is shown in Figure 12-9.

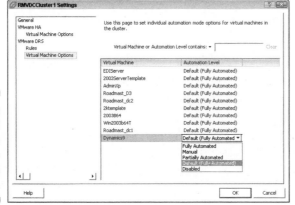

Figure 12-9:
Virtual
machine
DRS con-
figuration
page.

Using VMotion to Move Virtual Machines from One Host to Another

VMotion moves your machines from one clustered host to another without any downtime whatsoever. I have pinged a machine while it was moving and lost only a single ping. I know people who have watched streaming videos while a machine is VMotioned and didn't notice any anomalies.

You can use VMotion to improve overall hardware utilization or to move virtual machines from a piece of physical hardware to perform maintenance. VMotion is used both to load level virtual machines across cluster nodes and to move virtual machines if a hardware failure is detected.

Migrating virtual machines with VMotion

VMotion moves your entire virtual machine's state from one node to another. The state includes moving working processes, your virtual machines memory, and the virtual machine's hardware configuration. When initiated, VMotion does the following:

1. The virtual machine's memory is copied from the original node to the new node.

   At this point, the memory is frozen, but changes still need to be allowed because the virtual machine is running.

2. Any changed pages of memory after the initial copy has started are tracked in a memory bitmap on the original node.

3. The virtual machine is quiesced.

   At this point, no changes are allowed. This step is extremely brief and is the only moment when the virtual machine is actually inaccessible to users. Again, this step is so brief that you might not even lose a packet of information. The virtual machine's device state and the memory bitmap pointing to the changed memory pages are transferred to the new node.

4. The virtual machine starts running on the new node, and users can once again access it. Additionally, a Reverse Address Resolution Protocol (RARP) request is sent so the IP subnet knows that the virtual machine's MAC address is on a new switch port.

5. The changed memory pages pointed to by the memory bitmap are copied from the original node to the new node.

   If a dirty memory page (a page that has been changed but not written to disk) needs to be updated before it is copied over, it's fetched from the original node.

6. After the remaining memory is updated on the new node, the original node is notified that the migration is complete.

Only at this point is the virtual machine removed from the original node.

As an additional safety feature, the virtual machine is kept on the original node until it is fully moved and running on the new node. This is done in case something goes wrong with the migration, and the system needs to fail-back to the original node.

The two types of VMotion migrations are hot and cold:

✔ **Hot:** A *hot migration* occurs when the virtual machine is powered-on.

✔ **Cold:** A *cold migration* occurs when the virtual machine is powered-off.

In version 3.0.x, you can move the location of the virtual machine's files only with a cold migration. Version 3.5 allows you to move the virtual machine's files when it is running. This feature is called *Storage VMotion.*

What you need for VMotion to work

You need to meet several system prerequisites before you can use VMotion. When you issue a VMotion request, the prerequisites are checked. For VMotion to work, you need to meet the following conditions:

✔ **Each node needs to be able to access all SAN LUNs used by the virtual machine, whether they're Fibre Channel, iSCSI, or NAS.**

✔ **A gigabit (or greater) Ethernet connection between the source and target nodes.**

✔ **Connections to the same physical networks.**

✔ **Virtual switch port groups that have the same names.**

For example, if your virtual machine is connected to a virtual switch port group called Port Group 1, the target node needs to have a virtual switch with a port group called Port Group 1.

The virtual switches do not need to have the same name — only the virtual switch *port groups* have to have the same name.

✔ **CPUs that are compatible.**

Your hosts should generally have the same type of CPU — Intel or AMD — and all support the same instruction set (SSE) level.

You can mask CPU features to force VMotion compatibility if need be. This is done in the advanced option settings on a virtual machine. Make changes here only if absolutely necessary and speak with VMware technical support first.

Certain conditions will cause errors or warnings when you try to VMotion. Errors require repair before VMotion can continue. Warnings are informational and will not prevent a migration.

Error conditions include the following:

✓ **If the virtual machine (VM) has an active connection to a virtual switch with no uplink adapters**

This is referred to as an *internal virtual switch.*

✓ **When the VM is connected to a local floppy disk or CD-ROM and an image is mounted**

✓ **When a CPU affinity is set for the virtual machine**

✓ **When a virtual machine is set up in a Microsoft Cluster with another virtual machine**

Warning conditions are shown here:

✓ **The virtual machine is configured with an internal virtual switch but isn't connected to the internal switch.**

✓ **The virtual machine is connected to a local CD-ROM or floppy disk, but no image is mounted.**

✓ **If any snapshots exist of the virtual machine.**

✓ **If VMTools aren't installed or working properly on the virtual machine.**

You can visually check the VMotion constraints using the Maps tab after you're logged into VirtualCenter. For VMotion to work, the hosts and virtual machines need to be able to see the same data stores and network port groups. Figure 12-10 shows the Maps tab, and you can see the VMotion data store and network constraints are met for hosts and virtual machines. Notice that you can determine what you see by selecting and deselecting the check boxes for objects in the Map Relationships section. After you refresh your picture (by clicking the Apply Relationships button), you can click and drag it around to see what you need to see.

The Maps tab

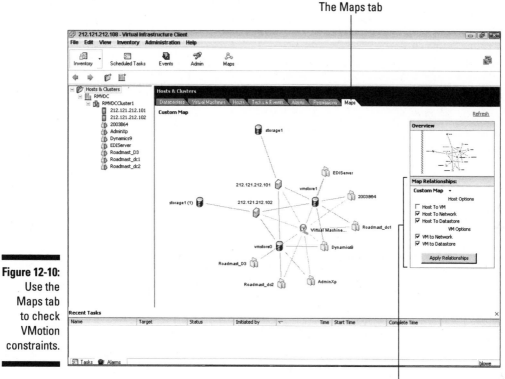

Figure 12-10:
Use the
Maps tab
to check
VMotion
constraints.

The Map Relationships section

Performing a VMotion migration

After the prerequisites are met, you can manually start VMotion to move a
virtual machine from one host to the next by following these steps:

1. **Log in to your VIC.**

2. **Right-click the virtual machine that you want to migrate.**

3. **Choose Migrate.**

   The Migrate Virtual Machine Wizard (as shown in Figure 12-11) starts.

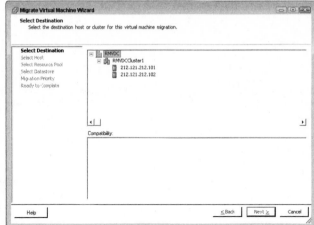

Figure 12-11:
The Migrate
Virtual
Machine
Wizard.

4. **Click your preferred destination host from the list of possible hosts.**

5. **After the validation process checks the prerequisites, click Next.**

6. **After resource pool validation process takes place, click Next.**

7. **Select High or Low priority and then click Next.**

   • *High-priority migrations* ensure the virtual machine remains
     available throughout the migration by reserving resources on the
     source and destination nodes before migrating.

   High-priority migrations can fail because of a lack of resources.

   • *Low-priority migrations* will always work, but the virtual machine
     might be briefly unavailable if resources are tight.

8. **Review your choices and then click Finish.**

Part V
Playing Virtual Administrator

The 5th Wave   By Rich Tennant

"We take network security here very seriously."

In this part . . .

This part analyzes the VMware security model and how it's similar to, yet different from, the Windows security model. You start by securing your system in Chapter 13. Resource pools are discussed in Chapter 14. Chapter 15 explores the various tools to use and ways to monitor your system. Preparing for disaster is covered in Chapter 16 and introduces various methods to backup your virtual machines. Lastly, Chapter 17 covers troubleshooting methodology as it applies to your virtual environment.

Chapter 13

Securing Your System

· ·

In This Chapter

▶ Looking at the VMware security model

▶ Seeing how Windows users and groups are used

▶ Discussing privileges and security roles

· ·

*A*ll systems need some sort of security model to prevent everyone from doing everything. Security models are usually made up of three things:

✔ Users and groups

✔ Rights and privileges

✔ Objects to which those rights and privileges apply

This is true in the physical world as well as the virtual computer world.

Take the simple example of a restaurant — say, Gordon Ramsay's The London in Manhattan (a fantastic restaurant where my friends and I actually met Gordon Ramsay after having dinner). There are three primary groups: the owners, the employees, and the customers.

The owners have the rights and privileges to go anywhere they want in the restaurant, can hire and fire employees, and most likely have the combination to the safe. They are the administrators and have rights to all objects: the restaurant, the bar, the kitchen, and the store rooms.

The employees are another group with more restricted rights. All employees likely have the rights to access the kitchen object. Waiters have the rights to the restaurant floor object. Bartenders have the rights to the employee-side-of-the-bar object. The maître d' has the rights to all the aforementioned objects. Yet, if you saw a waiter behind the bar, that might raise some questions, especially if he were having a drink!

Customers, on the other hand, have the most restricted set of rights. They have access only to their table object (reservations are recommended), the customer-side-of-the-bar object, and the restroom objects. They cannot go into the kitchen object or jump behind the bar object.

VMware Infrastructure 3 works the same way, with: users and groups, rights and privileges, and objects. In this chapter, VMware's security model is discussed. Users, roles, and privileges, and their applications are covered in detail.

Dissecting VMware's Security Model

Both VirtualCenter and ESX are organized hierarchically, based on objects. This is very similar to how Active Directory (AD) is organized. In AD, the object at the root level is the Forest. Then you have domains as the next hierarchical level. After that, you have organizational units; then you have leaf objects, such as users, groups, and computers.

As you look through your object hierarchies from the VMware Infrastructure Client (VIC), you see an object-based hierarchy similar to AD. In VirtualCenter, your root object is the Hosts and Clusters folder. Your next level in the hierarchy are datacenters. The next level are clusters, and then ESX hosts and virtual machines.

When connecting to an ESX host, the hierarchy is much smaller. You have the ESX host, and then virtual machines. The two hierarchies are shown in Figures 13-1 and 13-2. VMware applies security at the object level.

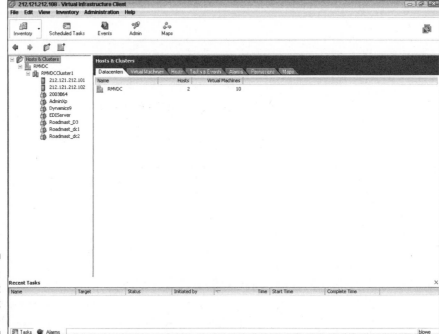

Figure 13-1:
An ESX host object hierarchy.

Figure 13-2:
An ESX host
object
hierarchy.

VirtualCenter and ESX use the same security model. The only difference is where the users and groups are defined:

> ✔ *VirtualCenter* **gets its users and groups from the Windows server on which it resides.**
>
> You can use domain or local users and groups.
>
> ✔ *ESX hosts* **pull from their local Linux users and groups.**

When you add an ESX host to a VirtualCenter server, VirtualCenter installs a proxy user onto the ESX host called VPXUSER. VPXUSER is an administrator on the ESX host. When you administer through VirtualCenter, the VirtualCenter server acts as a security proxy and restricts users from having full access to the ESX host through the VPXUSER account.

Users and groups are given roles. The roles determine what that user and group can do. Roles themselves are just sets of privileges. Privileges actually determine what can be done. Being able to take a snapshot of a virtual machines is a privilege, as is powering-on and -off a virtual machine. VMware has many privileges that are organized by functionality, as shown in Figure 13-3.

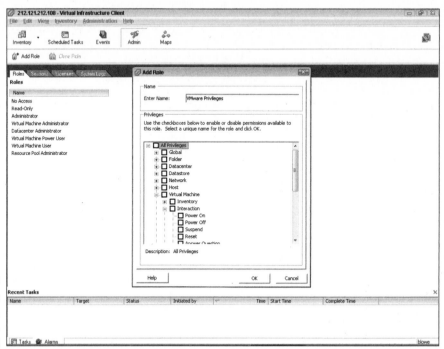

Security is defined by combining three things: the object itself, the user or group, and a security role. In other words, security is assigned at the object level by combining a user or group with a role and assigning the combination to the object. To make someone a virtual machine power user on a single virtual machine, you would add a permission to that virtual machine that combines the user (or a group the user is in) and the Virtual Machine Power User role. This is shown in Figure 13-4.

Assume you want to make a user, Bob, a Virtual Machine Power user on one of you VMs. Do the following:

1. **Login to VirtualCenter with your VIC.**

2. **Select the VM you want to give Bob the Virtual Machine Power user role for.**

3. **Click the Permissions tab.**

4. **Right-click in the User/Group area and select Add Permission.**

5. **Click the Add button under Users and Groups in the Assign Permissions window.**

6. **Select your user (or group), in this case Bob, by double-clicking on them and then click OK.**

7. Under Assigned Role, click on the drop down list and select Virtual Machine Power User. You should see a window similar to the one in Figure 13-5.

8. Click OK.

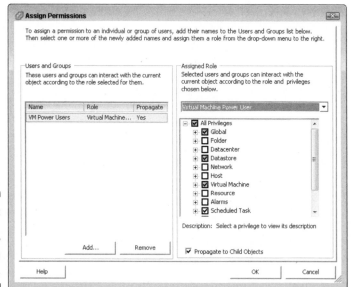

Figure 13-4:
Assigning security to a virtual machine.

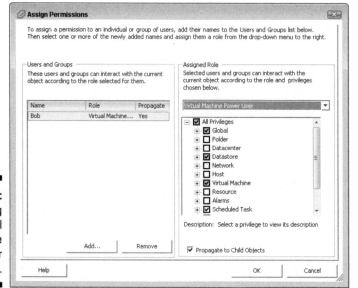

Figure 13-5:
Assigning the Virtual Machine Power User role to Bob.

By default, security is inherited by all child objects. Only administrators have full access to everything after an install. However, other default roles exist such as Read Only, No Access, Virtual Machine Administrator, Virtual Machine Power User, Virtual Machine User, Datacenter Administrator, Datacenter VM Manager, and Resource Pool Administrator; you just have to manually apply them.

Built-in roles

Several default roles are created when you install an ESX host or VirtualCenter. The default roles created on an ESX host are

- ✔ **No Access:** This role can be used to block inheritance.

- ✔ **Read Only:** As the name implies, you can look but you cannot touch!

- ✔ **Administrator:** Permissions are granted to all privileges that are available. If you're reading this book, this is likely the role you want!

The root account is given the Administrator role, and this combination is applied to the ESX host, which is the root object on an ESX host. Security is then inherited down to all virtual machines.

When you install VirtualCenter, the following roles are created by default:

- ✔ **No Access:** This role can be used to block inheritance.

- ✔ **Read Only:** As the name implies, you can look but you cannot touch!

- ✔ **Administrator:** Permissions are granted to all privileges that are available. Again, if you're reading this book, this is likely the role you want!

- ✔ **Virtual Machine Administrator:** This role has all the privileges that the Administrator role has except for the privileges required to modify security.

- ✔ **Datacenter Administrator:** This role defines a restricted administrator with fewer virtual machine privileges and no security modification privileges. This role has limited privileges when it comes to dealing with virtual networks and data stores as well.

- ✔ **Virtual Machine Power User:** This role grants all the privileges needed to work with existing virtual machines as well as the ability to take snapshots and schedule tasks. Snapshots are covered in Chapter 11.

- ✔ **Virtual Machine User:** This role provides the privileges needed to interact with an existing virtual machine and to schedule tasks. No snapshots are allowed.

- ✔ **Resource Pool Administrator:** This role can do most things to a resource pool. Resource pools are described in detail in Chapter 14.

Creating your own roles

You can create custom roles to suit your exact needs. To create a custom role, follow these steps:

1. **Log in to your VirtualCenter with VIC.**

   For this example, I'm creating a custom role to allow Bob to run a scheduled task.

2. **Click the Admin button.**

3. **Right-click the role that's the closest to what you want to create and then select Clone, as shown in Figure 13-6.**

   Optionally, you can right-click and create a new role from scratch. If you're creating a new role from scratch, like the one for Bob, you need to choose a role name and pick the privileges you want to assign a la carte as shown in Figure 13-7.

4. **Right-click the cloned role and choose Edit Role.**

5. **Provide a name for your role.**

6. **Add and remove the privileges (see Figure 13-8) as you see fit. Then click OK.**

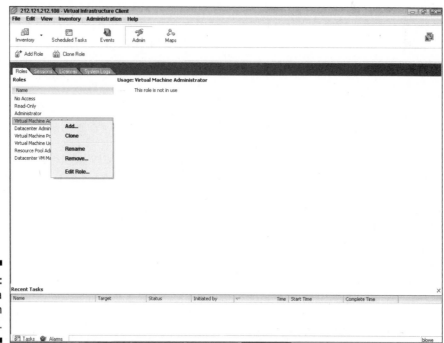

Figure 13-6:
Create a
role from
scratch.

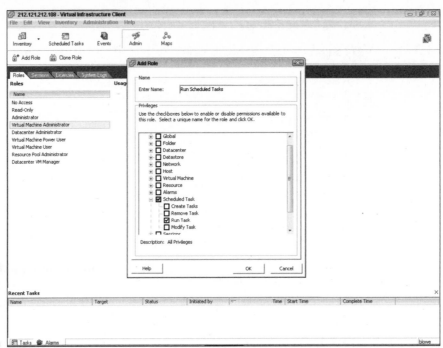

Figure 13-7:
Create a
role from
scratch.

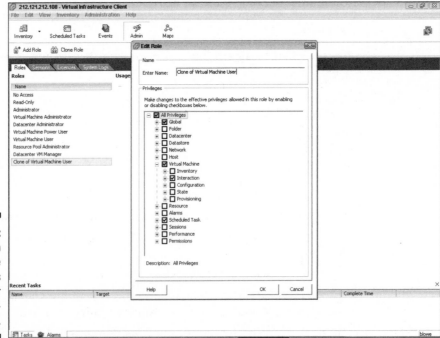

Figure 13-8:
Cloning an
existing role
to use as
a base for
customiza-
tion.

Combining users, roles, and objects for security

Suppose you have your VMware Infrastructure 3 objects set up as shown in Figure 13-9. You have two datacenters: one in New York, and one in California. Each datacenter has a two-node ESX cluster. You have a VMware administrator and a Windows administrator in each datacenter.

You want your VMware administrator to be able to do everything he needs to do in VMware for that datacenter. That includes the roles to add ESX hosts, configure Distributed Resource Scheduler (DRS) and High Availability (HA), view logs, and provision virtual machines. However, you don't want your VMware admin to be able to administer any virtual machines. You make a custom role called Datacenter VM Manager NY. Clone that role and call it Datacenter VM Manager CA.

You want your Windows administrator to be able to administer the servers, turn them on and off, modify their configurations, and set up alarms. Again, you create a custom role called Windows VM Administrator NY. Clone that role and call it Windows VM Administrator CA.

You now need to create four Windows groups to mirror the roles — Datacenter VM Manager NY and CA, and Windows VM Administrator NY and CA. These are the groups you will link with the security roles at the object level to apply your security design. Next, add the appropriate user accounts to the groups. Now you're ready to apply your security. To do so, follow these steps:

1. **After logging in to your VirtualCenter, click the Inventory button.**

2. **Click the CA Datacenter object.**

3. **Click the Permissions tab.**

   Notice that this area shows what object the permissions are originally set on. This comes in handy if you want to change permissions.

4. **Right-click in the empty space under any of the already assigned permissions and choose Add Permission.**

   The Assign Permissions window appears, as shown in Figure 13-10.

5. **Click the Add button (bottom left of the screen under Users and Groups).**

6. **Choose the Datacenter VM Manager CA group and the Windows VM Administrator CA, and then click OK.**

7. **Click the Datacenter VM Manager CA group.**

8. **On the right side of the screen (under Assigned Role), choose the Datacenter VM Manager CA role from the drop-down list.**

9. **On the left side of the screen, click the Windows VM Administrator CA group.**

10. **On the right side of the screen, choose the Windows VM Administrator CA role.**

11. **Make sure the Propagate to Child Objects check box is selected. Then click OK.**

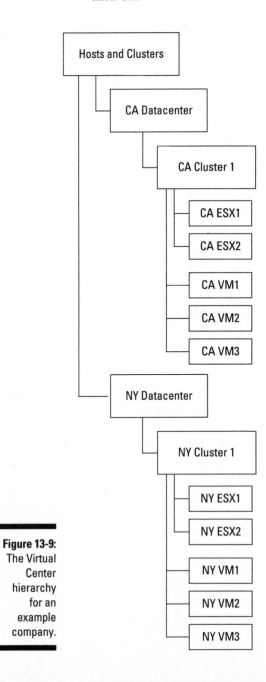

Figure 13-9:
The Virtual
Center
hierarchy
for an
example
company.

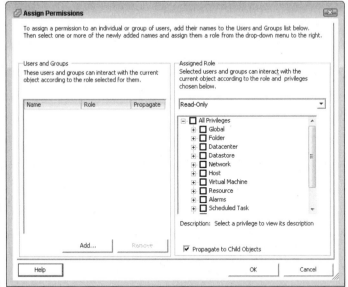

Several Examples of Applied Rights

The way inheritance works is similar to Windows, but there are differences. Several examples will illustrate how inheritance works, how to block it, how multiple roles combine, and what happens when a user role conflicts with a group role.

Be careful when applying rights. Unlike Windows, there is no option to Take Ownership if need be. If you accidentally remove the rights that you have as an administrator, you will have a very hard time getting them back.

Inheriting security roles

By default, if you apply rights to a parent object, all child objects that already exist (as well as new ones you create) get the same security applied to them. You can stop inheritance by right-clicking the parent permission, choosing modify, and deselecting the Propagate box, as shown in Figure 13-11. Another way to block inheritance is to apply the No Access role to an object. Again, the warning in the previous section applies.

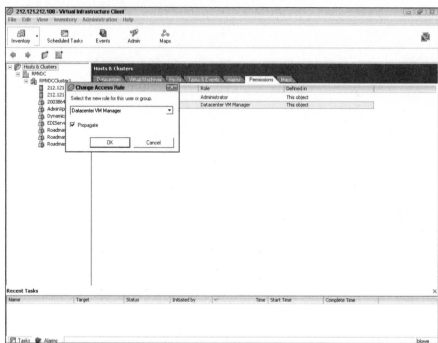

Figure 13-11:
Turning off
inheritance.

Roles and users in multiple groups

If a user is in multiple groups, here are the two cases to consider:

✔ **Permissions assigned to different groups on different objects**

✔ **Permissions assigned to different groups on the same object**

In the first case, rights assigned directly to an object override inherited rights. In Figure 13-12, assume that Bob is a member of the Windows Administrators group as well as a member of the Windows VM Read Only group. The CA datacenter has the administrator's role assigned to the Windows Administrators group with inheritance on. At this point, Bob is a full administrator of everything in the CA Datacenter. If the Read Only role were combined with the Windows VM Read Only group and applied to the VM1 object, Bob's rights would change slightly. He would have full a dministrator rights to everything in the CA Datacenter except VM1. Bob would have read-only rights to VM1.

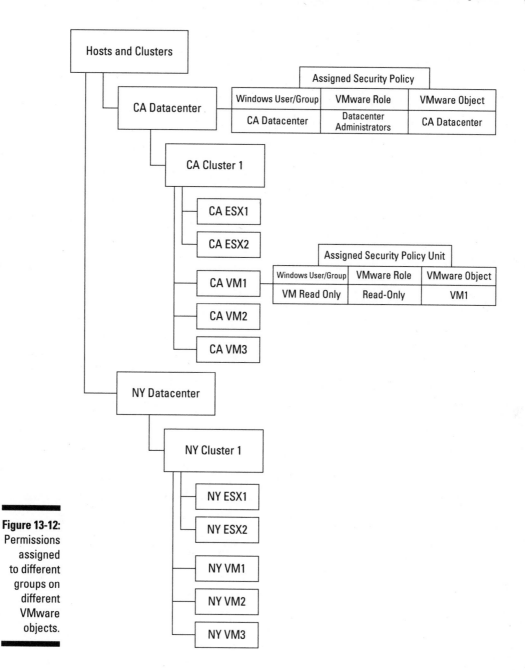

Figure 13-12:
Permissions assigned to different groups on different VMware objects.

Think of it as the same way that Windows applies share-level security and file-level security. If the share level is set to read-only and the file level is set to full control, the user has read-only rights when accessing the file over the network.

In the second case, the roles are combined. This works the same way as a member in two Windows groups that have file rights to the same object: The user has the combined rights of the two groups. In Figure 13-13, assume that Bob is now a member of the following Windows groups: CA VM Power User and CA Datacenter Administrator. In VirtualCenter, the roles Virtual Machine Power User and Datacenter Administrator are combined with the Windows groups CA VM Power User and CA Datacenter Administrator. Because Bob is in both groups, he has all the privileges assigned to both VMware security roles. If inheritance is enabled, Bob has those privileges on all child objects in the CA Datacenter.

Conflicting user and group roles

If you assign a role to a user, it will override any group role assignments to which the user is a member. For example, if Bob has the Datacenter Administrator role assigned to him on the CA Datacenter through a group and also has Virtual Machine Power User assigned to his Windows account on the CA Datacenter, Bob only has the privileges assigned to the role Virtual Machine Power Users and none of the privileges assigned to the role Datacenter Administrators. See Figure 13-14.

Role conflicts and inheritance

If a role is assigned to an object based on inheritance and a conflicting role is assigned directly to an object, the role assigned directly to the object overrides the inherited role. Say Bob has the Read Only role on VM1 through inheritance and the Administrator role assigned directly to VM1. Bob's effective rights are Administrator on VM1. See Figure 13-15.

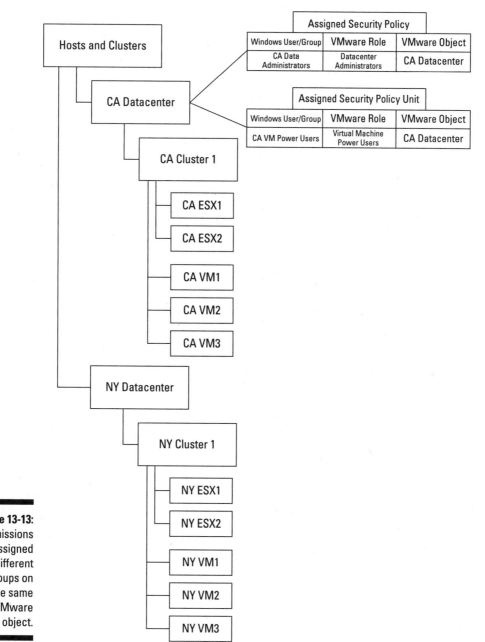

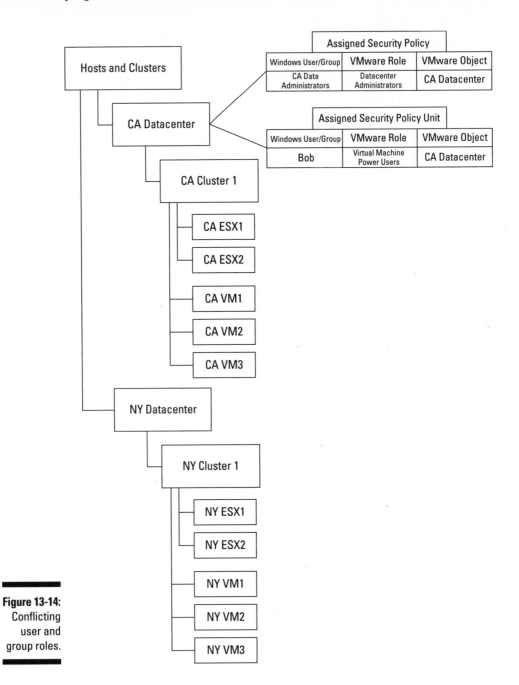

Assigned Security Policy		
Windows User/Group	VMware Role	VMware Object
CA Data Administrators	Datacenter Administrators	CA Datacenter

Assigned Security Policy Unit		
Windows User/Group	VMware Role	VMware Object
Bob	Virtual Machine Power Users	CA Datacenter

Figure 13-14:
Conflicting
user and
group roles.

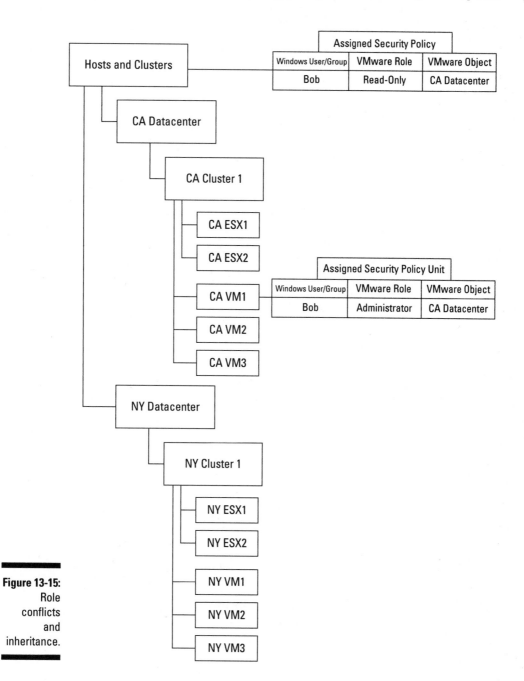

Assigned Security Policy		
Windows User/Group	VMware Role	VMware Object
Bob	Read-Only	CA Datacenter

Hosts and Clusters

CA Datacenter

CA Cluster 1

CA ESX1

CA ESX2

Assigned Security Policy Unit		
Windows User/Group	VMware Role	VMware Object
Bob	Administrator	CA Datacenter

CA VM1

CA VM2

CA VM3

NY Datacenter

NY Cluster 1

NY ESX1

NY ESX2

NY VM1

NY VM2

NY VM3

Figure 13-15:
Role
conflicts
and
inheritance.

Chapter 14

Swimming in Resource Pools

. . . .

. . . .

*V*Mware is designed to use computer hardware more efficiently. Just like anything else, though, this becomes too much of a good thing at some point. If you keep adding virtual machines without increasing the available hardware, you eventually have *hardware contention:* Suddenly there will not be enough CPU, memory, network, or disk resources available to support all of your virtual machines at the same time.

In this chapter, we first look at what resource pools can do for you. Next, we examine how resource pools work their magic. Finally, we discuss setting up and using resource pools.

Sharing and Playing Nicely with Resource Pools

Hardware contention really becomes a "race" condition. You need more memory than you physically have, or you need more CPU cycles than you physically have. By default, all virtual machines get more-or-less equal hardware access, but you can manually tilt the scale in favor of some machines at the expense of others. The way to do this is with *resource pools*.

Understanding what resource pools do

Tilting the scale in favor of some machines reminds me of the old airline joke about what to do if the oxygen masks fall from the ceiling when you're in a plane:

1. Put the mask on yourself first.

2. If you have a child with you, put her mask on after yours.

3. If you have more than one child with you, decide which one you like best!

Likewise, resource pools let you favor some virtual machines over others. Although folks argue that test and production machines should be on separate networks and isolated from each other in the physical world, you can easily run them both on the same physical hardware yet keep them isolated in the virtual world.

However, you definitely want to ensure that your production machines always have enough hardware. In essence, you give them a guarantee to a minimum amount of hardware in case an errant process sends a test machine off into a resource-intensive, infinite loop.

If you set up one resource pool for test and one for production, you can allow the test pool a maximum of 10 percent of your resources and the production pool the remaining 90 percent. That way, your test environment can use, at most, 10 percent of what's available to all the virtual machines.

Another possible use for resource pools is to sell a percentage of capacity in some sort of chargeback system. This allows you to dilute the cost of information technology over several departments. Thus, departments that use a higher percentage of resources buy (in essence) a bigger slice of the pie. There are even add-on utilities to manage chargebacks if you want to implement a system in this manner. A quick Google search for VMware Chargeback will provide a great starting point for your research.

Examining how resource pools work

All virtual machines have a minimum and maximum level for memory and CPU resources. A virtual machine won't start unless it can get the minimum amount of resources promised. Similarly, a virtual machine can never exceed its assigned maximum. It is the area in between that's open for contention. This is shown in Figure 14-1.

When two virtual machines are in *contention,* they both want the same hardware resource. This is a *race condition:* That is, whoever wins the race is a matter of probability. You can modify any virtual machine's probability so that it "wins" the race more often than other machines.

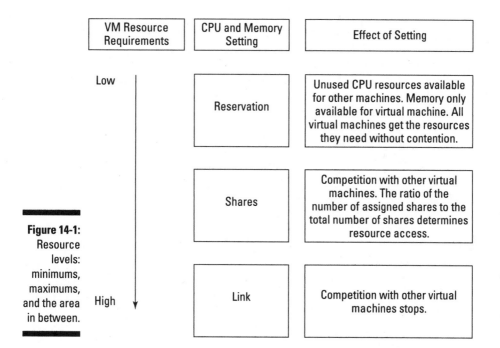

VM Resource Requirements	CPU and Memory Setting	Effect of Setting
Low	Reservation	Unused CPU resources available for other machines. Memory only available for virtual machine. All virtual machines get the resources they need without contention.
	Shares	Competition with other virtual machines. The ratio of the number of assigned shares to the total number of shares determines resource access.
High	Link	Competition with other virtual machines stops.

Figure 14-1: Resource levels: minimums, maximums, and the area in between.

Think of the hardware between the minimum and maximum area as a big pie. Everyone likes pie. Each virtual machine gets one or more slices of the pie. The more slices of pie you have, the higher your probability of winning a race condition, and the more resources you can use.

For example, in Figure 14-2 you can see three virtual machines with a pie of ten slices. VM1 has only one slice, or ten percent of the pie. VM2 has 3 slices, or 30 percent of the pie. VM3 has the remaining 6 slices, or 60 percent of the pie. In this scenario, VM3 has six times more access to hardware than VM1 and two times more access to hardware than VM2. This model for managing resources is a *proportional share system.*

The only part of the pie analogy that doesn't fit well is that when you power-on another virtual machine that has pie slices, no existing virtual machine gives up any of their existing slices of pie. Your pie simply gets cut into a greater number of smaller slices. Figure 14-3 shows what happens when you power on VM4, which is a virtual machine with three slices of pie. Your total pie now has 13 slices; and of course, each slice is now smaller than when it was cut into only 10 slices.

Now VM2 and VM4 have three times more resources than VM1 because they each have three slices of pie compared with the one slice allotted to VM1. VM3 still has two times the amount of resources of VM2 and VM3 and six times the resources of VM1.

The opposite is true when you power-off a virtual machine. If you were to power off VM1, you'd have 12 outstanding slices of pie instead of 13. Each slice is slightly bigger. VM3 still has two times the amount of resources that VM2 and VM4 have. This is shown in Figure 14-4.

Of course, VMware doesn't allow you to actually feed your virtual machines pieces of pie. In fact, there is probably no food allowed in your server room at all! Instead, you assign *shares* to your virtual machines. Shares work just like slices of pie. The more shares a virtual machine has, the higher its probability of winning a race condition and the more hardware access it has. Separate numbers of shares are assigned for memory and CPU resources. And that brings you to using *resource pools,* which are groupings of memory and CPU shares made available to virtual machines.

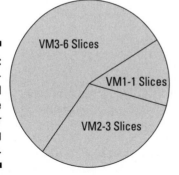

Figure 14-2:
Use a pro-
portional
share
system for
managing
resources.

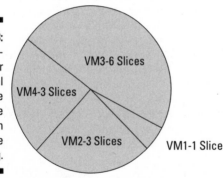

Figure 14-3:
Powering-
on another
virtual
machine
and the
effect on
resource
sharing.

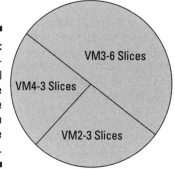

CPU and Memory Resource Pie
With 12 Slices

VM3-6 Slices

VM4-3 Slices

VM2-3 Slices

Figure 14-4:
Powering-
off a virtual
machine
and the
effect on
resource
sharing.

The share mechanism for dealing with race conditions doesn't become active until contention for a resource arises.

Sharing memory resources

Each virtual machine has four settings that determine how much memory is available in times of contention. They are

- **Available Memory:** This is the amount of memory you assign to a virtual machine via its hardware Properties page. This is the maximum amount of memory a virtual machine can use.

- **Limit:** This is the maximum amount of memory that can actually live in RAM instead of a swap file. Unless you change this setting, it is equal to the available memory.

- **Memory Reservation:** This is the minimum amount of memory a virtual machine is guaranteed. It is always available to the virtual machine, and no other machine can use it.

- **Memory Shares:** The more memory shares a virtual machine has compared with other virtual machines, the more often it wins memory resources when contention for memory happens.

    Suppose you have three machines with a total of 100 shares available to them. If one machine has 75 shares, the lucky machine with most of the shares will win races for memory 75 percent of the time.

When you think about the memory settings in the preceding list, you realize that you can allocate more RAM than you physically have in your ESX host or cluster. If you wanted to run 20 virtual machines on an ESX host with 10GB of RAM, you can set each virtual machine with a reservation of 500MB of RAM. That allows all the virtual machines to start. Next, you can limit all the machines at 1GB and assign them 2GB total. (You assigned 20GB of RAM on a physical machine that only has 10GB of RAM.) The limit gives each machine the potential to use 1 full GB of physical RAM and have a 1GB RAM swap file that's invisible to the other guest operating system(s) running on the physical server(s). No matter what the physical reality is, each guest OS thinks it has 2GB of RAM. VMware calls this Memory Overcommitment.

The limit can never be greater than the available memory a virtual machine has. It can, however, be less. Whenever a difference exists between available memory and the limit, VMware creates a RAM swap file that's the size of the difference. The swap file is created on a machine-by-machine basis.

Sharing CPU resources

Here are the three settings used to control CPU resources in cases of hardware contention:

- ✔ **Limit:** This is the maximum amount of CPU resources that a virtual machine can use, measured in MHz.

- ✔ **CPU Reservation:** Measured in MHz, this is the minimum amount that a virtual machine is guaranteed. If the virtual machine is using less than its reservation, the excess is available for other virtual machines until the virtual machine with the reservation needs it back.

- ✔ **Shares:** Shares are used to determine how often a virtual machine gets CPU resources between the reservation and limit when contention exists. The more shares a virtual machine has, the more often it will win the competition for CPU resources.

All CPUs in a virtual machine need to be scheduled at the same time. However, multiple virtual CPU machines split the number of shares over the number of virtual CPUs. So, if a machine with two virtual CPUs has 1,000 MHz, each virtual CPU has 500 MHz allocated to it. Because both virtual CPUs need to be physically scheduled to run at the same time (or during the same CPU time slice if you prefer), VMware does lose some flexibility.

A multiple CPU virtual machine often runs slower than a single virtual processor machine. You can potentially slow your entire infrastructure if you have several multiple, virtual CPU machines. You should use multiple virtual CPUs only if you can prove that they provide a performance boost.

Divvying resources with resource pools

You can create a resource pool on a standalone server or in a cluster. On a standalone server, the total amount of CPU and memory resources shared is whatever the server has. If your resource pool is part of a cluster, the total amount of CPU and memory resources are the sum of all the servers in the cluster. Distributed Resource Scheduler (DRS) will move resources to different ESX hosts to maintain the utilization rules defined in your resource pools. Your resource pools are named objects in your VirtualCenter hierarchy that allow you to define the following:

- Minimums for memory and CPU resources
- Maximums for memory and CPU resources
- Security permissions for the resource pool

Resource pools can be *nested*. In other words, your resource pool can have one or more sub-resource pools, as shown in Figure 14-5. In fact, your cluster is the parent of all resource pools below it and represents full access to all resources for all child virtual machines. The only time this does not hold true is if you define resource limits on the virtual machines themselves.

Notice how nesting affects your slices of the overall pie. Your cluster is divided into two pools: Sales and Accounting. If Sales has 65 percent of the shares, Accounting has only 35 percent. Accounting is then split into Test and Production. Test has 10 percent of the shares, and Production has 90 percent. In the overall cluster, Test has 10 percent of the 35 percent of the overall cluster resources. In other words, Test has a maximum of 3.5 percent of the clusters resources after contention begins. Production has 90 percent of Accounting's 35 percent of cluster resources, or a total of 31.5 percent of the entire cluster's resources after contention begins.

All in all, resource pools allow you to guarantee virtual machines a minimum amount of resources, limit the maximum amount of resources, and contend for access to resources when in between the two limits. The contention process allows you to stack the deck to favor some virtual machines over others.

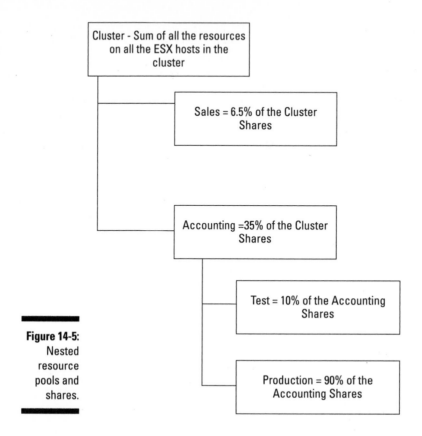

Cluster - Sum of all the resources on all the ESX hosts in the cluster

Sales = 6.5% of the Cluster Shares

Accounting =35% of the Cluster Shares

Test = 10% of the Accounting Shares

Production = 90% of the Accounting Shares

Figure 14-5:
Nested
resource
pools and
shares.

Expandable Resource Pools: Borrowing from Your Parents

Expandable resource pools are like children — they borrow from their parents. The only difference is the child resource pools always pay you back! When you set up a resource pool, you can allow it to borrow unused resources from its parent pool. This allows you to better utilize your overall resources systemwide as long as the parent pools aren't maxed out.

Say you have four machines using all the reserved resources in a resource pool and want to power-on a fifth machine. If you set the resource pool as expandable, the fifth machine can borrow resources from the parent pool if it has them to spare. As soon as you power-down a machine , borrowed resources are returned.

If you borrow resources from a parent for a virtual machine, those resources aren't available again until you power-off the virtual machine. This can prevent virtual machines in the parental pool from starting if they can't meet their resource reservation.

With *expandable reservations,* one child can be greedy and take all the parent's spare resources, leaving their sibling resource pool with no resources to borrow from the parent pool if needed. This can prevent virtual machines from powering-on.

The power-on algorithm is shown in Figure 14-6. As soon as you try to power-on a virtual machine, the system asks, "Are there enough resources to meet the virtual machine's reservation?" If so, it can start. If not, your system asks, "Can resources be borrowed from the parent pool?" If not, the virtual machine won't start. If resources are expandable and resources are available in the parent pool, the virtual machine can borrow them and start. Otherwise, the virtual machine can't power-on because its reservations have not been met.

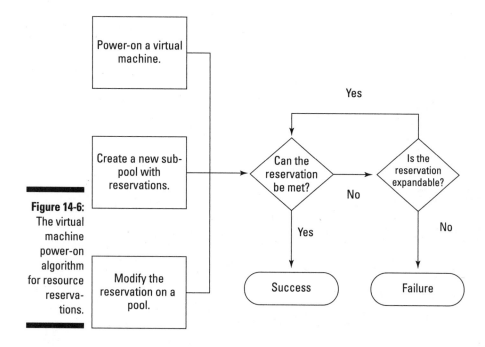

Figure 14-6: The virtual machine power-on algorithm for resource reserva-tions.

The following example is very detailed and provides one mathematical example of how a resource pool can be set up to meet resource utilization goals.

This example is based on a single cluster that has 10,000 MHz of CPU resources and 10GB of RAM. You create a parent resource pool that's not expandable but reserves the available resources in the cluster. You have test and production machines that you want to put in separate resource pools to ensure the production machines always have adequate resources available to them.

Here are the parameters:

- ✔ **You want to keep 20 percent of the resources floating between the test and production resource pools.**

    That translates to 2,000 MHz of CPU and 2GB of RAM.

- ✔ **You want the production machines to always have a minimum of 70 percent of the resources available to them and the test machines to always have a minimum of 10 percent of resources.**

- ✔ **When either pool needs more, you want the production pool to win 75 percent of the time and the test pool to win 25 percent of the time.**

To implement these settings, create the following resource pools (covered in the next section):

- ✔ **All Cluster Resources:** This is the parent pool and has the full cluster resources reservation of 10,000 MHz CPU and 10GB of RAM. This pool is not expandable because there are no more resources: This pool has them all reserved. There are no virtual machines in this pool.

- ✔ **Production:** This resource pool reserves 70 percent of CPU and memory; or, 7,000 MHz of CPU and 7GB of RAM. To ensure that this pool can get more resources from the parent if needed, leave the default setting as Expandable. You also give this resource pool 3,000 shares to use when competing with Test.

- ✔ **Test:** This resource pool reserves 10 percent of CPU and memory; or, 1,000 MHz and 1GB of RAM. You also leave this pool as Expandable and give it 1,000 shares to use when competing with Production. In case there is an errant runaway process on a test machine, you also limit the maximum CPU resources to 2,000 MHz and the maximum RAM to 2GB.

Similar resource pools are shown in Figure 14-7.

To see how they work, boot up all your test and production machines. Assume that they're not that busy at first, but then get busier over time until they eventually use up all the resources available in the cluster. You need to examine several resource-related system state changes:

- ✔ **Below Reservation:** In this state, all the machines are running, but the total amount of resources the Test and Production machines use is less than the amount of resources reserved for each resource pool. Production machines are using less than 7,000 MHz of CPU and less than 7GB of RAM. The Test machines are using less than 1,000 MHz of CPU and less than 1GB of RAM.

✔ **Reservation Threshold:** As the machines get busier and busier, they eventually use all the resources reserved for their resource pools.

✔ **Contention for Expandable Resources Before Limit Is Met:** After each group needs more resources than reserved for its resource pool, each group starts tapping into the excess 20 percent of resources that the parent pool has. Both pools are competing for the same spare capacity. Because the Production pool has 3,000/4,000 shares assigned to it and the Test pool has 1,000/4,000 shares assigned to it, the Production pool gets access to the spare capacity three times as much as the Test pool, meeting the 75 percent win requirement.

✔ **Limit Met:** As your Test machines use more and more resources, they will eventually hit their limit of 2,000 MHz and 2GB of RAM. You know the excess resources in the parent pool total 2,000 MHz and 2 GB of RAM. The reserved amount for the Test pool is 1,000 MHz of CPU and 1GB of RAM, and the limit is 2,000 MHz of CPU and 2GB of RAM. This means that the maximum amount of expandable resources the Test pool can take is one-half: 1,000 MHz of CPU and 1GB of RAM. The two pools are in the last state until Test reaches its limit. At that point, there is no contention for the remaining half of expandable resources: 1,000 MHz CPU and 1GB of RAM. The last bit of available resources just goes to the Production pool.

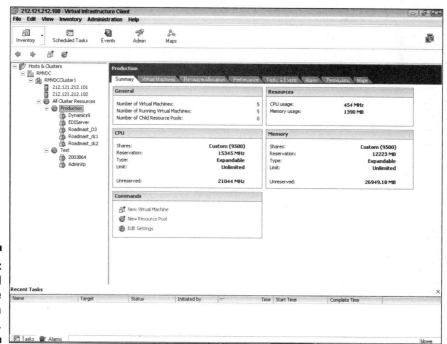

Figure 14-7:
Nested resource pools in a cluster.

The various system states are shown in Figure 14-8. Bear in mind that each virtual machine can be assigned varying numbers of shares to compete for the resources that its resource pool has won. This allows you to give your favorite machines more resources when things get tight.

Pool's State	Result of State	State Name
Production and Test using less resources than pool reservations.	Each virtual machine gets all the resources it needs.	Below Reservation
Production and Test use all the hardware they have reserved.	Each virtual machine gets all the resources it needs.	Reservation Threshold
Production and Test compete for the first half of the expandable resources of 1,000 MHz CPU and 1 Gig RAM.	Production wins the competition for the first half of the expandable resources 75% of the time.	Contention for Expandable Resources Before Limit Met
Test stops competing for expandable resources once it reaches the limit of 2,000 MHz and 2 Gigs of RAM. Production still needs more resources.	Production gets the last half of the expandable resources without contention. However, Production still competes with Test for the first half of the expandable resources.	Limit Met

Figure 14-8: Resource-related system states.

Setting Up Resource Pools: Which Machine Do You Love More?

Because resource pools are meant to favor some machines over others when there are not quite enough resources to go around, you need to give some thought as to which machine(s) you want to favor. Mission-critical machines are a good choice to assign more resources. Just remember that you're not actually assigning more resources — you're just assigning a better chance of winning access to resources.

Creating a resource pool

To create a resource pool, follow these steps:

1. **Log in to your VMware Infrastructure Client.**

2. **Right-click your cluster and choose New Resource Pool.**

   The Create Resource Pool window opens, as shown in Figure 14-9.

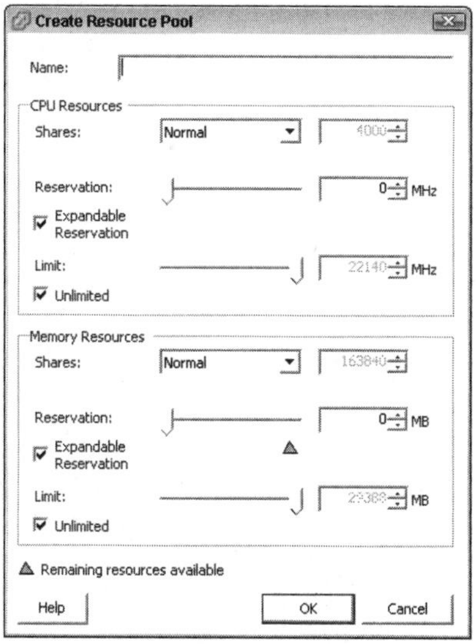

Figure 14-9:
Start creating a new resource pool here.

3. **Enter the name of the pool, the reservation information, and the share information, as shown in Figure 14-10.**

4. **Decide whether you want the pool to be expandable.**

   If so, leave the Expandable Reservation boxes selected. If not, deselect them.

Edit Settings

Name:	Production

CPU Resources

Shares: Custom 3000

Reservation: 7000 MHz
☑ Expandable Reservation

Limit: 22140 MHz
☑ Unlimited

Memory Resources

Shares: Custom 3000

Reservation: 7000 MB
☑ Expandable Reservation △

Limit: 29388 MB
☑ Unlimited

△ Remaining resources available

Help   OK   Cancel

Figure 14-10:
Enter the criteria for the new resource pool.

   5. **Click OK.**

Securing resource pools

By default, any resource pool you create will inherit its parent object's security. You can modify a resource pool's security settings the same way you modify any other object's security settings to meet your needs. Read through Chapter 13 for more information on security.

Moving machines into resource pools

A resource pool with no machines in it doesn't really provide you with any benefit. The two ways to populate resource pools with virtual machines are by

  ✔ Dragging and dropping a machine into a resource pool
  ✔ Creating a new machine in a resource pool

To create a machine in a resource pool, just pick the pool as the deploy point during setup. You can also drag and drop existing virtual machines onto a resource pool.

You don't have to power-off a virtual machine to drag and drop it into a resource pool.

Chapter 15

Monitoring Your System

· ·

· ·

*H*ere are two important reasons why you should monitor any system:

> ✔ **Proactive problem prevention:** *Proactive problem prevention* revolves
> around capacity, security, and software problems.
>
> ✔ **Estimation:** *Estimation* allows you to make an educated guess as to the
> effect of a change, see the effect of a change, and capacity-plan for the future.

In the physical realm, you need to watch each and every machine. In the
virtual realm, what you watch depends on what you're checking.

For example, you still need to check the logs of all your virtual machines on
a machine-by-machine basis. Even if you centralize monitoring to accomplish
this, you're still looking for software and security issues on a machine-by-
machine basis. On the other hand, you can look at hardware on a cluster
basis or an ESX host basis, depending on whether you're looking for resource
utilization metrics or a failed piece of hardware.

In this chapter, we discuss the various ways to measure performance and
create useful baselines.

Monitoring VMware Infrastructure 3

You can choose from several points of view when it comes to monitoring.
You can look at the virtual machines for logs and utilization stats. You can
look at the clusters and individual ESX hosts they run on. You can view usage
by subsystem, such as network and storage. VirtualCenter and VMware
Infrastructure Client (VIC) can aid in most monitoring tasks.

Monitoring metrics

Outside of checking the logs on your virtual machines — which does need to be done periodically — here are four metrics you want to consistently watch:

- ✔ **CPU usage**
- ✔ **Memory usage**
- ✔ **Disk usage**
- ✔ **Network usage**

Fortunately, VMware has built-in tools to help with this endeavor, such as performance charts and alarms. However, monitoring is both a point-in-time and a trending exercise. Any time you take a reading, you have a picture at *a point in time.* When you combine many point-in-time readings, you get a *trending* picture. It is important to have both because it gives you a picture of utilization over time. This allows you to predict when you need to add new hardware to your system.

To get a point-in-time reading, do this:

1. **Log in to your VirtualCenter with VIC.**
2. **Select your object of interest (say your cluster) by clicking on it.**
3. **Click on the Performance tab.**
4. **The CPU usage metric is shown in Figure 15-1.**

Creating a baseline

A *baseline* is simply a collection of point observations over time and becomes your current trending picture. Establishing a baseline can not only aid you in future capacity planning, but also help you proactively find problems before they affect your users. For example, if your current baseline says everything is running smoothly and then suddenly your available CPU resources drop off or your network queues start backing up, you know you have a problem to solve.

Additionally, as you add more and more virtual machines to a cluster, you can use your baselines to determine when and how much hardware you need to add. This can include a new ESX host, more disk space, RAM, or even another network card. Baselines allow you to prepare your budget more effectively.

Similarly, you can use your baselines as part of your charge-back mechanism to proactively alert departments that they need to purchase more computing resources or change their usage patterns. Baselines show you where you are today so you can get to where you want to be tomorrow.

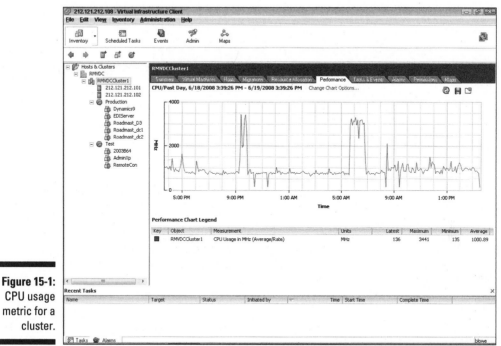

Figure 15-1:
CPU usage
metric for a
cluster.

Many Levels of Monitoring Performance

As I mentioned earlier in this chapter, instead of looking at everything on each machine (as you would in the physical world), in the virtual world, you look at different levels of your system. You can examine from the cluster level down to the virtual machine level. Each level and what you can see is described in the following sections.

The hosts and cluster level

The top of your virtual hill is the Hosts & Clusters folder. Your Hosts & Clusters folder contains all your clusters, hosts, resource pools, and virtual machines. You can view several metrics on your datacenter to evaluate its overall health. To get to these metrics, log in to your VIC and click your datacenter. You can examine the following tabs to get the metrics:

✓ **Datacenters:** As shown in Figure 15-2, your Datacenters tab summarizes the datacenters in your VMware Infrastructure 3. From the example in the figure, you can see one datacenter with two hosts and ten virtual machines.

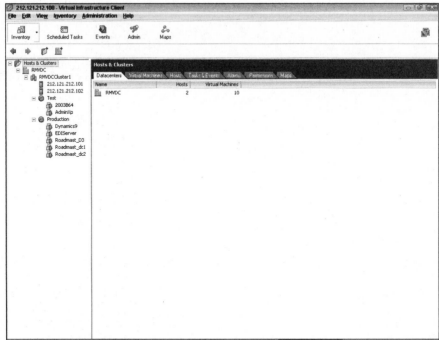

Figure 15-2:
The Data-
centers tab.

✔ **Virtual Machines:** This tab (see Figure 15-3) shows you all the virtual machines you have running, their IP addresses, and the amount of resources they're using. The Status column will quickly alert you to a problem: A problem exists if there is anything but a green dot. This tab also shows all your templates. You can add several other information columns (such as Uptime, IP Address, Memory, and DNS Name) by right-clicking any of the existing ones and choosing what you want from the drop-down list that appears.

VMware uses a color system with its alarms that match a traffic light. Green means everything is good, yellow is a warning, and red is bad. Virtual machines, by default, will trigger a yellow alarm when their CPU usage passes 75 percent and a red alarm when it passes 90 percent.

✔ **Hosts:** Figure 15-4 shows the Hosts tab. Here, you can quickly see whether a host is running low on memory or CPU resources by looking at the percentage used. Again, anything other than a green dot in the Status column is a cause for alarm.

✔ **Alarms:** The Alarms tab (see Figure 15-5) is actually broken into two separate sections. The Definitions link shows alarm definitions, and the Triggered Alarms link shows any alarms that have been triggered. You want to investigate any triggered alarms. The default alarms are shown in Figure 15-4.

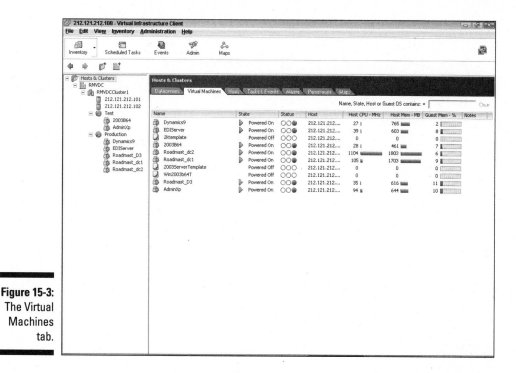

Figure 15-3:
The Virtual Machines tab.

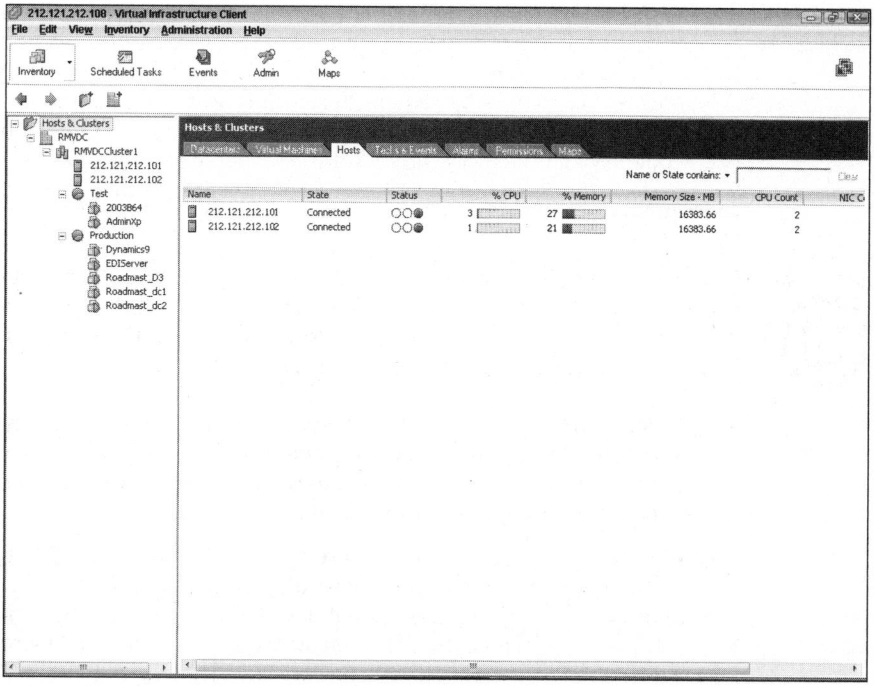

Figure 15-4:
The Hosts tab.

The Triggered Alarms link

The Definitions link

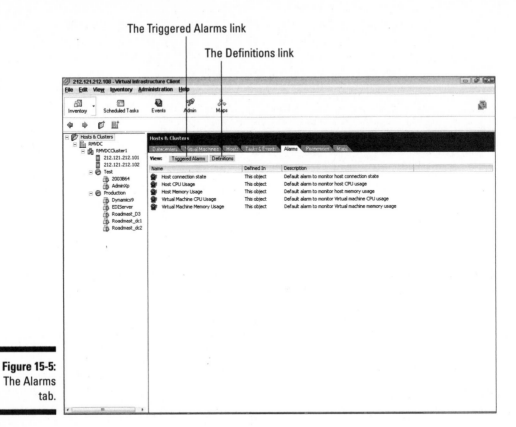

Figure 15-5:
The Alarms
tab.

The datacenter level

The datacenter-level performance monitoring tabs are the same as the Host & Clusters tabs. The only difference is they reflect only the clusters, hosts, and virtual machines in one datacenter.

The cluster level

The cluster level offers more monitoring options. You can still look at virtual machines and hosts, but you can also view resource-utilization graphs and Distributed Resource Scheduler (DRS) actions (DRS is covered in Chapter 12). You can examine this information on the following tabs:

✓ **Virtual Machines:** This is similar to the Hosts & Clusters level Virtual Machines tab in Figure 15-2. The exception is that this tab doesn't show templates but only lists virtual machines in the cluster.

✓ **Alarms:** Again, this tab is the same as the Hosts & Clusters level Alarms tab except it only lists alarms triggered in the particular cluster.

✓ **Summary:** The Summary tab allows you to see how many cluster resources you have — that is, if you have High Availability (HA) and DRS enabled — as well as how DRS is configured. Figure 15-6 shows the Summary tab for an example cluster.

- The *Utilization Percent graph* shows that 0–10 percent of the cluster's CPU resources are used and that 20–30 percent of cluster's memory resources are used.

- The *Percent of Entitled Resources Delivered graph* shows that 90–100 percent of the virtual machines are getting the resources they're entitled to. If this percentage is lower, DRS might be set too conservatively, you might have too many virtual machines on one host, or you might have small chunks of available resources on each host that are too small to satisfy a large virtual machine's requirements.

✓ **Migrations:** This tab (see Figure 15-7) shows any DRS migration recommendations and any migrations that happened recently.

✓ **Resource Allocation:** This tab can show different things, depending on how you're set up. Figure 15-8 shows the configuration of two example resource pools. If you have one or more virtual machines in your cluster at a sibling level to the resource pools, you would see them on this tab as well. The tab allows you to see the resource-use configuration for CPU and memory. Reservations, limits, share information, and expandability are also listed.

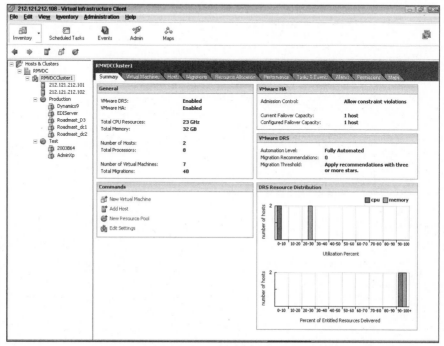

Figure 15-6:
The Summary tab for a cluster.

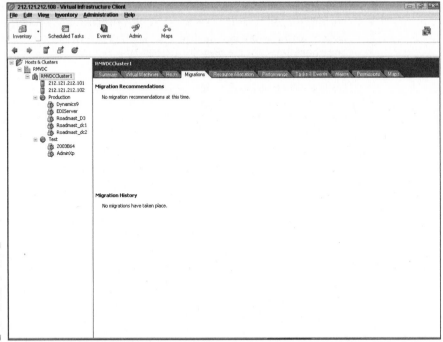

Figure 15-7:
The
Migrations
tab for a
cluster.

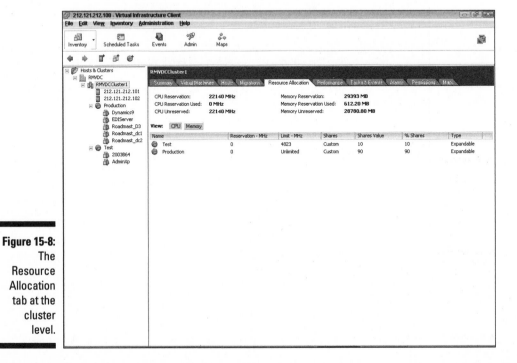

Figure 15-8:
The
Resource
Allocation
tab at the
cluster
level.

✔ **Performance:** This tab is the best place to get a handle on what's going on with memory and CPU resources in your cluster. It provides a real-time and historical view of your data, which makes it a great place to create your baselines. Figure 15-9 shows one year's worth of memory utilization.

You can customize the metrics you see by clicking the Change Chart Options link. Figure 15-10 shows one year's worth of CPU utilization. You can tell that seven machines are using a tiny fraction of the CPU resources. (Because there are eight 3 GHz cores and the machines are using 1 GHz over the last year, they're using only ¹⁄₂₄ of the CPU resources available.) You can also see that roughly 50 percent of the available memory is being used.

You can export a chart to Excel by clicking the icon that looks like a floppy disk. The icon to the right of the floppy disk (a box with an arrow in the upper right) allows you to "tear off" the chart, making it a floating chart that you can use to compare it with other charts.

The Change Chart Options link

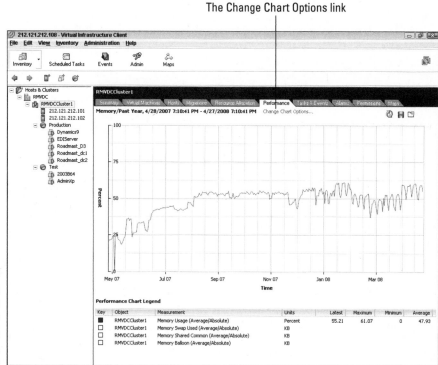

Figure 15-9:
Memory
usage over
one year's
time.

Click to tear off the chart.

Click to export chart to Excel.

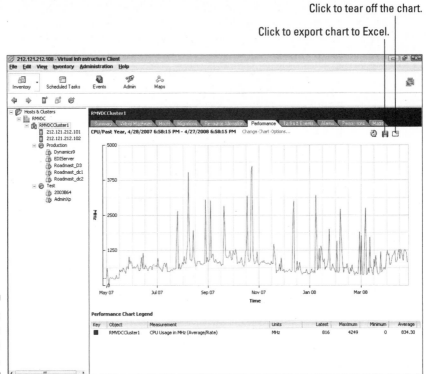

Figure 15-10:
CPU usage
over one
year.

The server level

You might have noticed that the cluster performance metrics have only cluster, CPU, and memory metrics. No disk or network metrics are available. This is because the disk and network metrics are specific to ESX hosts and are not pooled in the cluster, like memory and CPU resources. To see the server-specific metrics, click a server itself. The Virtual Machine and Alarms tabs are the same as the cluster level except that their focus is now in the server itself. However, two tabs are significantly different:

- ✔ **Summary:** The Summary tab (shown in Figure 15-11) shows server-specific information in the General section as well as utilization and storage information in the Resources section.

- ✔ **Performance:** The only two differences between this Performance tab and the cluster-level Performance tab are that the focus is set to a physical server, and there are more metrics you can measure. This is another good area from which to build a baseline. You have the additional metrics (available by clicking the Change Chart Options link) of Disk and Network, not to mention more granular CPU and memory metrics. Figure 15-12 shows the *disk* metrics for one year, and Figure 15-13 shows the *network* metrics for one year. The export and tear-off links work the same as the cluster level.

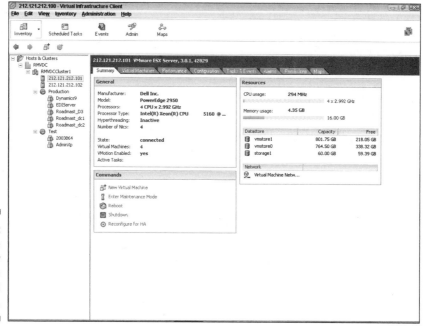

Figure 15-11:
The
Summary
tab at the
physical
server level.

The Change Chart Options link   Click to tear off the chart.

Click to export chart to Excel.

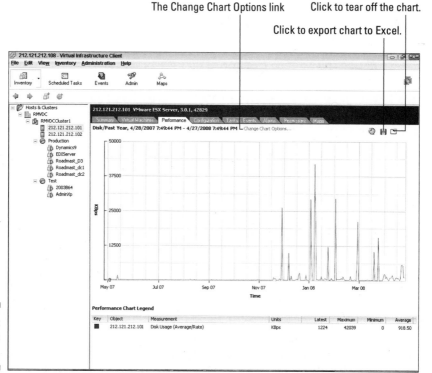

Figure 15-12:
Disk metrics
for one year.

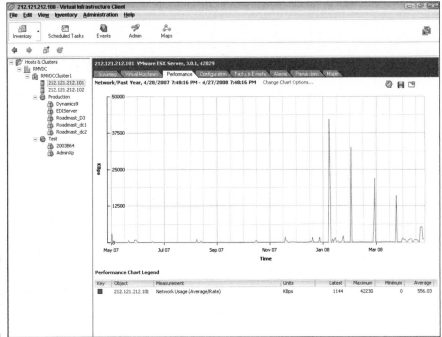

The resource pool level

At this level, all the monitoring tabs are practically the same except that the focus is on the resource pool itself. The Summary tab is different: It basically shows the settings for the resource pool broken into sections by functionality. The Summary tab is shown in Figure 15-14.

The virtual machine level

The only level left to look at is a virtual machine. Again, all the tabs are the same as the resource pool level except that the focus is on a single machine, and the Summary tab is different. This tab can be very handy for a granular view of which virtual machine is using what resources. Like the server-level Performance tab, you can look at CPU, disk, memory, and network metrics. The Summary tab is shown in Figure 15-15.

In addition to using the Summary tabs in VIC,, a command line resource-utilization analysis tool is available that you can run on the ESX host console. Just type in **ESXTOP**. Download the PDF for using ESXTOP from here:

    www.vmware.com/pdf/esx2_using_esxtop.pdf

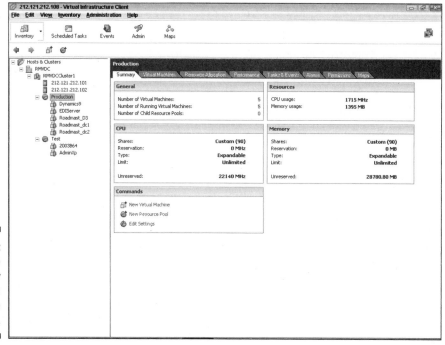

Figure 15-14:
The Summary tab for a resource pool.

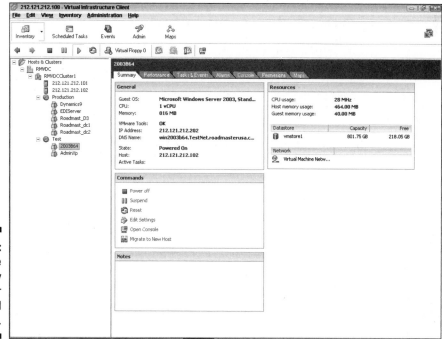

Figure 15-15:
The Summary tab for a virtual machine.

Proactive Monitoring with Alarms

Although VMware creates several default alarms like the ones for Virtual machine Memory and CPU when you install it, you can also create your own alarms. Additionally, you can add a little creativity by forcing actions to happen when alarms go off. Although you define alarms for any object the same way, virtual machine alarms give you the most configuration options. To create an alarm for a virtual machine, follow the steps below:

1. **Log in to your VIC .**

2. **Click the virtual machine you want to define an alarm for.**

3. **Click the Alarms tab.**

4. **Click the Definitions link.**

5. **Right-click in the free space below the defined alarms and then choose New Alarm.**

   The Alarm Settings dialog box opens, as shown in Figure 15-16.

6. **Keep the default settings in the Alarm Type and Trigger Priority sections, and leave the Enable This Alarm check box selected. Then click OK.**

   Leaving the Trigger Priority set to Red means this alarm will trigger before any green alarms. This means the danger alarm state changes have a higher priority than the non-danger state changes so you see them first.

7. **On the Triggers tab, click the Add button and then click the default trigger that gets added.**

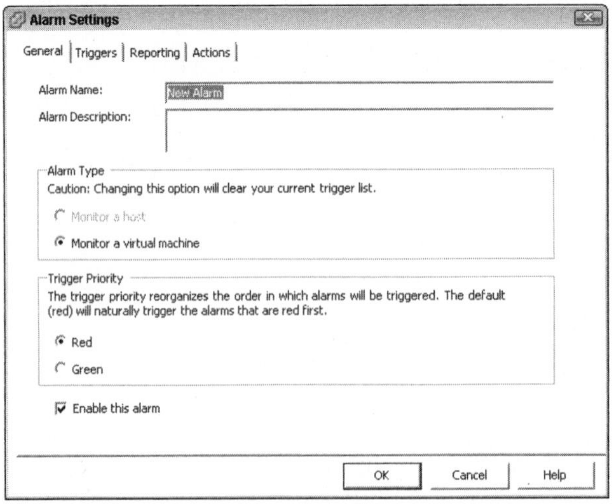

Figure 15-16: Set a new virtual machine alarm here.

8. **Select the Trigger Type from the drop-down list, as shown in Figure 15-17. Then click OK.**

   You can set the same alarm types for ESX hosts by clicking on one, selecting the Alarms tab, and adding an alarm.

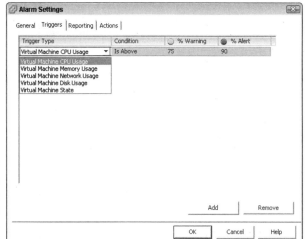

Figure 15-17:
Select the
trigger type
here.

9. **Click the Reporting tab, as shown in Figure 15-18.**

10. **Set the tolerance range.**

    A *tolerance range* prevents the alarm from triggering again until the alarm goes over or under the percent you enter here.

Figure 15-18:
The
Reporting
tab.

11. **Enter the time constraint and then click OK.**

   The alarm won't trigger again until the amount of time you enter here expires.

12. **Click the Actions tab.**

13. **Click Add.**

   A default Send a Notification E-mail action is added.

14. **Click the section and then select the action you want from the drop-down list shown in Figure 15-19.**

15. **Select the check box next to the state transition (from yellow to red for instance) that triggers the action, click OK, and close the Alarm Settings dialog box.**

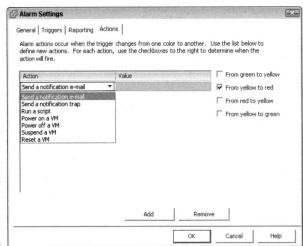

Figure 15-19:
The Actions
tab.

Chapter 16

Preparing for Disaster

· ·

· ·

*I*t is the day that no system administrator wants: For one reason or another, one of your systems has crashed and is in an unrecoverable state. Although this isn't the worst thing that can happen, it certainly constitutes a small disaster.

If you're working with physical servers, you might or might not have to spec out, order, and build new hardware. However, you will likely have to reinstall your operating system and patch it to the current level. And you'll probably have to reinstall your applications if you're not imaging your server. After all the preceding steps are completed, it's time to restore your system's data from backup.

If you're working with virtual machines, though, your machines are less likely to have problems in the first place — and, if a problem does arise, it's far easier to recover from. The worst case is that you deploy a new virtual machine from a template, patch the newly deployed machine, reinstall your applications, and restore data from your backup system. You can probably get to the point of data restore in less than one-half hour. The best-case scenario is just restoring an image of the virtual machine: that is, of course, if you can't just flip a switch on a separate disaster recovery system and bring the virtual machine back to life.

In this chapter, we discuss different ways to assess, prepare for, and recover from disasters. We also look at Virtual Consolidated Backups, a new ways to protect your data that uses snapshots to make recovery fast and effective.

Same Systems, New Choices

When you go virtual, you don't lose any existing backup functionality. Tape backup, disk-to-disk-to-tape, replication, or whatever backup method you use should still work after you virtualize. However, you do get some new tools to put in your backup tool bag.

The old ways to backup servers

Tape backups have been the staple of disaster recovery for a long time. Chances are that you still use tape. You may copy to disk first, but then you probably back that up to tape. Perhaps you use data de-duplication before backing up or just replicate to multiple different sites. Maybe you back up to a mainframe that then gets dumped to tape. I once consulted for a company that lost an entire building. There was a large datacenter in that site. If it weren't for the remote system backups to a mainframe several miles away, many systems would have been forever lost. These are several examples of pre-VMware backup methods.

Virtual Consolidated Backup: A new option

Disk-to-disk-to-tape backups are very popular. Part of the reason is because dumping your data to tape is slow and often subject to a backup window that's 8–12 hours long. Because of data-growth rates, many companies have more data to back up than they have time during their backup window. You might have experienced this firsthand.

By using disk-to-disk-to-tape, you can (in a sense) achieve an infinite backup window. Data is dumped to an intermediary store that can be backed up 24/7. When you copy your data and back up the copy, backup windows have much less influence on your overall disaster recovery plan.

VMware makes use of a disk-to-disk-to-tape backup framework called *Virtual Consolidated Backup (VCB)*. Implementing this framework requires the following:

- ✓ **A backup proxy server:** A backup proxy server can be your regular backup server if you want, as long as it is running Windows Server 2003, so check the compatibility guides before deploying. The backup proxy needs to have access to a SAN LUN that your ESX hosts — and, ideally, your tape drives — also can access.

- ✓ **Backup software that can support VCB:** As long as your software can execute pre-backup and post-backup script files, it should work.

  ✔ **A license to use VCB**

  ✔ **VCB software**

Setting up VCB will vary, depending on your backup software. You can back up an entire virtual machine image or a subset of its files. You can even combine using backup agents and VCB. For instance, you can make periodic backups of full machine images with differential file backups in between.

Dissecting VCB: How it works

Your 20,000-foot view of VCB is as follows:

1. The pre-backup script takes a snapshot of a virtual machine and dumps it to a SAN volume.

2. The snapshot is then merged back into the virtual machine, but the files dumped to the SAN still remain.

3. Your backup software copies the dumped snapshot to tape.

4. A post-backup script removes the snapshot files from disk to reclaim the space.

Pretty easy, right?

Figure 16-1 shows the connectivity diagram for VCB. Notice that the backup proxy server has both a LAN and a SAN connection to VirtualCenter or an ESX host. Also, you need to make sure that the LUN ID is the same on both the backup proxy and your ESX host or VCB will not work.

You can significantly increase the speed of your backup if your backup tape drives are connected to your SAN fabric instead of a slow SCSI connection to your backup server. See Chapter 8.

When you use VCB, the network connection initiates the snapshot, and then the SAN controls the file creation, storage, and deletion. This is called a *LAN-free backup* because the files are copied from the SAN and not over your network connection.

Now that you've seen the 20,000 foot view, it's time to see exactly what happens when you use VCB to back up a virtual machine:

1. Your backup software starts the backup job for a virtual machine.

2. The pre-backup script runs.

3. Virtual Consolidated Backup runs a VMsnap VCB Mounter command.

4. The virtual machine's file system is quiesced and then briefly frozen.

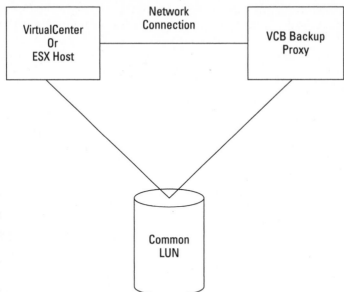

Figure 16-1:
VCB
connectivity
diagram.

5. A snapshot is taken.

6. The machine is unfrozen so it can now apply changes, which are tracked in a differential file. See Chapter 11 for more information on snapshots and differential files.

7. A block list is created. The list is just pointer to the blocks of data that make up the VMDK file. See Chapter 10 for more information on VMDK and other files that make up virtual machines.

8. The virtual machine's block-level information is copied to the backup proxy over the SAN. The information shows up as files on the backup proxy.

9. The delta file is applied to the virtual machine as the snapshot is removed.

10. The pre-backup script is finished and control is given back to your backup software.

11. The virtual machine information is copied from the mount point to tape.

12. The backup is verified (optional, but a good idea).

13. The post-backup script runs.

14. The snapshot files are deleted from the mount point to clean it up.

15. The backup job is complete.

You can see that a lot happens when you back up a virtual machine. Every now and then, the job will likely fail. Sometimes the backup does not complete and the snapshot is not deleted. If that happens, you have to manually go in and clean house. This can involve deleting the snapshot and/or the snapshot files in the mount point. If either exists, they can cause your next backup of the virtual machine to fail.

Be careful with database servers. Even though VCB Mounter can quiesce the file system, active databases can become corrupt when a post-snapshot differential file is applied to the virtual machine. To avoid this risk, you can run a script to stop the database or suspend the virtual machine during the snapshot process.

Setting Up Virtual Consolidated Backup

Setting up your backup software to use VCB is a tricky subject to cover because this varies, depending on the backup software you use. I use Symantec Backup Exec so the directions, examples, and screenshots in this section reflect this software.

After your VCB proxy server is set up to meet the prerequisites (see the "Virtual Consolidated Backup: A new option" section earlier in this chapter), you have a few other tasks to perform. The following sections discuss each step in this process in more detail.

1. **Using either Windows archive bits or Change Journal, make sure your backup software is not altering the file system.**

   The virtual machine's file system cannot be altered through snapshots.

2. **Disable automatic drive letter assignment.**

3. **Install the Consolidated Backup Framework.**

4. **Add your backup software Interoperability Module.**

   Not all backup software requires this step. Some integrate with the VCB framework natively.

5. **Customize your `config` file.**

Verifying that backup software isn't altering the file systems

With Backup Exec, you can base your backups on archive bit, file modify time, or just copy the files. Copying the files is the best bet because it does not try to modify the file system by resetting the archive bit.

Disabling automatic drive letter assignment

Disabling automatic drive letter assignment prevents corruption when backing up virtual machines that use RDM. You can do this by shutting down your backup proxy server, removing your SAN connections, restarting, and then running the `diskpart` command line utility. The commands you need to run are in the following steps:

1. **At the command prompt, type** Diskpart **and then press Enter.**

   The command prompt changes to what you see in Figure 16-2.

Figure 16-2:
The
`diskpart`
utility
screen.

2. **Type** Automount Disable **and then press Enter.**

3. **Type** Automount Scrub **and then press Enter.**

4. **Type** Exit **and then press Enter.**

   At this point you can shut down your backup proxy, reconnect the SAN hardware, and reboot.

Installing the Virtual Consolidated Backup Framework

This part is easy. All you need to do is run the setup program on your VCB disk. You should go with the default installation directory because VMware engineers expect the installation to be in the default directory. When they write an update or add some functionality down the road, they work from the assumption that VCB is installed in the default directory.

Adding your software interoperability module

You need to download and add the interoperability module for your backup software from VMware. For Backup Exec, after the module is downloaded, you need to add it to the VCB install directory, as shown in the following path:

```
C:\Program Files\VMware\VMware Consolidated Backup Framework\backupexec
```

Not all backup software requires this step. Some natively integrate with the VCB framework.

Customizing your config file

The VCB install directory contains a folder called Config. In that folder is the config.js file. You need to open the Config.js file and customize a few options VCB knows how to work. The options are as follows:

- **Backuproot:** The mount point for backups, this is the LUN that your VMware Infrastructure 3 and your backup proxy server can both access. This is also where the snapshot files are copied. The default is C:\mnt. Since you don't want to allow any machine but your proxy server to write to the drive that contains its operating system, this option needs to be changed.

  Remember you need to use a LUN that is visible to both the proxy server and your ESX hosts. Assign this LUN a drive letter in Windows (I use B:\) and create the mnt directory on it. Then set this option to match your drive letter\mnt. Mine is set to B:\mnt.

  The size of the backup lun should be at least as big as the sum size of your biggest virtual machine's hard disks so you can fit all the data on it.

- **Host:** This is the machine that you want your backup proxy to connect to. It should be your VirtualCenter server. You can use an FQDN or the machine's IP address. There is no default setting for this option.

- **Port:** This is the TCP/IP port that your backup proxy should use for communicating with your VirtualCenter. The default is 902. Unless you changed the port, leave the default.

- **Username:** This is the username used to log in to your VirtualCenter. No default exists.

- **Password:** This is the password associated with the username. Again, no default is provided.

✔ **Snapshot Policy:** The default setting is automatic, but you have the following options:

- *Automatic:* Snapshots are created but then deleted on demand by the backup proxy. This is what is usually used.

- *Manual:* No snapshot is created or deleted by the backup proxy server. Instead, it expects to see a snapshot called _VCB_BACKUP_ and uses that for backup purposes.

- *Createonly:* This option creates a backup snapshot but does not remove it after backup. This option is useful when doing verifications.

- *Deleteonly:* This option assumes that a snapshot called _VCB_ BACKUP_ already exists and doesn't try to create it. This leaves the post-backup command in charge of deleting the snapshot.

Setting up your backup scripts

For Backup Exec, you need to configure one job per virtual machine. You also need to customize each job and decide whether you want to back up an image of the virtual machine or just its files.

In the mount point, if you back up an image, you will see that a lot of files get created for each disk the virtual machine has. If you back up the files, you see a directory for each drive letter and then the files that are on each drive. To set up a backup job for Backup Exec, follow these steps:

1. **Log in to Backup Exec.**

2. **Create a new backup job by clicking on File and selecting New Backup Job.**

3. **In the Source section, choose Selections.**

   What you put here varies, depending on the type of backup you're performing. If you're backing up an image of the entire virtual machine, you select your mount point, as shown in Figure 16-3. Notice the selection is B:\mnt.

   If you're performing a file backup, you need to click the View Selection Details tab and insert a selection for each drive in the virtual machine. Notice in Figure 16-4 that the selections include the mount point, the machine's IP address or FQDN, the subdirectory letters, and the drive letter.

4. **The next setting that VCB cares about (and that you need to enter) is the Job Name, found by clicking the General option under the Settings section on the left of the window.**

   You need to use this name in the Pre- and Post-commands fields in the next two steps.

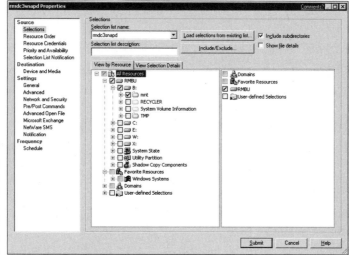

Figure 16-3:
Backup
selection for
an image-
based
backup.

The View Selection Details tab

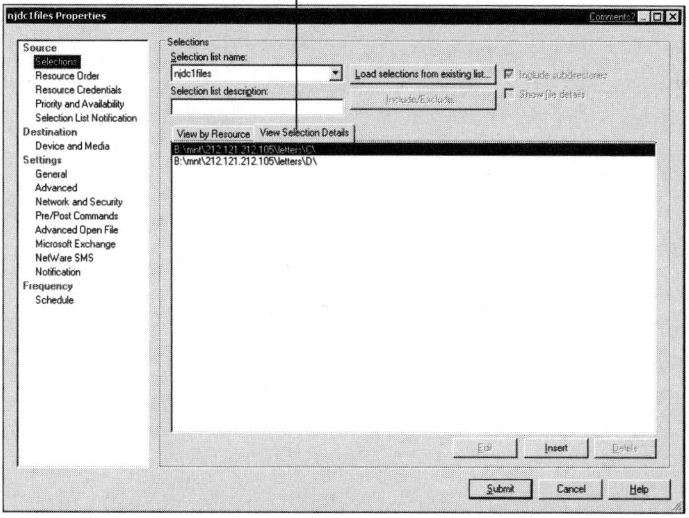

Figure 16-4:
Backup
selection for
file-based
backups.

5. **The last setting requiring modification is the Pre/Post Commands options under the Settings section on the left of the screen.**

   Again, the pre-commands vary, depending on your backup type. If you're performing an image-based backup, the command includes the full path to the `Pre-backup.bat` file, a space, the backup job name from Step 4, and the machine name or IP address concatenated with `-fullvm`. Here is a sample command:

```
"c:\program files\vmware\vmware consolidated backup framework\backupexec\
             pre-backup.bat" rmdc1snapw 212.121.212.75-fullvm
```

If you're performing a file-based backup, the command does not use the
-fullvm switch. Here's the file-level command:

```
"c:\program files\vmware\vmware consolidated backup framework\backupexec\
             pre-backup.bat" njdc1files 212.121.212.105
```

6. Enter the post-command, which is the same regardless of backup type.

The post-command has the full path to the post-backup.bat file, a
space, and the job name from Step 4. Here's a sample:

```
"c:\Program Files\VMware\VMware Consolidated Backup Framework\backupexec\
             post-backup.bat" njdc1files
```

**7. In the same screen, select the first four Pre/Post Command options, as
shown in Figure 16-5.**

Select these four options.

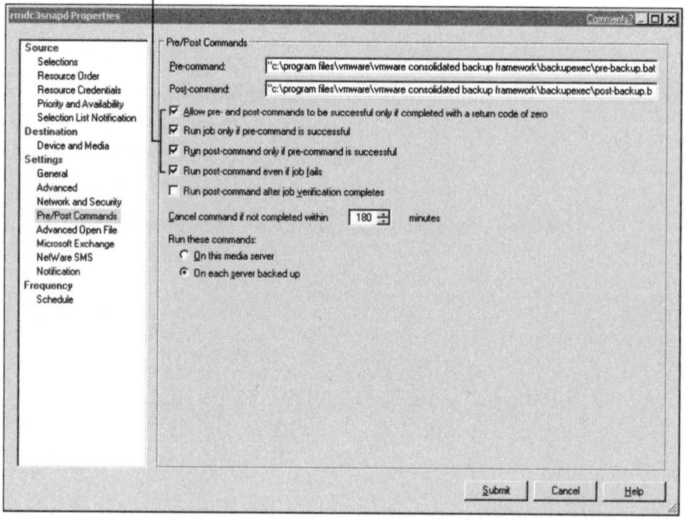

Figure 16-5:
Select these
Pre/Post
command
options.

8. Set up your job schedule and then click the Submit button.

Repeat the process for each server you want to back up with VCB.

Restoring from backups

Restoring from backups is extremely easy, be it an image restore or just a single file. To restore an entire virtual machine from an image, follow these steps:

1. **Restore the most recent image-based backup files to your mount point.**

2. **Launch VMware Converter.**

3. **Use VMware Converter the same way as I outline in Chapter 11, except that now you select Standalone Virtual Machine, Backup, or Disk Image for your Source option, as shown in Figure 16-6.**

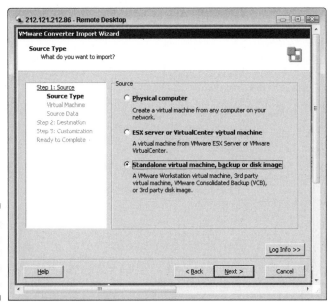

Figure 16-6:
Restoring an
image with
VMware
Converter.

If you're in need of only a file or two, just restore those files to your backup proxy server and copy them to your Virtual Machine over the network. Optionally, if you have backup agents installed on the virtual machine, you can restore the file directly to the virtual machine.

The VCB Framework offers you some new tools to add to your backup toolbox. Depending on your situation, you might want to exclusively use VCB, use only backing up over the network through backup agents, or use a combination of the two. Sometimes agents are an à la carte option for backup software, so depending on your number of servers, you might see significant savings by not buying backup agents in the first place.

Chapter 17

Troubleshooting

In This Chapter

▶ A systematic approach to troubleshooting

▶ Looking at example problems

▶ Taking a proactive stance

roubleshooting is both an art and a science. The more artistic ability you develop, the faster you can fix problems. However, there is no escaping the science part of the equation. Troubleshooting is an applied scientific method with a divide-and-conquer approach.

With that in mind, you need to pool all your technical knowledge about how your subsystems work and interact with each other. When you encounter a problem, you need to put on your scientist's lab coat and hypothesize where that problem is coming from. If you combine the scientific method of testing your hypothesis (make only one change at a time, please) with the concept of divide and conquer, you can isolate the problem to a subsystem. Repeat the process and isolate the problem to part of a subsystem. Keep repeating the process until you know exactly what the problem is. That is a systematic approach to troubleshooting.

In a best-case scenario, taking a random approach will take you longer to isolate and fix the problem. And in a worst-case scenario, your problem will get worse.

In this chapter, we examine a systematic approach to troubleshooting. Additionally, we discuss taking a proactive stance to prevent problems before they happen.

Asking Murphy What Can Go Wrong

Not to sound like a pessimist, but Murphy's Law applies to computers. Design your system with that in mind, and your problems will be few and far between. VMware is extremely dependent on its connected subsystems because a change in one subsystem can affect your entire VMware Infrastructure 3. This is a *tightly coupled system.* Thus, the first step to troubleshooting is always finding the subsystem that has the problem. The two types of problems are internal and external problems.

Identifiying internal problems

Internal problems are problems within the virtual realm itself. Many of these problems are the result of software or a misconfiguration. You generally see internal problems like

- **Problems with virtual machines:** These types of problems can include network problems, crashing software on a VM, and configuration errors. Any problem that can happen on a physical server can also happen on a virtual server.

- **Problems with VMotion:** These types of problems can include ping ponging your servers from one node to another repeatedly or servers not moving from one node to another when they should.

- **Problems with High Availability (HA):** These types of problems can include HA not working due to misconfiguration.

- **Problems with any system running on your virtual machines:** This can include domain name system (DNS), e-mail, Enterprise Resource Planning (ERP), or any other system.

Of course, some of the virtual realm problems can be hardware related. Because the focus is only on problems in the virtual realm right now, the hardware under consideration are your ESX hosts and your clusters. You might see the following two hardware-related issues:

- **Lack of resource issues:** These issues can include running out of disk space, network bandwidth, memory, or processing power.

- **Hardware failure issues:** These issues can include HBA card failures, network card failures, and entire server failures.

From speaking with VMware technical support personnel, the most common problems are caused by inadequate resources (which comes from inadequate capacity planning; see Chapter 2) and misconfiguring VMware settings. One common performance-killing mistake is to use multiple virtual CPUs. VMware is very good at sharing resources. Any setting that manually overrides the VMkernel's ability to be flexible results in some sort of performance hit. On the other hand, my Exchange server needs two vCPUs and a higher share allocation to prevent alarms from going off. It is the only server I have utilizing two CPUs.

Understanding external problems

External problems live in your subsystems, which VMware is dependent on for functionality. These include your physical network and storage subsystems. Generally, after these systems are set up in a fault-tolerant way and properly configured, they provide flawless and trouble-free service until one of three things happens:

✔ **Someone makes a change that has a negative effect on the subsystem.** For example, I once worked on a very large-scale Exchange deployment. The system was designed to be modular: Two node clusters connected to SAN storage, and each cluster would support roughly 20,000 users. One day, a consultant (panicking to solve a problem quickly) accidentally deleted one of the database files. This left a lot of people with a crippled system and made a bad problem far worse. This is an extreme example of how a change can cause a problem.

✔ **A piece of hardware fails: Murphy is always lurking around your hardware.** Sometimes, I think Murphy has a bunch of gremlins on his payroll! All your hardware will fail eventually. As long as your system is designed to be fault-tolerant, though, these issues are pretty easy to resolve, usually with no downtime.

✔ **Your capacity is exceeded.** This, thankfully, is an easy problem to solve as well: Just add more capacity. If you keep baselines and monitor your system (see Chapter 15), you can see this problem coming from a mile away. If your infrastructure is designed for modular expansion, you just need to add another module of capacity, be it a new ESX, another shelf of SAN disks, or NAS.

Examining Some Problem Scenarios

This section walks you through some common problems you might see. Divide-and-conquer, as well as the scientific method, are described. The examples range from simple to complex.

Virtual machine will not power on

If you start a virtual machine and get an error stating there are not enough resources, you know you have a problem. The error itself will tell you whether the issue is because of CPU or memory. You need to diagnose the issue in the following manner:

1. **Attempt to identify what might be causing the problem.**

   This is a prime example of divide-and-conquer. Say the error message says that the memory resources available are insufficient. You know that four areas provide memory resources:

   - Physical memory in your ESX hosts

   - The pooled memory of your ESX hosts in a cluster

   - Your resource pools

   - Your virtual machine settings themselves

2. **Isolate the problem.**

   This is the scientific method. You hypothesize that your cluster might not have enough memory to meet your virtual machine needs.

   a. You log in to your VMware Infrastructure Client (VIC) and look at the current cluster's memory statistics. You see that they're fine. You have plenty of memory left at the cluster level. This rules out your cluster resources as a problem. Of course, while you're looking at your cluster, you see an alarm icon on one of your ESX hosts.

   b. You look at the memory on the ESX with the alarm and find that memory is maxed out. You realize that all your virtual machines are running on this node. Now you have some additional information to throw in the mix. Your new clue leads to a new hypothesis: Memory is not the problem. Rather, the problem is that Distributed Resource Scheduler (DRS) isn't distributing the virtual machine load over all your ESX hosts.

   c. After digging a little deeper, you find the cluster has recommended many migrations, but none of them have been implemented. This reinforces your new hypothesis that DRS isn't moving machines. After checking the DRS configuration, you see that DRS is set to manual.

3. **Resolve the problem.**

   After you know what the problem is, solving it is usually pretty straightforward. In this case, you automate DRS with the migration threshold set to the middle. Now you monitor for both intended and unintended consequences. At this point, your virtual machine starts, and everything seems to be running well. Problem solved.

One word of caution: Before implementing the solution, think about any unwanted side effects it might have and document the change. At the bare minimum, the date, time, system, and change description should be recorded. If you have a fully functional system and a problem suddenly appears that is not hardware related, the first question you should ask is "What Changed?" If you track your changes, you can answer that question.

A virtual machine blue-screens

If one of your virtual machines blue-screens (BSOD), your first likely action is a reboot and check the virtual machine's logs. If the logs reveal no hints, there is a better chance the problem is hardware than software. It might be time to migrate all the virtual machines off that particular ESX host and run hardware diagnostics.

If, on the other hand, the logs reveal many application errors, you need to research those to find a possible solution. Google and Microsoft's TechNet, and Microsoft's Web site (support.microsoft.com) are great places to research errors and possible fixes. Also, never underestimate the benefit of purchasing technical support from a vendor. I know many proud system administrators that race the hold time for tech support against their ability to solve the problem. That's not a bad way to do it.

In general, if a single virtual machine has a problem, you troubleshoot it just like you would a physical machine. If several virtual machines are having a problem, you would likely look at your ESX host and network or disk subsystems. Remember that it's all about divide-and-conquer. Use the scientific method to isolate the problem, and then you can solve it.

Problems with VMware Infrastructure Client (VIC)

If you can't log into your VirtualCenter or ESX hosts, one of two types of problems is typically the culprit:

✔ **Security:** You might have an error with the username or password. The error you see tells you the problem, as shown in Figure 17-1.

✔ **Some type of connectivity issue:** A connectivity problem can live in only three places:

   • Your computer

   • The intermediary network

   • The machine you're connecting to

Ruling out your machine and the machine you're connecting to is easy — just try launching a Web browser or a `ping` command on each machine. That tests both outbound and inbound communications. If you have a machine problem, troubleshoot by pinging the loopback (127.0.0.1) and the default gateway and then look at the logs. If both machines work, the problem lies in the intermediary network.

When on a remote site without my VPN running, I get the error shown in Figure 17-2 when trying to connect. Other network errors can be because of name resolution. In that case, try to connect by using the IP address instead of the DNS name. If that still fails, you have to start standard TCP/IP troubleshooting procedures. Ping your loopback address, then your default gateway, then the next hop, then the next, and so on until you either connect or find where the problem is.

Figure 17-1: Username or password login error.

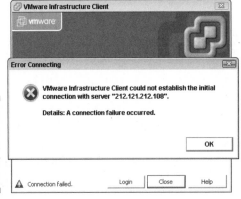

Figure 17-2: Error from network connectivity problems.

ESX host problems

Three things can cause ESX problems: inadequate capacity planning, misconfigurations, and hardware problems. If you've read this book to this point and followed its advice, the first two should never happen. That leaves hardware failure to discuss.

If an ESX host ever crashes with a Purple Screen of Death (PSOD), the first thing you should do is attempt to capture any error information you can. If you can take a screen shot, fantastic. Otherwise, take a picture of the screen. Most of the time, the error information is collected in the dump file, but there are no guarantees. I have never seen a PSOD, but they are usually caused by hardware failures. In fact, Machine Check Exception (MCE) errors point to some sort of hardware failure and can be any piece of hardware. Non Maskable Interrupt (NMI) errors usually point to RAM.Here are the three steps to follow after gathering the error information:

1. **Call VMware Technical Support at 877-486-9273, option 4.**

2. **Make sure that all your virtual machines are running on other hosts.**

   This assumes that you have a cluster with HA enabled on it.

3. **Check your Change log for the last change.**

   Some changes aren't applied until you reboot, so the symptom can appear long after a change occurs. Just to be safe, you should always reboot after a change to make sure there are no problems.

4. **Check to make sure that no hardware was accidentally unplugged.**

Technical Support will want to make sure you have VMware-certified hardware, but you do (right?), so that shouldn't be an issue. VMware technicians will help you diagnose where the problem is. They might have you run the `vm-support` command line utility on the ESX host (assuming that it reboots). They might also have you export diagnostic data. To do that, follow these steps:

1. **Log in to VIC.**

2. **Click File, then mouse over Export, and then click Export Diagnostic Data.**

3. **By default, all sources of data are selected. For troubleshooting, the more data the better, so stick with the default. choose a location to save the data, as shown in Figure 17-3.**

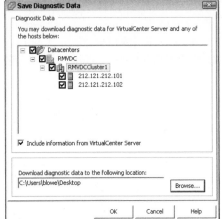

> **4. Click OK.**

VirtualCenter service problems

If your VirtualCenter services don't start, your virtual machines will still continue running. The risk is that HA and VMotion won't work without VirtualCenter. Here are the three places to check for errors if your VirtualCenter services don't start:

- ✓ **Your event logs**
- ✓ **Your database logs**
- ✓ **Your VirtualCenter log file (vpxd.log)**

In Summary

Toubleshooting is a very important topic — it can save you both a lot of time and money. That said, it can't hurt to repeat and highlight the critical information in this chapter.

The troubleshooting process

Your troubleshooting methodology needs to follow a well-defined process. Follow these steps:

1. Decide where the problem could be.

2. Divide and conquer your system by coming up with and testing your hypothesis as to where the problem exists.

3. Gather clues from logs and tests to further divide and conquer.

4. Isolate the problem.

5. Come up with a solution.

6. Think about potential side effects. If there are none, document and implement the solution.

7. Monitor the system for the desired — as well as undesired effects — from the problem resolution.

Maintaining a proactive stance

If you're proactive, you can see and prevent many problems before they happen. You can do several things to be proactive even if you don't have a Simple Network Management Protocol (SNMP) system set up. Here are a few suggestions:

✔ **Always know your baselines and trends so you can see resource constraints before they happen.**

✔ **Watch your disk space periodically.**

This goes for your virtual machines as well as your SAN and NAS. *I check my servers disk space daily and my SAN / NAS space weekly.* Even if your system warns you when you're running low on space, if you proactively watch it, you know far ahead of time and can be ready. This is much better than rushing a fix through at the last minute. Earlier in the chapter, I talk about what I saw happen when a panicky consultant rushed a solution.

✔ **Monitor your disk and network IO and lag times periodically.If everything is working fine, I only watch this monthly or right after a change.**

✔ **Set automated alarms on everything you can so if you're rapidly heading toward a problem, you will get an e-mail, a phone call, and a text message.**

Hopefully, you never experience this. But, if you do, you might be able to solve the problem before it affects your clients.

✔ **Monitor your server logs for errors.**

On a small system, you can do this manually. On a larger system, you want a centralized system to do this.

Part VI
The Part of Tens

The 5th Wave   By Rich Tennant

@RICHTENNANT

"Someone want to look at this manuscript
I received on e-mail called 'The Embedded
Virus That Destroyed the Publisher's Servers
When the Manuscript was Rejected?'"

In this part . . .

No *For Dummies* book would be complete without its Part of Tens section. In this part, Chapter 18 covers places on the Web that you can visit to learn more about VMware Infrastructure 3. Chapter 19 takes a look at other VMware products, and Chapter 20 discusses some cool virtual appliances.

Chapter 18

Ten Places to Discover More

As a whole, VMware Infrastructure 3 is a very complex product. Often, you need more information as you plan, deploy, and manage your virtual infrastructure. I have found the following ten sites very helpful. Some are subsections of the VMware Web site.

VMware Resources Page

`www.vmware.com/resources`

This link (see Figure 18-1) gives you access to VMware events, including tradeshows, seminars, and Webinars. Additionally, you can find white papers, technical papers, compatibility guides, and product documentation. The compatibility guides are updated weekly.

Figure 18-1:
VMware
Resources
page.

VMware Education Services

```
http://mylearn.vmware.com/mgrreg/index.cfm
```

If you want training on VMware or certification, this is the place to start (see Figure 18-2).

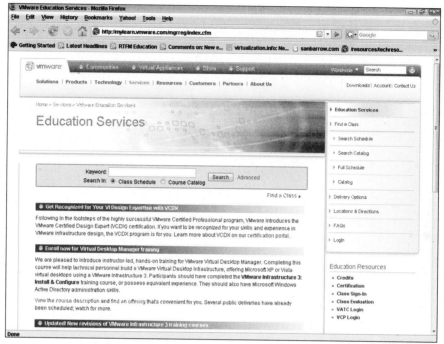

Figure 18-2:
The first place to go for VMware training certification.

VMware Product Index

www.vmware.com/products/product_index.html

Want to find out more about VMware products? Read the next chapter, and then go to this link (shown in Figure 18-3). It lists all VMware products from A to Z. VMware has several different families of products aside from VMware Infrastructure 3. Additionally there are desktop virtualization products like VMware Workstation and VMware Fusion. You can also get various management and automation products like Lab Manager.

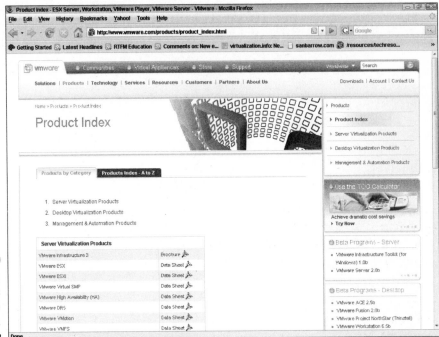

Figure 18-3:
The families
of VMware
products.

VMware Support

`www.vmware.com/support`

If you have a problem with your system, are getting a strange error message, or just want to figure out how to do something, this link is for you (see Figure 18-4). You can search the knowledge base or search through community forums. You can also find links, patches, documentation, and compatibility guides. You can also open a technical support call from this link.

Figure 18-4:
The first
stop when
trying to
solve a
VMware
problem.

VMX File Settings

http://sanbarrow.com/vmx.html

If you want to learn about VMX files, this is the link that will get you off to a
good start (see Figure 18-5). Because VMX files store all your virtual machine's
settings, you should get familiar with them. Occasionally you will find the need
to edit these files to apply advanced settings or remove hardware when you
can't through VIC.

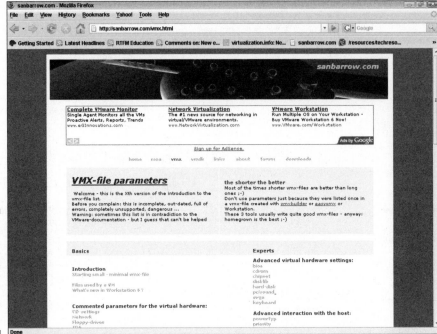

Figure 18-5:
Your one-stop shop for VMX file configuration parameters.

General Virtualization Information

http://vmblog.com

This is a good site (see Figure 18-6) to stay current on the virtualization industry. David Marshall is not only the author of this blog, he is also the technical editor of this book. He knows virtualization inside and out and selflessly shares his knowledge. Hopefully he will also shamelessly plug this book!

Mike Laverick's Web site/Blog

www.rtfm-ed.co.uk

Mike is a consultant and author who specializes in VMware and Citrix in Europe. He has written two advanced technical design books on VMware. Mike is also very active on VMware's forums and has been mentioned in VMware's newsletter. You can see Mike's Web site and blog in Figure 18.7.

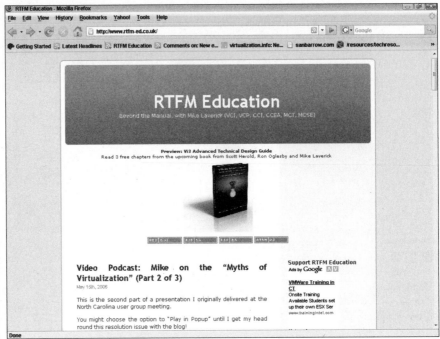

Figure 18-7:
Mike
Laverick's
RTFM
education
site.

EMC2

www.emc.com

EMC2 (see Figure 18-8) makes various SAN products and owns VMware. My understanding is that EMC2 does not interfere with VMware's management team or products. With VMware's sales doubling every year for the past couple of years, they have no reason to. If you are considering VMware, you need to consider EMC2's storage solutions.

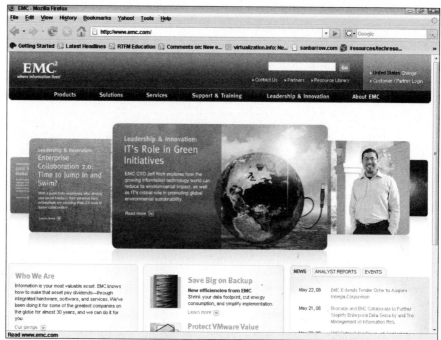

Figure 18-8:
The EMC2
Web site.

Search ServerVirtualization.com at Techtarget

http://searchservervirtualization.techtarget.com/

This is another good site (see Figure 18.9) to measure the pulse of the virtualization industry. This site also offers whitepapers and webcasts; links to other virtualization information hubs; and well categorized topics on various virtualization information like technologies, hardware, and strategies.

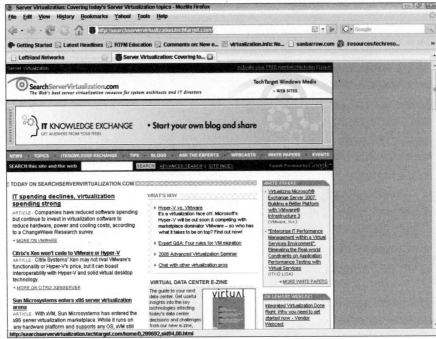

Figure 18-9:
The first
of two
TechTarget
sites.

SearchVMware.com at TechTarget

http://searchvmware.techtarget.com

This site (shown in Figure 18-10) provides a cornucopia of information on
virtualization with VMware. Unlike the first TechTarget site listed, which is
devoted to virtualization in general, this site is strictly devoted to VMware
virtualization information. Again, it has white papers and product news.

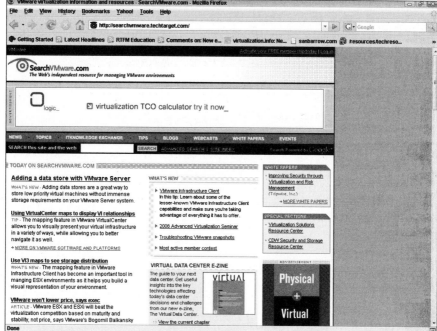

Figure 18-10:
The second
TechTarget
site.

Chapter 19

Ten Other VMware Products

▶ VMware products to introduce you to virtualization

▶ Virtual appliances to speed new system deployments

▶ Running Windows on a Mac without rebooting

*I*f you're as addicted to VMware as I am, you'll likely want to check out some of its other products. Take a look at the list in this chapter to see whether any of these products interest you. You can get a really good feel for virtualization using either VMware workstation or the free VMware server. If you need to run Windows on a Mac, VMware Fusion is a fantastic product. Virtual appliances are pre-configured servers that you can deploy in minutes. Virtualization opens up a whole new way of doing things.

VMware ACE

www.vmware.com/products/ace/

You can use ACE (see Figure 19-1) to distribute standardized and secured virtual desktops. It enables you to easily deploy and run a virtual machine that meets your corporate standards on any PC. Additionally, your users can bring their virtual machines with them on a thumb drive by using Pocket Ace.

Figure 19-1:
VMware
Ace
homepage.

VMware Fusion

www.vmware.com/products/fusion/

If you have an Intel Mac, you can run Windows on it by dual-booting with the Apple Boot Camp technology. Alternatively, you can run Windows at the same time via VMware Fusion (see Figure 19-2). You can also utilize snapshots with Fusion.

Figure 19-2:
A better
way to run
Windows on
a Mac than
Boot Camp.

VMware Player

www.vmware.com/products/player/

This free product (see Figure 19-3) lets you run pre-made virtual machines on your PC. It can run virtual machines created by VMware Workstation, VMware Server, and VMware ESX Server. It can even run Microsoft virtual machines and Symantec LiveState Recovery disks. VMware Player is also very handy for evaluating virtual appliances.

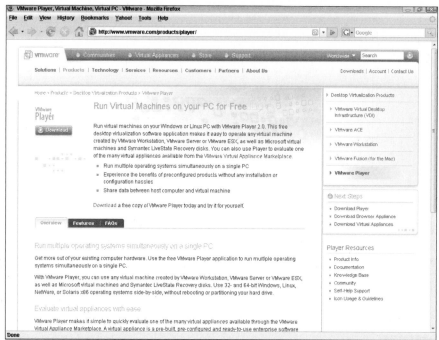

Figure 19-3:
A free way
to run
pre-made
virtual
machines.

VMware Server

`www.vmware.com/products/server/`

VMware Server (see Figure 19-4) is a free virtualization product that allows you to run multiple virtual machines on a single Windows or Linux server. This is a great product for testing patches, programs, and software development. Try this VMware Server to get a taste of virtualization. Before you try this product, I just have to warn you: VMware is extremely addictive!

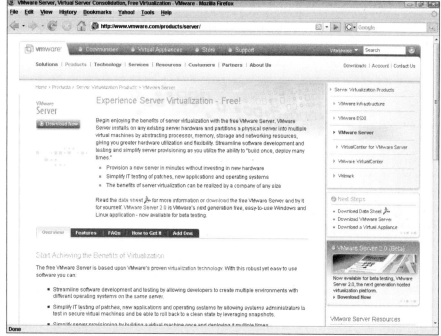

Figure 19-4:
VMware
Server's
home page.

VMware ESXi

```
http://www.vmware.com/products/esxi/
```

What if VMware put ESX on a chip in a physical server? You could deploy a new ESX from a diskless physical server in a very short time. In fact, a person with no understanding of virtualization could deploy a new server. And after deployment, you could connect to and manage the new ESX from VirtualCenter. Well, VMware did just that with ESXi (see Figure 19-5).

Figure 19-5:
VMware on
a chip.

VMware Update Manager

http://www.vmware.com/products/vi/updatemanager.html

New in Version 3.5, Update Manager (see Figure 19-6) automates patch management on ESX hosts and many Windows and Linux virtual machines. It can even update virtual machines that are powered-off! Update Manager works with Distributed Resource Scheduler (DRS) to migrate virtual machines off an ESX host before patching it, for zero downtime.

Figure 19-6:
Simplify
your patch
manage-
ment with
Update
Manager.

VMware Storage VMotion

http://www.vmware.com/products/vi/storage_vmotion.html

Before version 3.5, you could move a virtual machine's storage location only when the machine was powered-down. With Storage VMotion (see Figure 19-7), you can now relocate a virtual machine's storage location while it's powered-on.

Figure 19-7:
Storage
VMotion
home page.

VMware Capacity Planner

www.vmware.com/products/capacity_planner/

This product (see Figure 19-8) provides an in-depth capacity analysis of your non-virtual infrastructure. It is an agent-free program that runs in your data center. This is usually used by VMware consultants and is a good idea to use if you're planning on doing a large-scale virtualization project.

Figure 19-8:
Help
automate
your
capacity
planning.

VMware Converter

www.vmware.com/products/converter/

VMware Converter (see Figure 19-9) is the fastest and easiest way to migrate your physical machines to virtual machines. Additionally, you can use it to recover virtual machines from consolidated backups. You can choose from free and purchased versions. They do the same thing, but the for-fee version has a far-richer feature set.

Figure 19-9:
An absolute
necessity
for
moving from
physical to
virtual.

VMware Workstation

www.vmware.com/products/ws/

VMware workstation (see Figure 19-10) is what started x86 virtualization. This was the product that eventually grew into ESX host. The product allows you to run multiple virtual machines on your desktop or notebook. The uses are endless. You can setup an entire network to test new software. Tons of sales people use it to demo client server applications. If you're a programmer, you will love this product. Each virtual machine is stored in a file so it is easily backed up. Additionally, you can make snapshots before changing a VM.

Figure 19-10:
A product
with endless
uses.

Chapter 20

Ten Cool Virtual Appliances

*V*irtual appliances are a really cool idea. If you drink coffee, think about your coffee machine for a moment. It is a single device that is preconfigured to perform the glorious function of making coffee. It's a *coffee appliance.*

Virtual appliances are very similar. They are preconfigured virtual machines that perform a certain function. I haven't tried many appliances on this list, but they did catch my interest and appliances can get certified by VMware. Many appliances are free and some are available for purchase. Here are some virtual appliances that I found interesting. Bear in mind that most appliances are Linux-based to skirt vendor licensing costs.

There are two things that make virtual appliances beneficial:

✔ **The are free or low-cost systems.**

✔ **They are already designed and built so you do not have to spend time doing that yourself.**

Just because you don't have to design the application and server itself does not mean you are off the hook. You still need to carefully design the integration of virtual appliances into your existing environment.

PostPath Server

www.vmware.com/appliances/directory/1089

PostPath (see Figure 20-1) is a Linux-based, e-mail and collaboration platform. It natively supports Active Directory, Exchange, and Outlook. It can also be used with Active Sync and BlackBerry devices. This appliance is described as a drop-in replacement for Exchange that uses native Exchange protocols for complete integration at roughly 1/5 of the cost.

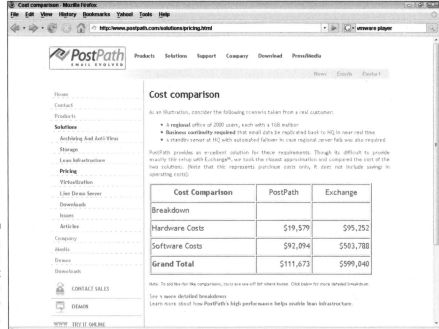

Figure 20-1: PostPath's own cost comparison to Exchange.

Akorri BalancePoint

www.vmware.com/appliances/directory/1084

This cross-domain performance planning and optimization program (see Figure 20-2) analyzes servers and storage. It understands virtual servers and virtual storage as well. This is one of a new breed of applications designed to help utilize and manage virtual infrastructures. With everyone catching the virtualization bug, I suspect you will see more and more applications designed to help you leverage your virtual infrastructure.

Ubuntu JeOS with VMware Drivers

www.vmware.com/appliances/directory/1136

This appliance (see Figure 20-3) is a stripped-down Ubuntu server designed to take up a very small amount of disk space. It is designed to be a platform on which to build your own appliances. Any drivers that probably won't be used on a server like audio and USB have been removed to reduce the server disk and memory footprint.

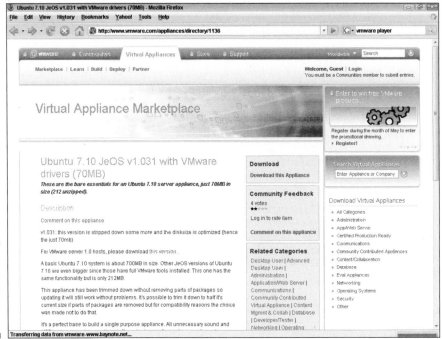

Figure 20-3:
Ubuntu
appliance
download
page.

VMware Infrastructure Perl Toolkit 1.5

www.vmware.com/appliances/directory/1026

Although this appliance (see Figure 20-4) is generally for developers, it's designed to allow you to take advantage of the Virtual Infrastructure API for management and control through scripts. If scripting and automation is your thing, or you are developing applications that utilize virtual infrastructure, this toolkit is something you should try. The download link allows you to get SDKs and APIs with their documentation.

Figure 20-4:
Pearl Toolkit
download
page.

VKernel

www.vmware.com/appliances/directory/881

Often IT is a centralized resource that all departments use. The question becomes "Who gets to pay for the technology?" Many companies work on a chargeback system that allows the costs of IT to be disbursed on a usage basis. If you use departmental chargebacks for computing resources, this appliance (see Figure 20-5) might interest you. It tracks ESX resources and generates chargeback reports. So, if sales uses twice as many resources as logistics, their bill is twice the bill of logistics. Bear in mind you can use Resource Pools (Chapter 14) to strictly enforce resource utilization limits if you want to.

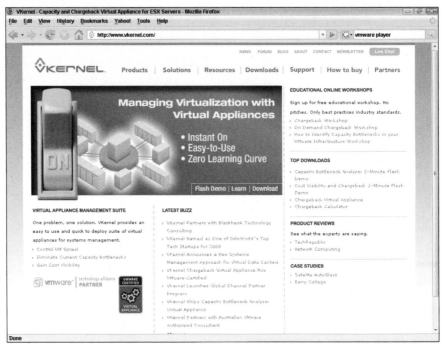

Figure 20-5:
VKernel
homepage.

vmSight

www.vmware.com/appliances/directory/1197

Are you wondering what goes on in your virtual network? vmSight is a
Big Brother appliance that watches and reports. This is an entire suite of
modules that allow you to analyze application performance and uptime;
perform capacity planning; control VM sprawl by identifying unauthorized
VMs; provide chargebacks; and provide regulatory compliance reports.
The modules themselves are described in Figure 20-6.

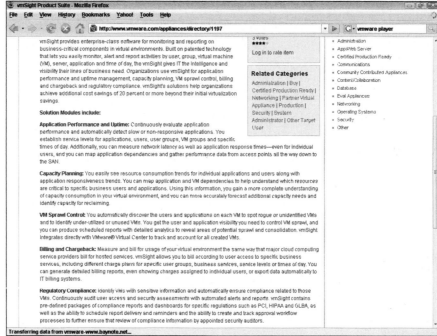

Figure 20-6:
vmSight
module
descriptions.

JumpBox for SugarCRM 4.5.1h

www.vmware.com/appliances/directory/883

"CRM in a box" best describes this appliance (see Figure 20-7). Sugar is a fairly feature-rich program, and JumpBox appliances all feature simple Web-based configurations. I asked my programmer to test this application and he liked it quite a bit. He said there was a great deal of functionality and a very clean interface. Additionally, it was fairly easy to configure.

Figure 20-7:
Jumpbox for
SugarCRM
homepage.

Proficient Software

www.vmware.com/appliances/directory/744

This project-management appliance (see Figure 20-8) also provides team collaboration, issue tracking, sales pipeline, and file management functionality. It seems to have many workflow capabilities such as task delegation and approvals. I am currently looking for a workflow/project management/ collaboration application for a department where I work and will be taking a closer look at this appliance.

Figure 20-8:
Proficient
home page.

JumpBox for Twiki 4.2

www.vmware.com/appliances/directory/1007

Download and start this appliance (see Figure 20-9) to discover the fastest way to deploy a wiki. With a *wiki,* your users can create and edit Web page content from any browser. This can be used as a simple and efficient collaboration tool. And, like all JumpBox appliances, it is designed for easy deployment.

Figure 20-9:
JumpBox
Twiki
product
page.

MindTouch Deki Wiki

www.vmware.com/appliances/directory/705

Another wiki appliance (see Figure 20-10) for you to check out. It is free and has an API for programmers to extend its functionality. It has WYSIWYG editing; file upload capability; a security framework; and an extensive search engine.

Figure 20-10:
MindTouch
home page.

Index

• X •

Notes

Notes

Notes

BUSINESS, CAREERS & PERSONAL FINANCE

Fundraising FOR DUMMIES
0-7645-9847-3

Investing FOR DUMMIES
0-7645-2431-3

Also available:
- Business Plans Kit For Dummies
  0-7645-9794-9
- Economics For Dummies
  0-7645-5726-2
- Grant Writing For Dummies
  0-7645-8416-2
- Home Buying For Dummies
  0-7645-5331-3
- Managing For Dummies
  0-7645-1771-6
- Marketing For Dummies
  0-7645-5600-2

- Personal Finance For Dummies
  0-7645-2590-5*
- Resumes For Dummies
  0-7645-5471-9
- Selling For Dummies
  0-7645-5363-1
- Six Sigma For Dummies
  0-7645-6798-5
- Small Business Kit For Dummies
  0-7645-5984-2
- Starting an eBay Business For Dummies
  0-7645-6924-4
- Your Dream Career For Dummies
  0-7645-9795-7

HOME & BUSINESS COMPUTER BASICS

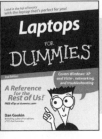

Laptops FOR DUMMIES
0-470-05432-8

Windows Vista FOR DUMMIES
0-471-75421-8

Also available:
- Cleaning Windows Vista For Dummies
  0-471-78293-9
- Excel 2007 For Dummies
  0-470-03737-7
- Mac OS X Tiger For Dummies
  0-7645-7675-5
- MacBook For Dummies
  0-470-04859-X
- Macs For Dummies
  0-470-04849-2
- Office 2007 For Dummies
  0-470-00923-3

- Outlook 2007 For Dummies
  0-470-03830-6
- PCs For Dummies
  0-7645-8958-X
- Salesforce.com For Dummies
  0-470-04893-X
- Upgrading & Fixing Laptops For Dummies
  0-7645-8959-8
- Word 2007 For Dummies
  0-470-03658-3
- Quicken 2007 For Dummies
  0-470-04600-7

FOOD, HOME, GARDEN, HOBBIES, MUSIC & PETS

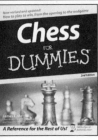

Chess FOR DUMMIES
0-7645-8404-9

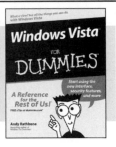

Guitar FOR DUMMIES
0-7645-9904-6

Also available:
- Candy Making For Dummies
  0-7645-9734-5
- Card Games For Dummies
  0-7645-9910-0
- Crocheting For Dummies
  0-7645-4151-X
- Dog Training For Dummies
  0-7645-8418-9
- Healthy Carb Cookbook For Dummies
  0-7645-8476-6
- Home Maintenance For Dummies
  0-7645-5215-5

- Horses For Dummies
  0-7645-9797-3
- Jewelry Making & Beading For Dummies
  0-7645-2571-9
- Orchids For Dummies
  0-7645-6759-4
- Puppies For Dummies
  0-7645-5255-4
- Rock Guitar For Dummies
  0-7645-5356-9
- Sewing For Dummies
  0-7645-6847-7
- Singing For Dummies
  0-7645-2475-5

INTERNET & DIGITAL MEDIA

eBay FOR DUMMIES
0-470-04529-9

iPod & iTunes FOR DUMMIES
0-470-04894-8

Also available:
- Blogging For Dummies
  0-471-77084-1
- Digital Photography For Dummies
  0-7645-9802-3
- Digital Photography All-in-One Desk Reference For Dummies
  0-470-03743-1
- Digital SLR Cameras and Photography For Dummies
  0-7645-9803-1
- eBay Business All-in-One Desk Reference For Dummies
  0-7645-8438-3
- HDTV For Dummies
  0-470-09673-X

- Home Entertainment PCs For Dummies
  0-470-05523-5
- MySpace For Dummies
  0-470-09529-6
- Search Engine Optimization For Dummies
  0-471-97998-8
- Skype For Dummies
  0-470-04891-3
- The Internet For Dummies
  0-7645-8996-2
- Wiring Your Digital Home For Dummies
  0-471-91830-X

Separate Canadian edition also available
Separate U.K. edition also available

Available wherever books are sold. For more information or to order direct: U.S. customers visit www.dummies.com or call 1-877-762-2974.
U.K. customers visit www.wileyeurope.com or call 0800 243407. Canadian customers visit www.wiley.ca or call 1-800-567-4797.

SPORTS, FITNESS, PARENTING, RELIGION & SPIRITUALITY

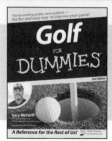

0-471-76871-5

0-7645-7841-3

Also available:
- Catholicism For Dummies
  0-7645-5391-7
- Exercise Balls For Dummies
  0-7645-5623-1
- Fitness For Dummies
  0-7645-7851-0
- Football For Dummies
  0-7645-3936-1
- Judaism For Dummies
  0-7645-5299-6
- Potty Training For Dummies
  0-7645-5417-4
- Buddhism For Dummies
  0-7645-5359-3

- Pregnancy For Dummies
  0-7645-4483-7 †
- Ten Minute Tone-Ups For Dummies
  0-7645-7207-5
- NASCAR For Dummies
  0-7645-7681-X
- Religion For Dummies
  0-7645-5264-3
- Soccer For Dummies
  0-7645-5229-5
- Women in the Bible For Dummies
  0-7645-8475-8

TRAVEL

0-7645-7749-2

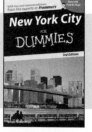

0-7645-6945-7

Also available:
- Alaska For Dummies
  0-7645-7746-8
- Cruise Vacations For Dummies
  0-7645-6941-4
- England For Dummies
  0-7645-4276-1
- Europe For Dummies
  0-7645-7529-5
- Germany For Dummies
  0-7645-7823-5
- Hawaii For Dummies
  0-7645-7402-7

- Italy For Dummies
  0-7645-7386-1
- Las Vegas For Dummies
  0-7645-7382-9
- London For Dummies
  0-7645-4277-X
- Paris For Dummies
  0-7645-7630-5
- RV Vacations For Dummies
  0-7645-4442-X
- Walt Disney World & Orlando
  For Dummies
  0-7645-9660-8

GRAPHICS, DESIGN & WEB DEVELOPMENT

0-7645-8815-X

0-7645-9571-7

Also available:
- 3D Game Animation For Dummies
  0-7645-8789-7
- AutoCAD 2006 For Dummies
  0-7645-8925-3
- Building a Web Site For Dummies
  0-7645-7144-3
- Creating Web Pages For Dummies
  0-470-08030-2
- Creating Web Pages All-in-One Desk
  Reference For Dummies
  0-7645-4345-8
- Dreamweaver 8 For Dummies
  0-7645-9649-7

- InDesign CS2 For Dummies
  0-7645-9572-5
- Macromedia Flash 8 For Dummies
  0-7645-9691-8
- Photoshop CS2 and Digital
  Photography For Dummies
  0-7645-9580-6
- Photoshop Elements 4 For Dummies
  0-471-77483-9
- Syndicating Web Sites with RSS Feed
  For Dummies
  0-7645-8848-6
- Yahoo! SiteBuilder For Dummies
  0-7645-9800-7

NETWORKING, SECURITY, PROGRAMMING & DATABASES

0-7645-7728-X

0-471-74940-0

Also available:
- Access 2007 For Dummies
  0-470-04612-0
- ASP.NET 2 For Dummies
  0-7645-7907-X
- C# 2005 For Dummies
  0-7645-9704-3
- Hacking For Dummies
  0-470-05235-X
- Hacking Wireless Networks
  For Dummies
  0-7645-9730-2
- Java For Dummies
  0-470-08716-1

- Microsoft SQL Server 2005 For Dummies
  0-7645-7755-7
- Networking All-in-One Desk Reference
  For Dummies
  0-7645-9939-9
- Preventing Identity Theft For Dummies
  0-7645-7336-5
- Telecom For Dummies
  0-471-77085-X
- Visual Studio 2005 All-in-One Desk
  Reference For Dummies
  0-7645-9775-2
- XML For Dummies
  0-7645-8845-1

HEALTH & SELF-HELP

0-7645-8450-2

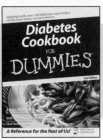

0-7645-4149-8

Also available:

- Bipolar Disorder For Dummies
  0-7645-8451-0
- Chemotherapy and Radiation For Dummies
  0-7645-7832-4
- Controlling Cholesterol For Dummies
  0-7645-5440-9
- Diabetes For Dummies
  0-7645-6820-5* †
- Divorce For Dummies
  0-7645-8417-0 †

- Fibromyalgia For Dummies
  0-7645-5441-7
- Low-Calorie Dieting For Dummies
  0-7645-9905-4
- Meditation For Dummies
  0-471-77774-9
- Osteoporosis For Dummies
  0-7645-7621-6
- Overcoming Anxiety For Dummies
  0-7645-5447-6
- Reiki For Dummies
  0-7645-9907-0
- Stress Management For Dummies
  0-7645-5144-2

EDUCATION, HISTORY, REFERENCE & TEST PREPARATION

0-7645-8381-6

0-7645-9554-7

Also available:

- The ACT For Dummies
  0-7645-9652-7
- Algebra For Dummies
  0-7645-5325-9
- Algebra Workbook For Dummies
  0-7645-8467-7
- Astronomy For Dummies
  0-7645-8465-0
- Calculus For Dummies
  0-7645-2498-4
- Chemistry For Dummies
  0-7645-5430-1
- Forensics For Dummies
  0-7645-5580-4

- Freemasons For Dummies
  0-7645-9796-5
- French For Dummies
  0-7645-5193-0
- Geometry For Dummies
  0-7645-5324-0
- Organic Chemistry I For Dummies
  0-7645-6902-3
- The SAT I For Dummies
  0-7645-7193-1
- Spanish For Dummies
  0-7645-5194-9
- Statistics For Dummies
  0-7645-5423-9

Get smart @ dummies.com®

- **Find a full list of Dummies titles**
- **Look into loads of FREE on-site articles**
- **Sign up for FREE eTips e-mailed to you weekly**
- **See what other products carry the Dummies name**
- **Shop directly from the Dummies bookstore**
- **Enter to win new prizes every month!**

* Separate Canadian edition also available
† Separate U.K. edition also available

Available wherever books are sold. For more information or to order direct: U.S. customers visit www.dummies.com or call 1-877-762-2974.
U.K. customers visit www.wileyeurope.com or call 0800 243407. Canadian customers visit www.wiley.ca or call 1-800-567-4797.